Nature Reborn

Then I saw a new heaven and a new earth . . .
And I saw the holy city, the new Jerusalem,
coming down from heaven.
—Rev. 21:1-2

Nature Reborn

The Ecological and Cosmic
Promise of Christian Theology

H. Paul Santmire

FORTRESS PRESS   MINNEAPOLIS

NATURE REBORN
The Ecological and Cosmic Promise of Christian Theology

Cover art: *Wheatfield with Crows*, Vincent van Gogh. Copyright © Art Resource.
    Used by permission.
Book design: Michelle L. Norstad

Library of Congress Cataloging-in-Publication Data

Santmire, H. Paul.
    Nature reborn : the ecological and cosmic promise of Christian theology /
H. Paul Santmire.
        p. cm. — (Theology and the sciences)
    Includes bibliographical references (p.) and index.
    ISBN 0-8006-3234-6 (alk. paper)
    1. Nature—Religious aspects—Christianity. 2. Human ecology—Religious
aspects—Christianity. I. Title. II. Series.

BT695.5 S253 2000
261.8'362—dc21   00-022295

The paper used in this publication meets the minimum requirements for American National Standard for Information Sciences—Permanence of Paper for Printed Library Materials, ANSI Z329.48–1984.

Manufactured in the U.S.A.   AF 1-3234

04   03   02   01   00   1   2   3   4   5   6   7   8   9   10

*To Jean C. Santmire
and in memory of
Harold C. Santmire*

Contents

Preface

For more than thirty years, I have been laboring in the field of the theology of nature. Things have changed. Whereas at first a few of us had to write, as with megaphones, to announce that theologians can and must be concerned with ecological issues and with related cosmic anxieties, now such matters are addressed in summer camps and Sunday schools. I would like to think that the labors some of us began more than three decades ago have indeed borne some good fruits.

Still, we have at best only just begun. Much, although surely not all, of the new growth of interest in theology and nature appears to be superficially rooted. I hope that the story this book tells, gleaned from those many years in the field, will serve to strengthen some of this new growth, where it is promising. At the same time, insofar as some of the new growth is not so promising, I hope that this volume will help with the weeding-out process.

I want to thank many people for their encouragement over these thirty years. I have learned a great deal from those who have taken the trouble to listen to the theological explorations that have, in a subsequently revised form, come to expression here. I have also learned much from the coworkers involved in the process of developing social statements on the environment first for the Lutheran Church in America (1972) and then for the Evangelical Lutheran Church in America (1993). I cannot begin to express the debt of gratitude I owe to my wife, Laurel, and to the members of the congregation I now serve, Trinity Lutheran Church, in Akron, Ohio, for their willingness to grant me time for my mind to labor, and often to wander, in this field.

This book is dedicated to my mother and in memory of my father, with profound gratitude. They led me into the liturgy of the church of Jesus Christ, and thenceforth into the liturgy of the cosmos. They taught me to appreciate the variegated beauties of fabricated nature, to love the disciplines of cultivating nature, and to stand in awe of the wilderness, all with a heart full of praise. They also instilled in my soul, at an early age, a tenacious sense of fairness, which led, I am now certain, to my preoccupation with social justice, as well as with nature.

The cover of this volume is graced with one of the great paintings of the nineteenth century, Vincent van Gogh's *Crows over the Wheatfield* (1890), completed just a few weeks before his suicide. While many interpreters of this majestic creation see a profusion of sinister meanings, especially in the images of the crows, I am convinced that Kathleen Powers Erickson's reading of the painting is at once the most compelling and the most revealing.[1] She points out that the painting consists of four major symbolic elements, wheat, crows, roads, and sky. "The roads," she observes, "weaving their way through the wheat, serve as symbols of the journey of life, while the wheat itself symbolizes renewal and rebirth in the cycle of life. The wheat is also a subtle reference to the divine presence, as it has been traditionally symbolic of the purest of Christian sacraments, the Eucharist." Even the crows, she suggests, by no means must be read nihilistically, as numerous critics have done. On the contrary, in van Gogh's work, crows are associated with the images of planting and harvesting wheat, allowing him to tie in "the religious connotation of the Eucharist as it recalls the death and resurrection of the Lord." Further, "the vast, turbulent skies of deep royal blue, which occupy almost half of the compositional space of the painting, are symbolic of the infinite, the ultimate goal of the artist's pilgrimage." In sum: "In the totality of its images, van Gogh's painting of crows flying among a field of golden wheat, over a series of country roads, under a mysterious indigo sky, is not a painting of psychological deterioration, but a work depicting the journey of life, with the hope of ultimate rebirth." The wheat, the crows, the roads, and the sky, I believe, forged into a transcendental unity by van Gogh's visionary hand, tell a story dramatically and visually that I seek to tell theologically and narratively, and much more modestly, in *Nature Reborn*.

Chapter 1

Revising the Classical Christian Story

The Theological Challenge before Us

*"We know that the whole creation has been groaning
in travail together until now." (Rom. 8:22)*

The Emerging Awareness of an Emergent Crisis:
Environmental Degradations and Cosmic Anxieties

When, on January 2, 1989, *Time* magazine refused to name any person Man
of the Year and instead named "Endangered Earth" as its Planet of the Year,
an anxiety surfaced for all to see that had been stirring in the American soul
for at least two decades. But this time it appeared that that anxiety had at
last become a permanent fixture in the consciousness of the nation.

The anxiety had surfaced earlier, amid the turbulent movements of the
1960s, coming to its first major cultural expression on Earth Day 1970. But
with the counterculture of the sixties waning, the interest in ecology and
the concern about the global environmental crisis waned, too. In the minds
of many, accordingly, the ecology movement was to be remembered only as
an interesting cultural phenomenon, even as a fad, alongside the Wood-
stock experience and popularizing testaments such as Charles Reich's *The
Greening of America.*[1]

Then the era of the 1970s and the 1980s was upon us, championed by
a Secretary of the Interior, James Watt, who in the name of Christian eschatology called for increased, not decreased, exploitation of nature, for the
sake of economic growth and profits. Culturally, these decades also witnessed a dissipation of the nation's moral ethos: the public sanctioning and
the domestic celebration of a hedonistic narcissism.[2] In the name of

1

national aggrandizement and creature comforts, the zealous exploitation of nature came to be a kind of national pastime, as it had been in earlier eras in American history when the spirit of unbridled greed had driven the nation into the allegedly beckoning arms of the great frontier.

But the anxiety that we are indeed living on an endangered earth, as *Time* proclaimed, and as cautious scholars and angry critics kept reminding the nation throughout the '70s and '80s, could not be forever repressed. Now, with the uncertain prospect of the new millennium much on our minds, it appears that that anxiety has indeed taken deep root, appropriately so, in the soul of the nation.

We *do* live on an endangered earth, as the distinguished professor of international law Richard Falk already argued in his 1971 study *Our Endangered Planet: Prospects and Proposals for Survival.*[3] Today, however, the prospects for human survival—which we should always take to mean *humane* survival of our species, a world that can reasonably promise some justice and some peace for all peoples, not merely a marginal biological existence for the masses—are much less cheering than they were in 1971. The circumstances surrounding these prospects have been documented in sobering detail by the yearly *State of the World* studies issued by the Worldwatch Institute.[4] It was also reflected in the somber mood at the 1992 United Nations Conference on the Environment in Rio.

Some popular pundits in the United States daily announce that the idea of a global environmental crisis is a fraud perpetrated by leftists. And a few environmental scientists produce a variety of books (frequently given extensive public exposure by the same pundits) that attempt to show that the notion of a global environmental crisis is confusing at best and misconstrued at worst. But the large majority of scientists *who publish their findings in refereed scholarly journals around the world* generally share the somber mood of the Rio conference and generally agree with the tenor and the substance of the findings summarized yearly by the Worldwatch Institute.

Some serious students of our global culture and its impact on the biosphere give us perhaps three decades before certain devastating environmental disruptions will become irreversible. They point to the much discussed and sometimes hotly debated "Greenhouse Effect," the warming of our atmosphere. They highlight continuing population growth, especially in the Two-Thirds World. They document the constant wasting of the planet's forest and soil resources, the global despoiling of water and air resources, the accelerated exhaustion of fossil-fuel resources, and the volatility of the relationships between the nations (and ethnic groups within nations), an increasing number of which are gaining the capability of waging thermonuclear warfare. The sociopolitical dynamics of the global environmental crisis, which prophets in the 1960s announced as the premier ethical challenge of our time, and which the high priests of the 1970s and 1980s denounced as a weak-kneed liberal idea, have apparently in this decade taken the human species as a whole—although not yet, it appears, the affluent elites who control most of the world's wealth—to the brink of radical environmental and social decline. Something is wrong, perhaps fatally wrong, with the way we human beings are living on the earth.

The causes for this crisis are complex and manifold, and widely discussed and debated. But behind it all surely lies what one pioneering church statement aptly called "the human crisis in ecology,"[5] namely, *a crisis in values.* That it has been permissible and even laudable for humans to exploit nature for their own ends, with little or no concern for their own ecological well-being, not to speak of the ecological well-being of future generations or of the natural systems themselves, has been a foundational assumption of modern Western society. Call this the spirit of domination.

This spirit has been described by a variety of historians and social critics. It is predicated on a profound alienation from nature. It is driven by a number of widely shared myths that have shaped both individual actions and social policy, whether socialist or capitalist, in the modern West: (1) the world of nature has no value in itself; it is a world of "mere things"; (2) the world of nature is given to us humans, either by evolutionary accident or by divine purpose, to exploit for our own projects, regardless of the toll such exploitation might take on natural systems themselves; (3) humans can in fact control and manage nature for the sake of virtually any project, in virtue of the understandings forged by the natural sciences and with the assistance of the immense and always progressive powers of modern technology. Nature in the modern West has been frequently regarded merely as "the means of production," given to humans to "conquer" at will. Nature has been widely regarded and treated—*dominated*—as a world of worthless things, even as "the enemy."

True, a whole range of prophetic voices have spoken against this spirit of domination. Throughout much of the modern period, romantic visionaries like Henry David Thoreau and John Muir in the nineteenth century, and ecological thinkers such as Aldo Leopold and Loren Eiseley in the twentieth, took strong and passionate issue with these myths of modernity, as have many other social critics, philosophers, and poets. Some theologians also addressed these issues critically. The whole modern project of domination was diagnosed profoundly, and with particular reference to the desecration of nature, by theologian Paul Tillich, as his essay "Nature and

Sacrament" shows.[6] But such voices did little to change the course or inhibit the power of the spirit of domination. Hence a deep-seated alienation from nature has remained a pervasive cultural force in the modern West.

In recent years, this alienation, mostly presupposed or unconsciously assumed during much of the modern period, has become more and more a matter of conscious awareness, witness the 1989 *Time* magazine cover article. By the end of the twentieth century, moreover, nature had even become in the public mind, more and more consciously, a *negative* force, surely in most developed countries: a huge and, so it is often perceived, mindless enemy that seems to be lashing out against human civilization. This is because natural systems have rebounded, rather like an abused child who in turn becomes abusive in relationships with others. The ecologist David Orr, and others, have described this fear of nature as "biophobia":

> The manifestation of biophobia, explicit in the urge to control nature, has led to a world in which it is becoming easier to be biophobic. Undefiled nature is being replaced by a defiled nature of landfills, junkyards, strip mines, clear-cuts, blighted cities, six-lane freeways, suburban sprawl, polluted rivers, and superfund sites, all of which deserve our phobias. Ozone depletion, meaning more eye cataracts and skin cancer, does give more reason to stay indoors. The spread of toxic substances and radioactivity does mean more disease. The disruption of natural cycles and the introduction of exotic species has [sic] destroyed much of the natural diversity that formerly graced our landscapes. Introduced blights and pests have or are destroying American chestnuts, elms, maples, dogwoods, hemlocks, and ashes. Global warming will degrade the flora and fauna of familiar places. . . . Biophobia sets into motion a vicious cycle that tends to cause people to act in such a way as to undermine the integrity, beauty, and harmony of nature, creating the very conditions that make the dislike of nature yet more probable.[7]

The growing consciousness of this crisis in Eden (Frederick Elder) has then resonated with still deeper cosmic anxieties. In our century, visions of cosmic immensities have shaken the complacent spiritual geocentrism that many had until very recently taken for granted, centuries after the death of Copernicus. Yes, they had known cognitively that the earth was no longer the center of the universe, but many had never really appropriated that knowledge existentially. But that spiritual complacency has now been shaken by highly publicized space probes. Now the visions of incomprehensible cosmic magnitudes—the billions and billions of galaxies—are inescapable. This growing awareness of cosmic infinities and apparent earthly insignificance has had the widespread spiritual effect of undermining, if not totally obliterating, longstanding socially constructed assumptions about the meaningfulness of human life on planet Earth. Given the unspeakable vastness of the cosmos, is human life anything more than an accidental organism riding out its fleeting life on a piece of cosmic dust?[8] Further, is it not possible, perhaps even likely, that some random asteroid or other cosmic body will plummet to earth, destroying life as we know it or wreaking such unimaginable havoc so as to make life not worth living? Such anxieties have been reflected and perhaps heightened by a host of immensely popular films about cosmic monsters and catastrophes.

These anxieties, taken together with perceived ecological threats to our whole earthly habitat, have driven an increasing number of thoughtful souls into a state of quiet cosmic despair. Nothing is safe anymore, it appears, neither the earthly "firmament," which we used to think of as our congenial home, nor the cosmic milieu, which we used to think of as the benign and beautiful scenery that secured and blessed our earthly tranquillity. No wonder that the spirituality of Gnosticism, which feeds on cosmic alienation, and which is fundamentally hostile to the material world, is thriving again in our time.[9] Hence, at the dawn of a new millennium, we are probably best advised to speak not just of a global environmental crisis, but of a crisis in cosmic meaning as well. What was once a proclamation of apostolic faith has become, in our time, a pervasive cultural experience: the sense that the whole creation is groaning in travail.

This, in turn, points to ambiguities in the very language that we use to speak about the crisis the human species is facing today. On the one hand, the crisis before us is very much terrestrial: it has to do with the ravages of human greed and ignorance on the natural systems of planet Earth, and the experienced or feared rebound of those natural systems, in turn, as they ravage human life or threaten to ravage human life, in terms of droughts and floods and plagues and heat waves and the like. On the other hand, the crisis before us has to do with our constantly expanding awareness of the immensities of the cosmos and of the apparent cosmic isolation and cosmic fragility of the human species. The one aspect of the crisis is perhaps most fittingly called ecological, the other cosmic. But they are indeed two aspects of the same crisis. We are probably best advised, therefore, to live with this terminological ambiguity, using the word *ecological* when the interrelatedness with our earthly habitat is most on our minds and the word *cosmic* when the immensities of our universe are the focus of our attention. We should never forget, however, that this is one and the same crisis: our alienation from nature.[10]

An Emerging Theological Response:
Reconstructionists, Apologists, Revisionists

In response to this situation, religious leaders of all persuasions, and in sizable numbers, have begun to address environmental issues and related questions about cosmic meaning in a concerted way. This was nowhere more apparent than at the Rio conference, where representatives from many of the world's religions were a noticeably visible presence. In the United States, especially in the wake of Earth Day 1990, a variety of religious voices have also been raised, in behalf of the environment and questions of cosmic meaning more generally. Among those advocates who speak self-consciously from the perspective of the Christian tradition in North America, we can instructively identify three "schools," although no single writer can easily be so classified.[11]

The *reconstructionists* generally believe that a new edifice of thought must be designed, from the ground up, with new foundations and new categories. These thinkers take it as a given that traditional Christian thought offers no—or few—viable theological resources to help people of faith respond to the ecological crisis and related cosmic anxieties today. Some, such as the various exponents of New Age thinking, have turned away from Western religious traditions with a passion, in favor of the insights they glean from primal and Eastern religions.[12] Typically, these protagonists syncretistically blend mystical and magical materials, such as Taoism from the East, alchemy from the West, or what they think of as a neolithic spirituality which they claim to find in pre-Columbian Native American traditions.

The most illustrious and in many ways the most illustrative of the reconstructionists who address a general audience today is the imaginative ecotheologian Matthew Fox. He draws extensively from mystical traditions in the Christian West, as well as from the spiritualities of primal religions. His thought will occupy our attention in the following chapter.

Other reconstructionists project theological arguments that are primarily based on findings of the natural sciences, enhanced, on occasion, by related philosophical or literary insights.[13] Still others have turned to the insights of feminist thought, often with the intent of breaking away altogether from what they perceive to be the patriarchal tyranny of classical Western theology. Ecofeminists characteristically commit themselves to a radical reconstruction of traditional Christian thought, sometimes to its total deconstruction. They find inspiration, typically, in the insights of primal religious experience, often invoking the name of a newly celebrated mother earth goddess.[14]

But whether the primary perspective be popular New Age thinking, the sophisticated insights of Western or global mystical traditions, the projections of a new scientifically oriented ecotheology, or the imaginative, groundbreaking constructions of ecofeminism, the result for the reconstructionists is generally the same. They consciously or unconsciously reject the classical kerygmatic and dogmatic traditions of Christianity as the primary matrix of theological knowing.

Not unaware of such developments, some defenders of the classical Christian tradition—call them the *apologists*—have sought to underline what they consider to be its positive ecological implications, above all the tradition's encouragement of "good stewardship" of the earth. The apologists have typically defined their discussions of environmental issues with reference to the themes of social justice. Wise management of the resources of the earth for the sake of the people of the earth, especially the poor—"ecojustice"—has been their primary concern. Thus the World Council of Churches (WCC) has called for a "just, participatory, and sustainable society" and has sought to focus the considerable resources of its ecumenical theologians on environmental issues, especially in the context of the great North-South divide between the rich and the poor. These concerns were given a public focus at the 1991 Seventh Assembly of the WCC in Canberra, Australia, when that ecumenical body lifted up the theme "justice, peace, and the integrity of creation," along with the prayer, "Spirit of God Renew the Whole Creation."[15] In addition, a whole range of sometimes highly sophisticated apologetic works have emerged in our time focusing on the theme of theology and science.[16] This kind of theological focus on science in general and scientific cosmology in particular has also been of concern to the international ecumenical community for some time.[17]

But the wide-ranging and imaginative explorations of reconstructionist discourse and the sometimes forceful but often conventional expressions of international ecumenical apologetics are by no means the only theological options available in Christian circles today. Relatively independent of the highly publicized claims of reconstructionist spirituality and the intramurally celebrated (if not always widely promulgated) claims of mainline ecumenical theology, a little noticed yet vigorous tradition of orthodox but innovative theological reflection about environmental and related existential issues has flourished at the edge of the public square, mainly in the United States, since the 1960s. Call this the revisionist tradition.

The *revisionists* have worked mainly within the milieu of classical Christian thought, as defined by the ecumenical creeds and, often, by the confessional theology of the Reformation era and beyond. Since, moreover, the Old and New Testaments are the font of the classical theological tradition in the West, and since these scriptures are taken as the chief norm for all teachers and teachings (*norma normans*) by the tradition itself, the revisionists, as a matter of course, also have given the highest priority to biblical interpretation. At the same time, however, the dynamics of the classical tradition, thus understood, constantly call forth a *re-forming* of the tradition itself, as that term itself historically has suggested. The revisionists have tended to see themselves, accordingly, as latter-day, albeit lowercase, reformers.

This revisionist tradition surfaced publicly at least as early as Joseph Sittler's 1961 address to the World Council of Churches in New Delhi, "Called to Unity."[18] It fell from public sight, by and large, during the 1980s, as did the ecology movement itself, but by no means did it die. Indeed, I believe that we can think of this tradition as the rebirth of nature within classical Christian theology. Call it "nature reborn."

By 1992, it had reached a kind of culminating point for its first three decades. It had come of age with the publication of James A. Nash's masterful study in environmental ethics, *Loving Nature: Ecological Integrity and Christian Responsibility.*[19] Among the several strengths of Nash's study is the author's empathetic familiarity with the revisionist discussion of ecological issues during the preceding thirty years, as well as his thoughtful understanding of the reconstructionist and apologist positions. The book's argument, moreover, is deeply rooted in the classical theological tradition, in particular as that tradition is mediated by the neoorthodox theology of Reinhold Niebuhr.

In recent years, a variety of revisionist studies in the field of theology and science have emerged, perhaps the most noteworthy of these being works by the theologian and physicist John Polkinghorne. He develops the argument of his book, *The Faith of a Physicist: Reflections of a Bottom-Up Thinker*, The Gifford Lectures for 1993–94, as a commentary on the Nicene Creed.[20] Also in the 1990s, signs that scholarly biblical exegesis had taken a major turn in the direction of affirming creation-history as the primary biblical "horizon," not just human redemption-history, were also in evidence. These revisionist trends came to their most insightful expression in North America in the programmatic exegetical essay by the Old Testament scholar Terrence Fretheim, "The Reclamation of Creation: Redemption and Law in Exodus," published in 1991.[21]

This reemergence of creation-theology in biblical studies was paralleled, and partially sustained, in recent decades by a more general expansion of scholarly interest in the biblical theology of wisdom, both in the Old and the New Testaments.[22] That interest, in turn, helped set the stage for new developments in theological reflection about nature. The most forceful and focused expression of the latter trend, firmly rooted in biblical exegesis, on the one hand, and in classical christological and trinitarian theology, on the other hand, was the 1995 study by the Australian Catholic theologian, Denis Edwards, *Jesus and the Wisdom of God: An Ecological Theology.*[23] We can think of Edwards's work as the emergence of a neo-Catholic revisionism in ecological theology. Edwards picked up and developed many of the themes that preoccupied Joseph Sittler thirty years before. As far as Edwards is concerned, however, his own theological heritage is rooted more self-consciously in the thought of one of the preeminent Catholic thinkers of the last century, Karl Rahner.

I would identify my own work in the theology of nature with that orthodox but innovative revisionist tradition, which stands over against the sometimes heterodox religious expressions of the reconstructionist position, on the one hand, and the often thoughtful, but typically conventional traditionalism of modern ecumenical theology, on the other.[24] The emergence of the global environmental crisis in our time, and the existential crisis that has accompanied it, has driven those of us who are revisionists back to the sources of the theological tradition, especially to the Scriptures and to certain premodern Christian thinkers, such as Irenaeus and Augustine, Luther and Calvin, and in the process we have discovered hidden ecological and cosmic riches that many modern Christian theologians mostly neglected.[25] We have wanted not to abandon or defend the classical theological tradition, but to *reclaim* it, and then to *reenvision* it, for the purpose of serving the worship, the teaching, and the public witness of the church in our own time of global environmental and existential crisis.[26]

But how to get from there to here, from the rediscovery of what the theological tradition has had to say, to the appropriation of the insights of the tradition as our own?

The ecologically and cosmically rich thought of traditional Christianity—*not* those strains in the tradition that have been essentially *un*ecological and sometimes *a*cosmic, which have been especially dominant in the modern period[27]—must be reformulated in the context of our own cultural situation and in our own public language, so that we can indeed make it our own, both practically and reflectively.[28] That is the challenge addressed by this book: to revise the classical Christian story to identify and to celebrate its ecological and its cosmic promise.[29]

The argument of this book corresponds to its purpose. As a revisionist theological project, the argument that follows is deliberately and self-consciously *circular.* It presupposes the faith of the classical Christian story at the center, sustained and proclaimed by the church in its worship.[30] At the same time, circumferentially, as it were, the argument follows a course that is intended to illuminate that center from several interconnected vantage points.[31] Owing to said interconnectedness, a number of themes will be touched on repeatedly, at various points along the way. But this will, I hope, serve my purpose of illuminating the center as clearly as possible within the compass of a single volume.

As the argument begins to unfold, in chapter 2, I seek to *reclaim* the classical Christian story historically, in its ecological and cosmic fullness, from the hands of its theological critics, focusing mainly on the work of theologian Matthew Fox. With the story thus reclaimed, I explore in chapter 3 some of the biblical roots of the story, in an effort to *rediscover* the ecological and cosmic breadth and depth of the biblical witness over against the anthropocentric bias of much traditional biblical interpretation, an essential operation for any theological revisionist. Then, in chapter 4, appropriating the visionary christocentric and cosmic schema of the theologian and paleontologist Pierre Teilhard de Chardin, and reshaping that schema along the way in order to overcome his anthropocentrism, I attempt to *retell* the classical Christian story narratively. Chapters 5 and 6 address the formative existential matrix of the story, without which the meaning of the story cannot be fully understood. In conversation with the eminent Jewish philosopher Martin Buber, and in response to the Gothic spirit in the West, I describe what it can mean to *reenvision* the story interpersonally and then to *reenact* the story ritually. Chapter 7 explores the meaning of the classical Christian story spiritually, drawing on the witness of the classical Celtic saints, in order to describe what it means to *reexperience* the story.

The circumferential process of reclaiming, rediscovering, retelling, reenvisioning, reenacting, and reexperiencing the classical Christian story brings me full circle to a discussion of *reliving* the story ethically, in chapter 8. These concluding explorations I project in the form of a personal testament of nature reborn.

The Emergence of a New Theological Paradigm: The Legacy of "the Lynn White Thesis"

But readers should beware, particularly those who are here encountering revisionist thinking for the first time. The theological paradigm many Christians have presupposed in one way or another for the last five centuries is changing. It is expanding, as a matter of fact. This is an insight many of the apologists have yet to grasp and most of the reconstructionists simply have taken for granted, without self-consciously exploring its historic significance. But any theology of nature projected from a revisionist perspective must presuppose more than a passing acquaintance with the new paradigm. For any revisionist theology of nature, indeed, this is the heart of the matter.

Because the very idea of any new paradigm is illusive—witness the complexities of the discussions that have followed the publication of what is perhaps the single most influential work on the topic, Thomas Kuhn's *The Structure of Scientific Revolutions*[32]—it probably is best to approach the matter historically. We can do this instructively, by reviewing the response to what must be ranked one of the most important formative essays in ecological theology in the last century, first delivered as a lecture by the historian Lynn White Jr., in 1966.[33] In that lecture, the then relatively unheralded historian took Christian theology to task for, he alleged, helping to cause and continuing to fuel the global environmental crisis.

The impact of White's lecture, "The Historical Roots of Our Ecologic Crisis,"[34] has been enormous. It calls to mind the influence of Martin Luther's "95 Theses," posted in 1517. While White was no Luther and the ecology movement then emergent in the 1960s was no Reformation, the discussion generated by White's modest talk has still not run its course more than thirty years later. The lecture has been reprinted in numerous volumes and continues to be cited wherever environmental and related theological issues are discussed. White's essay took on a kind of scriptural aura for the proponents of the ecology movement in the 1970s once it had been published in the first major manifesto of that movement, *The Environmental Handbook*.[35] White's essay was almost immediately greeted with sharp criticism and even some derision, however, by a number of scholars and popular church writers, preeminently by the apologist Thomas Derr several years later.[36] "The Lynn White Thesis" became, overnight, a cultural and theological event of some magnitude.

White began his lecture by calling for a clarification of the presuppositions that underlie modern science and technology. These cultural forces, he observed, are profoundly rooted in the values of Western culture, values that have been shaped by the Christian tradition. White maintained that exploitative attitudes toward nature surfaced widely during the Middle Ages and were encouraged and supported by the anthropocentric bent of the dominant theology of the time. He also argued that those theologically informed attitudes continue to shape our culture, however much we may have entered an era of self-conscious secularism. "Modern science is an extrapolation of natural theology," he argued, while modern technology "is at least partly to be explained as an Occidental, voluntarist realization of the Christian dogma of [human] transcendence of, and rightful mastery over, nature." If, therefore, modern science and technology are the cultural forces that have led us into the environmental crisis, then—and this phase is regularly quoted both by White's protagonists and by his critics—"Christianity bears a huge burden of guilt" for that crisis.

In White's view, it followed that if we are to confront the ecological threats of our time in an effective way, we will have to do something about the religious underpinnings of science and technology. At the end of his lecture, White therefore turned to the task of theological revision. He identified St. Francis as a "patron saint for ecologists," because Francis "tried to depose [humans from their] monarchy over creation and set up a democracy of all God's creatures." Francis's sense of solidarity with the whole creation, White suggested, can help us to discover the new values we need, which will allow us, in turn, to set aside the sometimes rapacious attitudes toward nature that inform the machinations of modern Western society.

Historically speaking, White's thesis is surely open to criticism from a number of vantage points.[37] The idea that the Christian faith could play such a singular role in "causing" the environmental crisis is surely suspect, especially given the fact that there is plentiful evidence that other cultures—shaped by other religions—also exploited nature, sometimes dramatically. Also, the most pervasive policies and practices of exploiting nature occurred in the modern era, when society at large, in the wake of the Enlightenment and developing industrialism, had already self-consciously *rejected* what Paul Tillich called the theonomous moral ethos of the premodern Christian tradition in the West, in the name of autonomous individualism and autonomous capitalism. These essentially secular forces in turn brought with them a flourishing of the spirit of domination in the modern era, for which Tillich used the term *heteronomy*. A case can readily be made that modern secularism, not traditional Christian faith, has been the major "cause" of the environmental crisis. But historical corrections of White's argument themselves do not yet take us to the most interesting aspect of his argument and its impact. For that, we must probe some of the critics' responses to White more deeply.

As we consider the attacks on White's argument by theologians in particular, we can note a certain emotional surcharge in many instances, even a tonality of vehemence. At the end of his otherwise thoughtful critique, for example, apologist Thomas Derr asserts that White, following the way of "paganism, authoritarianism, and brutality," is verging on the edge of proposing some "final solution" for humanity, according to which the numbers of humans on the planet would have to be reduced (killed?) in order to preserve the life of other species.[38] As Derr's passionate words suggest, it is not White's historical *descriptions* that most offend some of his critics, but his ethical *prescriptions*. By taking the side of St. Francis, by becoming the advocate of the whales and the birds, the mountains and the plains, the rivers and the oceans,

White was in effect lending support—so Derr reads him—to a whole range of serious thinkers and popularly celebrated prophets who want to defend "the rights of nature." And that theme, at least on first hearing, can sound profoundly misanthropic. Should we now try to save the whales and forget about the starving children? White's most ardent critics ask.[39]

This is the point at which we can see signs of the emerging paradigm shift, suggested explicitly, twenty-five years after White's lecture, by the title of Nash's major study, *Loving Nature.* In addition to everything else he may or may not have suggested, White was affirming that it is legitimate and also necessary to think theologically about loving nature as well as loving humanity. That is a new direction for modern Christian thought, which typically focused mainly on God and humanity and the bond of divine love between them as the chief theological data of theological reflection.[40] White's implication was indeed that the fundamental data for theological reflection have changed. This then is the new paradigm for theological reflection: the elliptical gives way to the triangular. The theology of two focal points gives way to the theology of three. The paradigm of God and humanity gives way to the paradigm of God, humanity, *and* nature, bonded together by the love of God. This, in turn, also explains the emotional surcharge that accompanies Derr's rejection of the White thesis, particularly as a prescriptive statement. Vehement rejection of new paradigms by the defenders of the old is to be expected, as Thomas Kuhn taught us to anticipate.

The significance of White's thesis, in this paradigmatic sense, can be set in clear relief if we read it as an expression of that Western prophetic tradition that has identified and criticized what I have already referred to as "the spirit of domination," only now read not just with regard to the environment in particular but more generally, functionally understood, as *structures of domination in the social order.* These structures can be viewed as the social expression of human sinfulness, as Reinhold Niebuhr interpreted them in *Moral Man and Immoral Society* in 1932. Throughout history, the structures of domination—which might be thought of in biblical language as the principalities and powers of this age—have supported the degradation of the powerless (slavery, child labor), the subtle and not-so-subtle practices of the genocidal mind (anti-Semitism), and the objectification of women (the "rape culture").[41] They have also undergirded the systematic exploitation of nature—the rape of the earth.

In response to these structures, the witness of the Church throughout the ages has typically been ambiguous, beginning with St. Paul himself. His fundamental faith commitments did prompt him to be opposed to the structures of domination, in the name of the love of God, mediated in Christ Jesus. This was Paul's faith, most fundamentally and most succinctly expressed in Gal. 3:28: "There is neither Jew nor Greek, there is neither slave nor free; there is neither male nor female; for you are all one in Christ Jesus."

Still, as Krister Stendahl pointed out many years ago, Paul did not consistently pursue the theological agenda he voiced in Gal. 3:28. Rather, he devoted most of his own attention to dealing with the first polarity, Jews and Gentiles.[42] Although Paul's faith in Christ's mission of love claimed other relationships, Paul never really allowed his core convictions to fully shape his articulations in those areas, as he did when he was dealing with the tensions between Jews and Gentiles. Indeed, some of Paul's comments about slaves or women sound rather traditional, even reactionary, and do not measure up to the Gal. 3:28 statement of his core convictions. It was only centuries later that the revolutionary dynamic of Paul's core convictions began to bear fruit in Christian opposition both to slavery and to the systematic exploitation of women.

Then there is the still more encompassing Pauline hope for the salvation of all the creatures of nature, along with the salvation of the whole of humanity: "For the creation waits with eager longing for the revealing of the children of God; . . . the creation itself will be set free from its bondage to decay and obtain the glorious liberty of the children of God" (Rom. 8:19-21). This utterance, like Galatians 3:28, is one of the linchpins of Paul's theology, as J. Christiaan Beker has demonstrated.[43] Beker holds that the theme of justification by faith, which has so dominated Protestant exegesis of Romans, is in fact central in Paul's theology, but only in the context of Paul's apocalyptic vision of "the triumph of God." That vision is finally theocentric, Beker shows, not anthropocentric. It points to the final outcome of the work of Christ in terms not unlike those taken for granted by the Book of Revelation: a transfigured world of glory, a New Jerusalem set in the context of new heavens and a new earth. That will be the day, in Paul's terms, when God will be "all in all" (1 Cor. 15:28).

The same motif appears in another distinct but related Pauline context, the Letter to the Colossians. The key text here is Col. 1:15ff., first brought to public ecumenical attention in our era by Joseph Sittler and much debated in recent decades. We will have occasion to return to it repeatedly in the ensuing explorations. Polemics apart, the words of the text—whether written by Paul, a Pauline redactor, a disciple of Paul, or some anonymous hymn writer(s)—undoubtedly state that Christ reconciles "all things," that his death inaugurates a cosmic peace. This sounds very much like the Hebraic-apocalyptic cosmic message of Rom. 8:19-21, only now expressed in the nonapocalyptic, syncretistic context of Hellenistic culture.

We can, in any case, legitimately view Paul's affirmations about the salvation of the whole creation in Rom. 8:19-21 as extensions of the core beliefs he announces in Gal. 3:28. Paul's was a universalizing gospel: it extended to the Gentiles as well as to the Jews, to slaves as well as free persons, to women as well as men, to the creatures of nature as well as human creatures. Those, in sum, were his core beliefs.

Strikingly, each of the dimensions of the love of God in Christ that Paul depicts in Gal. 3:28 had to be identified and defended with great effort against the protagonists of the received theological tradition. Paul himself valiantly and successfully struggled with the likes of Peter to make sure that the Gentiles were included within the scope of salvation. But it was left to later generations of Christians—generations well into the modern era, notwithstanding the witness of more or less solitary voices throughout the centuries—to reclaim the core convictions of Paul regarding the other polarities, slaves and free persons, women and men, abolitionists against defenders of slavery, feminists against defenders of patriarchy.

Ours is the day, it now appears, when the last extension of the Pauline vision of universal salvation, given voice in Romans 8—the inclusion of all the creatures of nature—is coming to the fore throughout the church, building on biblical and premodern Christian traditions that were given most dramatic expression along the way by witnesses such as St. Francis. Many voices within the church today are finally beginning to be raised on behalf of all the voiceless creatures of nature.[44] Is it any wonder, then, given this paradigm shift, that there should be passionate opposition to these new affirmations of the scope of God's love, as there were impassioned expressions of opposition, in earlier times, to extending understanding of the scope of God's love to Gentiles, slaves, and women?

Hence, although White raised a number of sharp historical questions about the Christian faith's historic impact on the world of nature, it now appears that the deepest significance of the Lynn White thesis lies not so much in what it describes as in what it prescribes or envisions: the end of theological legitimization of any structure of domination; the challenging of all master-slave relationships; the final inclusion of nature within the realm of grace; and the normative vindication of St. Francis and his life story.

The legacy of the Lynn White thesis is therefore primarily this: the disclosure of a new paradigm for theological thought about nature, extending our understanding of the love of God to nature. According to this new paradigm, nature is now a fundamental datum for theological reflection, along with God and humanity, no longer a matter of secondary or merely instrumental importance. This is the new paradigm that the following revisionist reflections about the theology of nature will constantly presuppose.

Chapter 2

Reclaiming the Story Historically

Beyond the Ecological Critique

"For in him all the fullness of God was pleased to dwell, and through him God was pleased to reconcile to himself all things, whether on earth or in heaven, by making peace through the blood of his cross." (Col. 1:19-20)

When Henry David Thoreau established his residence in Walden more than a century ago, he made a mythic statement that has echoed through American cultural and religious history ever since. Broadcast by popularizers such as the nineteenth-century champion of the American wilderness John Muir, and reinforced in our own time by the voices of many sensitive souls who stand in dread before the face of our global ecological crisis, that Thoreauvian echo has now become an uproar.[1]

What we hear, from many different places, is this: Christianity is ecologically bankrupt.[2] Christianity is predicated on a profound bias against the earth. Christianity heats up history over against nature. Christianity may not have caused the modern environmental crisis, as some believe, but to invoke its traditions in our situation of ecological crisis would be like trying to put out a fire by reaching for the kerosene. Particularly in its Protestant expressions in America, Christianity has, since the time of the Puritans, espoused a doctrine of human dominion over nature in a way that has left it thoroughly identified with those cultural and economic forces that have themselves fueled the fire of the ecological crisis, above all the philosophy of mechanism and the spirit of capitalism.

Today's situation of global ecological crisis, we are told, requires something else. It requires a religious worldview that cools down history, that shows us how to commune with rather than to dominate the earth. It requires us to be tutored by eccentric teachers such as Henry David Thoreau and John Muir, or by indigenous interpreters of primal religions who have kept alive a profound sense for the healing powers of nature. Better, then, repair to the cooling milieu of some Walden or the high sierra, where the experience of communion with nature is still alive, and begin to construct our religious worldview all over again.

In fact, however, our theological situation today is much more complex than advocates of the Thoreauvian vision generally seem to realize. It is one thing to set aside the anthropocentric and androcentric excesses of the kerygmatic and dogmatic traditions of Christianity. It is another thing to set aside fundamental elements of those traditions altogether, as some of these advocates appear to be doing, either consciously or by default.

We should at least realize what we may be losing if we decide to follow the shamans of the primal religious traditions or their fellow travelers, such as Thoreau and Muir. Indeed, it may be the case that the kerygmatic and dogmatic traditions of the Christian story are better equipped to guide the faithful in this ecological and cosmic era than the much-heralded primal religious traditions themselves. A much-neglected biblical text—the illusive Pauline witness in Colossians to the blood of the cross as God's way of making peace with all things—could be just what this generation, with its deep alienation from nature, urgently needs to hear.

But no one can legitimately entertain such thoughts in our time without taking into account the critique of classical Christian thought mounted by the reconstructionist theologian Matthew Fox, and the "creation spirituality" he advocates as a new, more ecologically viable form of Christian theology for our time. He is the most illustrious and the most illustrative spokesperson for the primal traditions and for Western mystical traditions in contemporary American theology. As such, he has lifted up what James Nash has called "the ecological complaint against Christianity" with an analytic consistency and a positive passion that are unequaled by any other theologian.[3]

We must address the critical theology of thinkers like Fox if we are to reclaim the classical Christian story historically. Left unaddressed, the charge that the classical Christian story is ecologically bankrupt will surely carry the day. Anecdotal evidence already suggests that in many respects, especially in college and university circles today, where the teachers who will teach our young are taught, and where the critical theology of Matthew Fox is often highly regarded, the claim that Christianity is ecologically bankrupt is widely assumed to be a self-evident fact.

The Critical Theology of Matthew Fox

Matthew Fox writes in a context entirely different from Thoreau's, but with a strikingly similar outcome.[4] The issue is no longer the artificiality of European culture and its denials of individual freedom. Now the issue is the perniciousness of what Fox calls the fall-redemption theology of the Christian West, and the possible destruction of the human species by environmental catastrophe or thermonuclear holocaust if the influence of that fall-redemption theology continues to hold sway.

The original sin, as Fox sees the matter, is for all intents and purposes the traditional Christian doctrine of original sin itself, as that doctrine has allegedly shaped the history of Western culture. In this sense, for Fox, a bad idea—theological dualism—is the root of all evil, rather than bad institutions, as Thoreau assumed. So Fox writes:

> I believe that an exaggerated doctrine of original sin, one that is employed as a starting point for spirituality, plays kindly into the hands of empire-builders, slave masters, and patriarchal society in general. It divides and thereby conquers, pitting one's thoughts against ones feelings, one's body against one's personal needs, people against earth, animals, and nature in general. By doing this it so convolutes people, so confuses and preoccupies them, that deeper questions about community; justice, and celebration never come to the fore.[5]

The perpetrator of this bad idea, in Fox's view, was St. Augustine, who, allegedly, had no positive regard for nature, whose thought from beginning to end was, allegedly, rife with sexual dualism and with an otherworldly, spiritualizing understanding of the world to come, that is, "last things" (eschatology).

Fox proposes to sweep away the dominance of this allegedly pernicious fall-redemption theology and to put in its place something else: a theology of original blessing and a theology of the coming Cosmic Christ. Fox wants to return, as it were, to the era of the garden, before the fall, much as Thoreau sought to establish the world of a New Adam at the edge of the wilderness, prior to the inroads and the corruptions of European civilization.

In this context, Fox believes, we can discover a new understanding of Jesus Christ. We can now encounter Christ as the eternal ground of creation, as the Cosmic Christ or Cosmic Wisdom.[6] Jesus Christ, in this sense, for Fox, is more the mystical, life-giving metaphysical source of all things than the particular historical person born in Bethlehem some 2000 years ago. As Fox explains his theological agenda: "What is needed . . . is a spiritual vision that prays, celebrates, and lives out the reality of the Cosmic Christ who lives and breathes in Jesus and in all God's children, in all the prophets of religion everywhere, in all the creatures of the universe."[7] Fox thus seeks to strip away what he considers to be the false theological constructions of so-called fall-redemption theology, in order to reveal the original blessings of God in the created order, through the marvelous activity and wondrous manifestations of the eternal Logos of God.

Note that the particular saving function of Jesus of Nazareth in this schema is to serve as the revealer or the teacher or the exemplar. Call this a *Christus Exemplar* understanding of salvation (soteriology). Jesus of Nazareth's role, as the mediator of salvation, is to reveal the universal functioning of the Cosmic Christ, manifest and operative, at all times and in all places, and in so doing to call us all to a greater awareness of the workings of the Cosmic Christ everywhere.

Thus Fox characteristically describes the role of Jesus in the Eucharist: "Like wisdom, the perfect hostess (Prov. 91, 92), he reveals in a banquet context the mysteries of our origin and of God."[8] Jesus, for Fox, is primarily understood as the New Adam,[9] who functions as "a poet, a storyteller, and artist," a kind of shaman figure who serves as "an awakener to the sacrament of the cosmos."[10] The cross of Jesus, accordingly, is seen by Fox, in the tradition of the medieval theologian Peter Abelard, mainly as a symbol of self-giving, as a revelation of the process that all the faithful must go through.[11] The historical Jesus remains mainly "a model and a teacher of letting go."[12]

And more: for Fox, the historical Jesus, revealer of the Cosmic Christ or Cosmic Wisdom, discloses to us, as we follow in his footsteps, that *we are also divine*, born of God, as Jesus of Nazareth himself was. In this way, Fox suggests, we "awake to our divinity."[13] Jesus' divinity, in this sense, is the prototype and exemplar of our own divinity.

As we thus awake to our divinity, according to Fox, our eyes are also opened and we see God in all things. Like St. Francis, Fox insists, as we are aware of our divinity we can lead an "enchanted existence," which is our salvation. Or, as Fox quotes the mystic Meister Eckhart: "This then is salvation: to marvel at the beauty of created things and praise the beautiful providence of their Creator."[14]

It goes virtually without saying, moreover, that this theology of original blessing must be in emphasis, if not totally in content, a theology of a *realized* eschatology, not a theology of "the last things"(*ta eschata*) yet to come. What else could Fox's theology be, since he predicates everything on his vision of cosmic origins, "first things" (protology). So Fox claims that the final fulfillment is *here and now.* God *is* "all in all."[15] This is to be contrasted with St. Paul's future reference to the final fulfillment: God *will* be "all in all" (1 Cor. 15:28). Fox reads Jesus' proclamation of the reign of God in much the same way: Jesus' theology was not a proclamation of a future redemption for the world, but "a kingdom come theology, a proclaiming of Good News and even Better News than creation had ever heard before, the news that humanity could, after all, learn here and now to enjoy creation rightly."[16]

On the basis of such mystical intuitions, Fox anticipates the dawning of a global renaissance in our time, as the subtitle of his book *The Coming of the Cosmic Christ* indicates: *The Healing of Mother Earth and the Birth of a Global Renaissance.*[17] This kind of anticipation is not unlike the speculations of the medieval visionary Joachim of Fiore, who projected a new age of the Spirit, when the sacramental ordinances of the church would no longer be the singular mediators of salvation. Accordingly, Fox envisions the emergence of an ever-increasing number of mystics and artists, shamans and gardeners, dancers and lovers around the globe, harbingers of the new age. Such individuals themselves will be exemplars of the Exemplar, Jesus Christ.

For Fox as for Joachim, a new kind of universal priesthood will emerge to initiate this global renaissance. "The creation tradition," Fox explains, "is essentially nonclerical because it recognizes existence, life itself, as the primary sacrament. This sacrament requires awareness and wakefulness, not ordination, to bring about its proper distribution and to elicit the sacrament from children and adults, workers, artists, lovers, citizens."[18] To this end, as a prescription for spiritual growth, Fox lifts up the fabled image of the noble savage, not unlike Thoreau's prescription of a Walden-immersion experience for all, or Muir's prescription of wilderness wandering for all. "Sweat lodges," Fox concludes, "ought to become a regular feature on the campus of every high school, college, and university, as well as every seminary, church, and synagogue."[19]

The Limits of Matthew Fox's Critical Theology

Fox's critique of some of the spiritualizing, anthropocentric excesses of the received theology of the Christian West is telling, in many respects. Likewise for his rejection of the theological tradition's patriarchal excesses and its marked rejection, on occasion, of creation spirituality. His explorations of the traditions of creation spirituality in the Christian West, moreover, particularly among the mystics, are also suggestive, and serve as a corrective to those readings of the Christian story that focus on kerygmatic and dogmatic motifs alone.

But Fox's critical theology also brings with it some serious liabilities. His approach resonates all too disquietingly with the anti-urban, romantic individualism of the Thoreauvian tradition. When all is said and done, Fox leaves us in the sweat lodge. His thought is not fundamentally at home in urban America. We can see this deficiency from the vantage point of any inner-city neighborhood.

Consider, for example, the world of Asylum Hill, located in Hartford, Connecticut, one of the innumerable inner-city neighborhoods that might be instanced here. What Good News does Fox's mystical theology really offer Asylum Hill? What does Fox have to say to the welfare mother in Asylum Hill who falls short on every initiative she conscientiously undertakes to better her life and the well-being of her family? What word of hope does he have to speak to the prospective teenage mother in Asylum Hill, who unknowingly awaits the ravages of an infant mortality rate that is higher than some Third World countries? What does he have to say to the unemployed, alienated African American males who hang out on the streets, not a few of them suffering from the delayed stress syndrome of the Vietnam War?

The message of Fox may speak to an elite, largely affluent few. What does it have to say to the impoverished urban masses around the globe, who must struggle every day for their sustenance, often against overwhelming odds? What does it say to a global society that is increasingly urban, for better or for worse?

It appears, regrettably, that Matthew Fox's strategy is to shoot the bearers of the bad news, in this case the theologians of the so-called fall-redemption tradition, such as Augustine. Soberingly, however, the real problem is not a bad idea, namely original sin, and its influence. The real problem is rather the finally undeniable reality of radical evil itself, to which the doctrine of original sin, in various ways, has historically—and sometimes inadequately—borne witness.[20]

Few among the masses who live in the Asylum Hills of this globe, most of whose citizens are impoverished and powerless, would for a moment deny the reality of radical evil. Only those intellectuals who live some distance from the streets would even feel called upon to have to argue the issue, pointing to Dachau and Buchenwald, Hiroshima and Nagasaki, apartheid and genocide, raping and battering, the millions of malnourished and starving children around the world, and the threat of global nuclear or environmental catastrophe.

Nor would it take a Martin Luther to convince the powerless and impoverished residents of these neighborhoods of the bondage of the will or the reign of the principalities and powers of death and destruction in this world. It all may look different from the bosom of some Walden or from the heights of the sierra, but radical evil looks starkly real and starkly inescapable for most of those who ply the streets of the Asylum Hills of this world. The problem is not the idea of original sin; the problem is the fact of original sin. As Reinhold Niebuhr liked to say, this would seem to be the one Christian belief that is empirically verifiable.

The fact of original sin, as Fox describes it, however, tends to be domesticated. Fox can catalog the works of the demonic in our history, but as he envisions human suffering it tends to be swept up quickly into the experience of cosmic redemption. It tends to become an occasion for mystical participation in the dark side of the cosmos, rather than an occasion to struggle with alien powers that wreak havoc in this world, come what may.[21]

Likewise, although Fox talks regularly about "justice-making," he chiefly seems to be thinking about a revolution of consciousness that is going to transform the world, not unlike the idea of "Consciousness III," proposed by Charles Reich in *The Greening of America* during the heyday of the 1960s. In Fox's major works we encounter little attention to the often stalemated, anguished struggles of the oppressed, which sometimes can last for decades, even longer, and then, with some regularity, still be lost.[22]

The Christian masses throughout the ages have likewise lived and died with the bitter reality of *struggle*. Struggle against overwhelming odds has been their daily bread. This is why they have turned again and again to the figure of the crucified, and have struggled all the more desperately in this instance to make sense out of this apparently senseless but nevertheless redemptive death. Historically, the vocation of Jesus Christ has been interpreted in at least three ways, as Gustav Aulen showed.[23] Matthew Fox seems to appreciate only one of these ways, which clearly does have roots in the Scriptures and which came to its classical expression in the teaching of Abelard, the *Christus Exemplar* theology of the atonement.

But the faithful throughout the ages, not just the theologians, have again and again turned to other approaches to the atonement also, in liturgical and martyrological praxis, as well as in theological reflection and mystical meditation, indicated by the expressions *Christus Victor* and *Christus Victim*.

This is the experiential matrix of the *Christus Victor* motif among the faithful throughout the ages. Given the reign of the principalities and powers of death in this world, a profound struggle had to be won by God at some point. Otherwise death would remain the final victor. We could not have won that struggle ourselves, moreover, nor could we simply have been taught how to win it ourselves. We mortals surely do not have that capacity.

This, similarly, is the experiential matrix of the *Christus Victim* motif among the faithful throughout the ages. Given the radical breach between us and God, an immeasurable price had to be paid by God at some point. Otherwise our estrangement from our Creator could and would not have been healed. We could not have paid that immeasurable price ourselves, nor could we simply have been taught how to pay it ourselves. We sinful mortals surely do not have that capacity.

To write off these experientially rooted fall-redemption motifs, however much they might be beyond our rational ken, and to do so as cavalierly as Fox does, is to show an innocence born of some protected cloister, certainly not the cruciform world of Asylum Hill or the miserable hovels of the downtrodden Christian masses throughout the ages. The faithful who live and groan for liberation in the Asylum Hills of this world live and groan in a world of struggle, and so they find empowerment in the figure of *Christus Victor.* The faithful who live and look for liberation in the Asylum Hills of this world live in a world that they find alienated from God, and so they find healing in the figure of *Christus Victim.* This is why they demand that the church minister the historical Eucharist, and not something else, to them. This is why some sweat-lodge experience, were it to be presented to them as a pathway to redemption, would appear baffling to most of them.

Further, the faithful in the Asylum Hills of this world are all too aware of their own mortality and their own sinfulness to make any sense at all out of the claim that they themselves, not just the Christ of their salvation, are somehow divine. They do not want to be told that they are divine. They *do* want to hear that they have been delivered and that they have been forgiven, so that they can then engage in the struggles for justice in this world, liberated from hopelessness and freed from the burdens of their own alienation.

Cosmic Christology must be an urgent theme for contemporary theology, precisely for some of the reasons Fox has articulated. Joseph Sittler made that point with resounding clarity in his World Council of Churches address on Col. 1:15ff. in New Delhi in 1961, and we will have reason to return to it often in ensuing chapters.[24] But a cosmic Christology must be predicated, as Sittler knew so well, and as Jürgen Moltmann has forcefully reminded us, on a theology of *the blood of the cross,* according to the witness of Colossians.[25] Otherwise we will end up with a so-called savior whose salvation is commensurate neither with the powers of evil nor with our alienation from God. The Gospels, after all, are, as Norman Perrin once observed, "passion stories with introductions." We ought not to forget that exegetical fact in our zeal to explicate the cosmic Christologies of Ephesians and Colossians.

In a certain sense the shadow of the cross falls upon the entire cosmos, not just on us humans, as the whole creation groans in travail under the weight of the principalities and powers of death. Because the creation itself longs for liberation, as Paul proclaims in Romans 8. For all its harmony and its healing power, indeed, nature can sometimes be a capricious friend: when the roar of the lion reigns in the night or when the tornadoes or the volcanoes block out the midday sun. Thoreau finally discovered this alien face of nature when he journeyed to Maine's great northern peak, Mount Katahdin, in the springtime—and encountered the blackflies. Wordsworth might have discovered the same insight had he been around long enough to read Aldous Huxley's striking essay "Wordsworth in the Tropics." Nature is full of suffering and death.

This is why the biblical prophets longed for a new day for the whole creation, for cosmic history as well as human history, a day when the lamb would finally lie down with the lion and all things would be made new.

Interestingly enough, the Bible begins with the garden and ends not with the garden but with the redeemed city, in the midst of a renewed creation. Biblical theology is not a theology of origins alone, but a theology of cosmic history oriented to the final manifestation of a glorified City of God and a glorified Cosmos of God. In between, however, the biblical narrators make sure that we hear the shrieking laments of human fratricide and the groaning cacophonies of cosmic violence, from Cain and Abel to Noah and Job, and above all the godforsaken silence of Golgotha.

Original blessing is not the ending, but the beginning for the Bible. Eschatology as a yet-to-be-fully realized dawning of a New Heaven and a New Earth, in the midst of which the New Jerusalem is to be situated—this is the driving biblical vision. But there is always what Ernst Käsemann called the "eschatological reservation," the witness to the "crucified God" (Jürgen Moltmann), as *the* sign of "God with us" in our struggle to hope and to love in the midst of this oppressed and alienated world God creates and blesses as good.

The question then remains whether this traditional eschatological theology of the cross, which witnesses so necessarily to a *Christus Victor* and a *Christus Victim* as well as to a *Christus Exemplar*, is also equipped to speak to the ecological and related existential issues that trouble us so profoundly in these times. Are the kerygmatic and dogmatic traditions of the Christian story, which attest catholicity in their theologies of redemption, also capable of attesting catholicity in their theologies of creation? This is the question, beyond everything else, that the critical theology of Matthew Fox bequeaths to us.

The answer to that question is yes. With some irony, this is apparent, richly apparent, in the thought of the very theologian who is the archdemon in Matthew Fox's theological Hades, Augustine.

The Ecological and Cosmic Promise of Augustine's Theology

The Augustine who emerges in Fox's major works is largely a caricature, an introspective, sex-obsessed cleric who hates the created world and wants to subject everybody to the authority of the church. The historical Augustine was, in fact, a much more complex, much more ambiguous, and much more instructive figure, as I showed in my study, *The Travail of Nature.*[26] There I argued, on the basis of a study of Augustine's theological development, that his mature theology represents a flowering of the ecological promise of Christian theology, which later was to be practically expressed in the life of St. Francis.[27]

True, Augustine began his theological career as a Manichaean, and he held an exceedingly negative attitude toward the material world. But, if anything, in his mature thought Augustine *overreacted* to his Manichaean past in celebrating the goodness of the earth. In his later years, he does not give much attention at all to what the biblical witnesses think of as the dark side of the creation, like the lion roaring in the night for its prey. At the same time, Augustine's positive evaluations of the world of matter in his mature thought allowed him even to overcome some of the sexual dualism that shaped his thought during his Manichaean period, particularly his negative attitudes toward the human body.[28]

That Augustine was almost immediately read by his followers more in terms of his early thought than his mature thought may well be true. Matthew Fox is by no means the first interpreter to do this. But to read Augustine's thought solely in terms of his early antinature bias and his fascination with the soul over against the body is to lay at his door a blame that more properly should be laid at the door of his less visionary and less biblically inspired disciples.

In Augustine's mature thought, in any case, we encounter a majestic, universal vision of cosmic history, predicated on the then-traditional idea of the six days of creation. This is the little-known, universal cosmic context of Augustine's otherwise celebrated theology of history, which focuses on the narrative of the City of God. The thought of God's overflowing goodness and immanence in nature shapes Augustine's mature understanding of cosmic history. He also envisions nature itself as a kind of universal process unfolding through time, according to his doctrine of the "seminal reasons."

Further, over against the Manichaeans and some other more mainstream theologians, such as Origen, he insists that the material order has *not* fallen. On the contrary, in its manifoldness and in its own history with God, in Augustine's eyes, the material cosmos as we know it to this day is resplendent with God's glory, as from the first day of creation. It portrays, fittingly, the beautiful providence of the all-transcending and all-nurturing Creator. So Augustine states characteristically:

> How can I tell you of the rest of creation, with all its beauty and utility, which the divine goodness has given to man [sic passim] to please his eyes and serve his purposes, condemned though he is, and hurled into these labors and miseries? Shall I speak of the manifold and various loveliness of sky, and earth, and sea; of the plentiful supply and wonderful qualities of the light; of sun, moon, stars; of the shade of the trees; of the colors and perfume of flowers; of the multitude of birds, all differing in plumage and in song; of the variety of animals, of which the smallest in size are often the most wonderful, of the works of ants and bees astonishing us more than the huge bodies of whales? Shall I speak of the sea, which itself is so grand a spectacle, when it arrays itself as it were in vestures of various colors, now running through every shade of green, and again becoming purple or blue? Is it not delightful to look at in the storm, and experience the soothing complacency which it inspires, by suggesting that we ourselves are not tossed and shipwrecked? What shall I say of the numberless kinds of foods to alleviate hunger, and the variety of seasonings to stimulate the appetite which are scattered everywhere by nature, and for which we are not indebted to the art of cookery? How many natural appliances are there for preserving and restoring health? How pleasant are the breezes that cool the air! How abundant the supply of clothing furnished us by trees and animals! Can we enumerate all these blessings we enjoy?[29]

With this vision of the infinite blessings of the Creator throughout the cosmos, Augustine also teaches what can be called a contemplative idea of human dominion over the earth. His assumption is not that humans are called to dominate the earth, but that by their knowing they are called to contemplate and give thanks for the wonders of the earth, as no other creatures are called to do in precisely that way. He also stresses that many creatures are brought into being by God with no human utility implied whatsoever, but solely for the sake of enhancing the beauty of the whole created order.

All this Augustine finally brings together with an all-comprehending vision of cosmic renewal in the end times. He depicts the coming day of universal fulfillment as it is envisioned in the Book of Revelation, not just as the consummation of the City of God, but also as the consummation of the entire cosmos.

Such is the grand sweep of Augustine's rendering of the Christian story. Notably, he projects that grand vision from the context of the city of this world, the *civitas terrena*. While Augustine is fascinated with the theology of origins, and never forsakes that theology in his mature thought, he takes his stand existentially not in the garden, not with a theology of original blessings, but in the midst of the brokenness of the human *polis*. So in addition to his celebration of the universal goodness of cosmic history, Augustine is also driven to trace a theology of fall and redemption, a theology that speaks to the realities of death and estrangement in human experience, a theology that addresses the particular human condition, as we find ourselves "condemned," as he says, and "hurled into these labors and miseries."

This is not to suggest that everything Augustine ever said or did is to go uncriticized.[30] The point here is not to argue that Augustine somehow transcended his sinful mortality or the limitations of his own historical particularity. The point rather is to show that this pivotal theologian, the *Doctor Gratiae,* historically speaking the single most important "father" in the Christian West (hence Matthew Fox is well-justified in singling him out for extensive attention) is at once the author of a highly suggestive theology of cosmic history—which Fox fails to see—right in the mainstream of the kerygmatic and dogmatic traditions of the Christian story.

That any contemporary theology of nature will seek to go beyond Augustine's constructions should also be clear. His grand cosmic theology can surely stand to be developed much more explicitly than it is in terms of the cosmic Christology of Colossians, and with more explicit treatment of the *Christus Victor* and *Christus Victim* themes. We will have occasion to revisit these topics at later points in these discussions. Other concerns of importance to us in the twenty-first century, which were of little concern to Augustine (such as the preservation of species or the rights of all creatures), must also be given explicit attention.

But we have seen enough of this Augustinian theology of the City of God and the Cosmos of God to be able to say that those who would follow Matthew Fox in claiming that the kerygmatic and dogmatic traditions of the Christian story are ecologically bankrupt should take another, more careful look, especially in light of the catholicity of these traditions as they come to expression in Augustine's theology of redemption and in his vision of the city and the cosmos as partners in the unfolding universal history of God. Notwithstanding the sometimes trenchant critique by Matthew Fox, we now are in a position to reclaim the classical Christian story historically. While there are surely grounds for declaring the story ecologically bankrupt at some points, there are also grounds for proclaiming the story's rich ecological and cosmic promise.

Chapter 3

Rediscovering the Story Biblically

Beyond Anthropocentric Interpretations

"The earth is the LORD's and the fullness thereof." (Ps. 24:1)

In his *History of Redemption*, eighteenth-century American theologian Jonathan Edwards surveyed the eternal purposes of God, traced the broad sweep of God's saving activity in history, and then brought that universal story to an astounding conclusion by telling of recent events in Northampton, Massachusetts. We can call this *the scandal of particularity*, a term given public prominence by Emil Brunner four decades ago, precisely to describe this kind of remarkable theological affirmation. Everything hinges on what happens in Northampton!

This is a venerable "hinge" for theology written in the tradition of the Reformation. Unless salvation is *pro me*, as Luther taught us, the door to salvation will not swing open. Faith will remain locked in itself, mere "historical faith" (*fides historica*). The moral of this Reformation story is this: unless biblical interpretation can speak to Northampton, it cannot really speak a word that makes any difference to me.

That powerful, if scandalous, particularism has fatefully influenced the Reformation tradition's reading of the biblical theology of creation. Luther stated the matter most revealingly in his Small Catechism, in his lead statement interpreting the First Article of the Creed, which has to do with the work of "God, the Father Almighty": "I believe that God has created me together with all that exists." The *pro me* of Reformation existential faith as a matter of course tended to produce an *anthropocentric* reading of creation texts as well as redemption texts.

The time has come to make some corrections, better, some extensions: to rediscover the biblical roots of the classical Christian story as those roots are nourished by a vision of the whole creation, according to the witness of the psalmist: "The earth is the Lord's and the fullness thereof." The proper word at this point is *rediscover*. Premodern Christian exegetes such as Augustine already had learned to interpret the Scriptures in terms that comprehended God's history with the whole creation, as we have seen. But that universalizing interpretive frame of reference began to recede from the theological consciousness by the time Reformation exegetes, like Martin Luther and John Calvin, had finished their labors.[1] They took the Augustinian interpretive framework for granted, but they were not its self-conscious champions. Issues of human salvation, not so much cosmic meaning, preoccupied the reformers. Their biblical interpretation, as a result, took on an anthropocentric focus. In this respect, their theological exegesis coalesced with a longstanding anthropocentric bias in traditional biblical interpretation in the West, notwithstanding major exceptions to that rule, such as the exegetical work of the mature Augustine.

That *pro me* theology of creation and redemption that the reformers championed surely had—and has—its validity. But it should no longer be read as the whole biblical truth, nor as the biblical truth that the Northamptons of this world truly need to hear. In this global age when the universal questions of justice and ecology ring from every mountain and wetland, from every tumultuous city and sequestered village, and when believers themselves sometimes survey "the starry skies above" with fear or even dread, our faith communities can no longer afford to stay at home with the particularistic theology of yesterday. Firm in our knowledge of what the evangelicals in our midst call personal salvation, we must now venture forth to contemplate a new universal horizon in our interpretation of the Scriptures.

The Genesis creation narratives are a critical case in point, as they already were for Augustine, who wrote no fewer than five commentaries on Genesis, each of which was a kind of milestone for him, as he moved from an early anthropocentric focus on God and the soul, to his mature, universalizing vision of the City of God and the Cosmos of God. If we cannot move beyond anthropocentric interpretations of these key creation texts, instructed wherever appropriate by the insights of Augustine, the cause for a broader, more ecological and cosmic reading of the whole Bible will surely be rendered exceedingly difficult, if not totally impossible.

For any revisionist theology, which is methodologically bound to take the witness of the Scriptures with utmost seriousness, a fresh, universalizing reading of Genesis chapters 1 and 2 is therefore of the highest importance.

To that end, we need an interpretive framework that, together with the most rigorous forms of historical study, will help us to hear the witness of the Scriptures as Augustine heard that witness. This framework cannot be justified in advance. It can only be justified in terms of its legitimate exegetical fruits. This is the interpretive framework (or hermeneutic) I propose, informed by the approach of the mature Augustine: from "first things"(protology) to "last things" (eschatology), or, in more rhetorical terms, the future and the fullness thereof.

Strikingly, that is how the Bible itself is put together. It begins with the creation of all things, but it does not end in Northampton. It ends with the New Jerusalem and the New Heavens and the New Earth. A Martin Luther or a Jonathan Edwards knew that, of course. But characteristically they focused their biblical interpretation on the anthropocentric particulars. We no longer have to do that—that theological victory has been achieved, however much it still needs to be defended and proclaimed. Nor can we do that only—since we are facing theological challenges that differ radically from the ones they faced.

"The Future and the Fullness Thereof" as an Interpretive Horizon

Luther's interpretive approach to the Scriptures is best summarized by his oft-quoted words: "what focuses our attention on Christ" (was Christum treibt). The Bible is to be read, for him, as a collection of texts that point to and reveal the meaning of Jesus Christ.[2] I will come back to this central principle, and reaffirm it, at the end. But to begin, I am suggesting this more explicitly universalizing interpretive horizon, highlighting "what focuses our attention on 'last things' and 'all things'" (was ta eschata und ta panta treibt).Which is to say, when we turn to biblical texts, we will be looking for meanings that point to the future and the fullness thereof.

This two-dimensional horizon—the future and the fullness—is by no means arbitrarily chosen. On the contrary, it is a summary of two central theological motifs in the Old Testament. Claus Westermann has called these two motifs the theology of deliverance and the theology of blessing.[3] The theology of deliverance looks forward to the future of God's liberating activity, from the perspective of some kind of bondage. The theology of blessing surveys the fecundity of God's creative activity, from the perspective of some kind of celebration. We will see that these two theologies overlap and complement each other in significant ways, and therefore, together, can provide an interpretive framework for the Old Testament as a whole—and, it would appear, for the New Testament as well.

Note at the outset the earth-related character of the theology of deliverance, as we see it coming into view especially in Deuteronomic texts. The *terminus ad quem* of this deliverance theology is *a land of fecundity,* the promised land. Yes, we are talking about historical liberation here, but note that it is not history over against nature. The Exodus story is about deliverance from oppression, through nature (the waters and the wilderness), into an experience of the fecundity of nature (the promised land). This is not a dialectic of "nature as the servant of history," as G. Ernest Wright used to say.[4] Rather, this is a dialectic of nature as a divinely shaped universal process that includes God's liberating history with the human creature.[5]

Deliverance in this sense, as tending to a fecundity experience in the land, is a central, if not *the* central, motif of the Old Testament, as Walter Brueggemann has shown.[6] "It will no longer do to talk about Yahweh and his people," Brueggemann states categorically, "but we must speak about Yahweh and his people and his land."[7] This land, moreover, is richly construed: "It fulfills every anticipation of the wilderness: water—brooks, fountains, springs; food—wheat, barley, wines, fig trees, pomegranates, olives, honey; plenty—without scarcity . . . , without lack . . . ; minerals— iron, copper. The water does not need to come at the last moment, incredibly from a rock. Its sources are visible and reliable."[8]

Deliverance to this land of fecundity is also, emphatically, in Old Testament traditions, deliverance to a land of justice. We have thereby identified a kind of double canon in this deliverance theology, the canon of fecundity in the earth and the canon of justice in the earth.

This is the scope of justice in the earth. The land is the Lord's first and foremost. It does not belong to the people. It is the "common-wealth," in the sense that all are to have equal access to the fruits of its fecundity (this thought lies behind the Jubilee traditions[9]), but only insofar as that commonwealth is and remains the gift of God. The land is never the property of the people. It is intended for all the people in equal measure, appropriate to their needs. It is surely not intended as a resource available for the amassing of wealth, either individually or collectively.

It is in this context that the voice of prophecy is heard in its sharpest form, because, historically, some did in fact try to lord it over others, by amassing the wealth of the land as their own. As Brueggemann explains: "The land creates a situation in which the new decisive word of Yahweh must be made visible to Israel. It is the condition of being in the land which creates a prophetic situation."[10] The protagonists of the monarchy became the champions of an unjust established order, while the prophets became the champions of God's good, promissory order. The monarchists defended social stability in the land, predicated on injustice. The prophets called for justice in the land, especially for the poor, and trust in God by all, no matter what social instability might arise. "The history of Israel in its classical period," Brueggemann states, "is presented as a tension between royally secured land and covenanted precarious land."[11]

This theology of deliverance to the land of fecundity and justice was developed with a universal scope by later prophets, such as the school of Isaiah, and by the apocalyptic writers. The return of the exiles to Zion is understood in this context as the center of an entirely renewed creation, which is also to be a light to the nations, where the hungry will be fed, the deserts will blossom, and the lamb will lie down with the lion. This is the theme in one of the latest of those Old Testament expressions:

> On this mountain the LORD of hosts will make for all peoples
>   a feast of rich food. . . .
> And he will destroy on this mountain
>   the shroud that is cast over all peoples,
>   the veil that is spread over all nations;
>   he will swallow up death forever.
> Then the Lord GOD will wipe away tears from all faces.
> (Isa. 25:6-8)

The theology of blessing, in turn, can be read in some respects as a complementary expression, and something of an extension, of the theology of deliverance, given the latter's sometimes elaborate accents on the theme of fecundity. The theology of blessing blossomed, although it did not originate fully, with the coming of the Davidic monarchy and its cultic activities.[12] This theology was construed with reference to the fullness of creaturely being (the cosmos), rather than with reference to the promise of justice and fecundity in the land. "The main axis of Davidic (royal) covenant theology," Bernhard Anderson explains, "was vertical (cosmic) rather than horizontal (historical). According to this circle of tradition, the security, health, and peace of society depend upon the cosmic, created order, whose saving benefits are mediated through the Davidic monarch."[13]

In this context, writings, such as Genesis 1 and Psalm 104, could emerge that ostensibly had no relationship to the theology of deliverance and its traditions of the land of justice and fecundity. Both the compact cadences of the Genesis text and the gracious poetic elaborations of that psalm, which celebrate the fullness of the creation, may have served originally as librettos for festivals in the Jerusalem Temple.[14] These texts make no direct mention of Israel but instead celebrate all the glories of the fullness of God's good earth.[15]

Further, the canonical arrangement of creation (Genesis) preceding redemption (Exodus) is to be read as giving voice to ancient theological commitments, as Terrence Fretheim has argued.[16] Both the Priestly writers and the Yahwist began their narratives of the activities of the God of redemption with accounts of the same God as the God of the whole creation. For the Hebraic mind, moreover, redemption presupposes that God's universal creative activity continues, while God's redemptive purposes unfold, at first particularly, then more universally.[17] This theology of blessing through God's history of creation thus forms the framework for understanding all his redemptive activity, for major Old Testament traditions.

Although by itself this theology of blessing could surely be carried to excesses, and it sometimes was (e.g., the sanctification of injustice in the name of cosmic order, which was precisely what many champions of the monarchy apparently attempted to do), it could and did function as a "friendly amendment" to the theology of deliverance, since the latter was from the first a theology that presupposed the universal creational activity of God (Fretheim) and that envisioned a future of creational fecundity in the land (Brueggemann), as well as a theology of justice. The canon of justice thus harmoniously embraced the canon of fecundity, since the latter was already given in significant measure with the former. The theology of the land of fecundity and justice could readily accommodate a much more elaborate theology of fecundity.

It was no accident, therefore, that prophets of the exilic and postexilic school of Isaiah could seize upon the traditions of the theology of blessing as one way of pursuing their agenda of universalizing the themes of the land and of justice, most dramatically evident in their depiction of the new Zion as the center of worldwide political and cosmic upheaval and renewal.[18]

In this sense, then, we have identified a universalizing interpretive horizon in the Old Testament texts themselves: in terms of the Old Testament theologies of deliverance and blessing, with their overlapping themes of the Creator giving the people a fecund land of promise and the Creator blessing the whole earth with fecundity. This horizon highlights the theme of the future and the fullness thereof (*was ta eschata und ta panta treibt*).

When we read Old Testament texts in this manner, in a certain sense we know, before we turn to the texts themselves, where their particular meanings will ultimately take us: to grasp more fully the universal meanings of God's deliverance and God's blessing, the unfolding promissory saga of the divine justice and the divine fecundity throughout the earth.

Now it remains to illustrate how this universalizing interpretive framework, the future and the fullness thereof, can make a difference in our interpretation of the Genesis creation narratives.

The Future and the Fullness Thereof as An Interpretive Framework for Genesis 1 and 2

Commentary on Genesis 1 and 2 has preoccupied Western theology from its very beginnings. Many theological giants and lesser lights wrote extended treatments of these chapters, including Origen, Basil the Great, Ambrose, Augustine, Thomas Aquinas, Martin Luther, John Calvin, and Karl Barth.[19] With some notable exceptions (such as the mature Augustine), however, this great tradition of theological interpretation was often highly anthropocentric, as was in some measure the case with the reformers, due to this tradition's preoccupation with the questions of human salvation.[20]

From the outset, the primary text in the eyes of many traditional interpreters was the garden narrative of Genesis 2 and 3, since that focused on the story of the human creature, particularly the aftermath, the fall. Genesis 1 was read mainly as a prologue: it described the stage on which the divine-human drama depicted by Genesis 2 and later chapters was to unfold. Sometimes that anthropocentric alignment of the two narratives even led to literal distortions, as when Ambrose commented that God looked *at the human creature* and then saw that everything was very good, while the text itself (Gen. 1:31) clearly states that God looked at *everything* he had created and saw that it was very good.

Likewise, the "image of God" (*imago dei*) was frequently interpreted in highly spiritualistic terms, setting the human creature anthropocentrically over against all other material creatures, thus blurring the Priestly writers' assumption of a certain commonality between humans and animals (created together on the sixth day). With this spiritualizing reading of the *imago dei*, moreover, many commentators as a matter of course interpreted the idea of human dominion over the earth as a kind of license for domination. In the same spirit, the *imago dei* was interpreted individualistically, often with gender differentiation, so that the male was given precedence over the female, in anticipation of the "Adam's rib" theology of domination, male over female, that these commentators would then espouse in their ensuing discussions of Genesis 2.

Then commentators would turn with enthusiasm to interpret the text that usually fascinated them the most, Genesis 2 and 3. Adam's naming the animals would generally be highlighted, characteristically in terms of power, while the theme of Adam's earthly origins (*adam* from *adamah* or "dirt") would often be underplayed. Much would be made of the man being created before the vegetation, the animals, and the woman, as a sign of the man's ontological priority in the created order. The harsh reading of dominion over the earth in Genesis 1, moreover, in the sense of "subdue," would often be carried over to commentary on Genesis 2, to the neglect of the softer nuances there, concerning caring for the earth. "What a marvelous house God has created for us humans to use!"— that was the typical reading of Genesis 2 in many traditional commentaries. Given the patriarchal assumptions of the tradition, moreover, such sentiments frequently meant in effect: "What a marvelous house God has created for us men to use!"[21]

It should be apparent how this tradition of interpretation could play into the hands of those who, for their own reasons, would want to champion the exploitation of the earth and the exploitation of women—and other so-called lesser human creatures, such as slaves. Whether, however, we should seek to blame this tradition of interpretation for the modern environmental crisis and for the violence of our own "rape culture" in the West is another question, which we can cautiously leave unanswered here.[22]

What do we see, in contrast, then, when we look at Genesis 1 and 2 not through the anthropocentric lenses of many classical Western interpreters, but through the eschatological and ecological lenses of the universalizing hermeneutic of the future and the fullness thereof, attentive to the land of fecundity and justice, on the one hand, and the fecundity of the earth, on the other hand?

To begin with, Genesis 1 now becomes the primary text for our understanding of the divine creativity, no longer Genesis 2 and 3.[23] Interpreters such as Augustine already moved in this direction when they used the idea of the six days as a framework for interpreting the universal history of God as it moves toward its final fulfillment in the New Heavens and the New Earth in which righteousness dwells.[24] Gerhard von Rad, in his Genesis commentary, suggests that the Sabbath rest of God on the seventh day is intended by the Priestly writers as *the future,* that is, as the eschatological fulfillment of the whole creation.[25] We are to understand, then, that we are living in the sixth day, awaiting the dawning of the final fulfillment of the whole creation—the day of perfect universal peace, *shalom.*

In this connection, we can read the proclamations of prophetic texts such as Isaiah 11 as a kind of commentary on the Priestly traditions that envisioned the seventh day as future:

> The wolf shall live with the lamb,
> the leopard shall lie down with the kid,
> the calf and the lion and the fatling together,
> and a little child shall lead them. . . .
> They will not hurt or destroy
> on all my holy mountain;
> for the earth will be full of the knowledge of the LORD
> as the waters cover the sea (Isa. 11:6-9).

Much the same can be said about the more proximate Genesis texts of the "rainbow covenant," in which a certain violence is permitted between humans and the animals in this world (Gen. 9:1-7), but where the divine will for the future of the whole creation is emphatically proclaimed to be shalom, a will which is sealed by the divine covenant with all creatures (Gen. 9:8-17)

During this sixth day, which is the time for human history, the goodness of the creation and the underlying divine intention to bring into being and to bring to fulfillment a fullness of creatures, does not change. Especially in light of a parallel text such as Psalm 104, we can see that a kind of continuous creativity is presupposed here, that the divine creativity by no means is seen as belonging to the past only. God speaks, to be sure, and those divine words accomplish what they say. But those creative words of God remain creative words. God does not withdraw from that creative engagement.

Also the Priestly traditions depict here a world of glorious beauty and harmony.[26] Implicit at this point, surely, are nuances dramatically expressed elsewhere in Israel's liturgical language, such as Ps. 19:1: "The heavens are telling the glory of God; and the firmament proclaims his handiwork." Accordingly, there is *no cosmic fall* even implied here, as traditional commentaries sometimes suggested (a point to which we will return when we consider Genesis 2 and its aftermath). Augustine, in contrast, read this text correctly. For Genesis 1, all the communities of created beings, from the creeping things to the stars, are created and continue to be created because the Creator wishes to bring these creatures into being and to fulfillment. Hence the cadence: "and God saw that it was good."

It appears that the Priestly writers even envisioned a certain aesthetic delight on the part of the Creator at this point, with regard to the daily fruits of the Creator's activity.[27] That is akin to the theme of Ps. 104:21, in which God is depicted as creating the sea monsters in order to play with them, or to take delight in them. The Creator, in other words, is not in a hurry to get to the human creature. Without the human creature, to be sure, the whole creation would not be "very good," but it is precisely the fullness of the creation, everything, that the Creator sees as very good, not just the arrival of the human creature.[28]

When during the sixth day the human creature is called into being, this happens *with* the animals. The envisioned original state of *shalom* unambiguously entails a certain commonality of life between the humans and the animals, not only in terms of the single day of their origin, but also insofar as both are given vegetation for food. A state of *shalom* with the animals is depicted here, since no killing of animals for food is envisioned. Luther, strikingly, imagines that Adam and Eve enjoyed a common table with the animals "before the fall." It could be, moreover, that this creation text is in some sense to be read in this respect as a foreshadowing of the seventh day, since the Priestly writers clearly understand that, under the later covenant with Noah, killing of animals is to be permitted in the present epoch of the creation, although with certain limitations (Gen. 9:1-7).

Whatever the extent of the commonality of the animals and the humans, however, the human creatures are also clearly set apart from the animals. Only the humans are created according to the "image of God" (*imago dei*). Only humans are created for a special relationship of hearing, trusting, obeying, and praising the Creator—nuances here, which are explicated in Genesis 2. This is signaled by the fact that only at this point in Genesis 1, when speaking to the human creature, does the Creator speak in the first person. The human creature, in turn, appears to be called to a special vocation of worship, among all other creatures, which also praise God, although they are, in a certain sense, mute.[29]

Without beginning to explicate the extensively debated meaning of the *imago dei*, two comments need to be made here. First, it is generally noticed now, following the insights of Dietrich Bonhoeffer and Karl Barth, that the *imago dei* is intended to refer to the relationship between male and female: that this is a community text, not an individualizing text. What we see here is the coming into being of creatures meant for life with God in a communal world, such as the people of God later on or, by extension, all the nations of the world being gathered together in justice and fecundity at Mount Zion. Had there been no fall, according to this way of thinking, the descendants of Adam and Eve would have lived justly and harmoniously in a communal world of *shalom*, not a world of individualizing aggrandizement and domination.[30]

The much-discussed dominion text of Gen. 1:28f. must then be read in this context, surely not in the context of the ideology of modern industrial society. It may be the case that harsh language is used here; it may be the case that the individual word *subdue* means "tread upon."[31] But that kind of language should not be allowed to shape our interpretation of the text exclusively. The apparently harsh language that gives voice, in part, to the theology of dominion here, must be read in the context of that all-pervading, harmonious world of *shalom,* which Genesis 1 presupposes, a world where the humans and the animals enjoy a marked commonality and where the Creator clearly has purposes for the whole creation that transcend instrumental human needs.

Further, Anderson has noted that "dominion," whatever else it might mean, clearly seems to refer to "the human capacity to multiply and fill the earthly [habitat], even as the fish multiply and fill their habitat (waters) and the birds theirs (sky)."[32] Dominion in this sense is an ecological construct. It refers to humans assuming their divinely given niche in the earth, alongside other creatures, which also have their divinely given places.

Another comment about the *imago dei:* there is some exegetical evidence that, in addition to the thought of relationality, this idea also gives voice to the nuance of corporeality. The human body is included in the imaging forth of God envisioned here.[33] If this is indeed a correct reading of this text, as it appears to be, this would lend further credence to the theme that the human creature is of the earth essentially, indeed created with legitimate physical needs, and also created to live in solidarity with the likewise embodied animal creatures.

Genesis 2 and 3 is to be understood, in turn, as it actually appears in Genesis, as a secondary text.[34] Its story is to be read in the context of the sixth day of a universal process of divine creativity, which is moving toward the seventh day. In this context, several verses merit direct comment, in terms of what they add to the meanings of Genesis 1. In general, we see once again that the creation is a world of rich fecundity, this time depicted as a royal garden. The word *Eden* means "place of delight." The trees of the garden are in themselves pleasurable to see, as well as producing fruits that are good to eat.

More particularly, the earthliness and the earth-relatedness of the human creature, already implied in Genesis 1, are here clearly expressed: *adam* is from the *adamah,* the earth. This earthly creature is then commanded to serve and to protect its earthly home. This is no command to exploit, although it has often been interpreted this way. Rather it is a command to care for the garden, presumably by being attuned to the needs of the garden, as any good gardener was surely understood to be in biblical times as in our own. Phyllis Trible has pointed out that the Hebrew word *'bd* is appropriately translated "to serve," rather than the more conventional "to till": "it connotes respect, indeed, reverence and worship." Likewise the word *smr,* usually translated "to keep," is much more adequately rendered "to protect."[35] Serving and protecting the garden, moreover, is depicted as "a pleasurable and loving activity—pleasurable and loving both for the doer and the receiver."[36]

Given with the earthliness and earth-relatedness of the human creature, moreover, is the clear reality of *limits*. The human creature is a creature, not a god. Human creatures can neither know all things nor accomplish all things. That is signified dramatically by the placing of the tree of good and evil in the garden. In this sense the human creature is created to be humble in the root sense of that word, close to the ground (*humus*).

Further, the Creator's bringing of the animals to Adam for him to name need no longer be read as an act of will-to-power.[37] In a certain sense, the Creator does withdraw and leave this responsibility to the human creature. But that can be read as a withdrawal to encourage creaturely bonding, rather than a deistic withdrawal to relinquish divine authority. The naming itself, moreover, can be understood as an act of affection on the part of the human creature, akin to the notion that Yahweh gives Israel, his beloved, a name (see Isa. 56:5). Comradeship on the part of Adam with the animals seems to be implied here in this naming scene, perhaps even with nuances of friendship and self-giving.[38]

That the human creature does not meet an equal until Adam meets Eve, moreover, by no means undercuts the idea that the animals were creatures in their own right in that primeval human world, offering the human creature a certain comradeship—a thought that will reemerge in the Noah story, when Noah is commanded to take the animals with him on the ark, along with his family. Presumably the animals in Genesis 2—akin to the thought of their commonality with the human creature on the sixth day in Genesis 1—are partners with the human creature, not mere instruments posited for the sake of the human's well-being, although they surely do not offer Adam the partnership that Eve will.

To comment on Eve as the helper (NRSV) or, better, the companion of Adam is to enter an exegetical morass equaled only by the bewildering exegetical history of the *imago dei* in Genesis 1. But at least this single observation may be permitted. That the "Adam's rib theology" of male ontological predominance over the female—which even a modern commentator like Karl Barth took for granted, as had many other traditional commentators—is an accurate reading of the so-called rib text is by no means obvious. Could it not just as readily suggest equality, intimacy, and partnership rather than dominance, distance, and servitude? *Helpmeet* or companion, as Phyllis Trible has observed, is a word that is used elsewhere of the creative and redeeming activity of God, certainly not one that suggests subservience.[39] Such an egalitarian approach to the rib text is also to read it more in consonance with its Old Testament setting, as an early Yahwistic statement of the theology of relationality expressed later by Priestly writers, in exilic and postexilic times, in Genesis 1, and as a foreshadowing of the partnership attested by exilic and postexilic prophetic traditions among all humans in the universal *shalom* of the nations at Mount Zion.

The story of the sixth day, of course, does not end at the end of Genesis 2. It is ongoing until the dawning of the seventh day. All the more poignant, it is immediately ongoing in the direction of destruction. That is the lesson we learn from the next eight chapters of Genesis. Adam and Eve are banished from the garden. The earth does not fall, significantly, but the earth is cursed because of them. They and their descendants are left to eat the bitter fruits of their own disobedience. Self-conscious violence now invades the human world in the form of fratricide. In response, the Creator struggles to keep from destroying the whole earth, but then decides to initiate a new and everlasting covenant of *shalom* with the whole earth, following the chaotic times of the flood.

Then, and only then, in that world held in check from chaos and destined for universal peace by the divine covenant, does the story of human redemption begin, with the promise to Abraham. But that story is not intended to be an end in itself either, separated from the narratives of Genesis 1 and 2. Rather, the story of redemption that commences with Abraham is understood to be a narrative about how God struggles to get the whole of human history back on track, so to speak, through the vocation of Israel and the blessings of the land of promise, so that the Noachic covenant with all flesh might finally be realized, and the perfect *shalom* of the seventh day might finally and perpetually be a blessing to all creatures, on the day when the nations gather at Mount Zion in the middle of the land of promise, surrounded by an entirely renewed cosmos.

From Genesis to the New Testament

While there are themes in the New Testament that are not "earth-friendly" and some texts that seem to sanction a certain indifference to the structures of injustice, such as slavery, the New Testament can also be instructively read from the perspective of this universalizing hermeneutic of the future and the fullness thereof.[40]

One can see the theology of the land and its justice emerging especially in the Gospel of Luke, in the form of its picture of Jesus in Jubilee terms:[41]

The Spirit of the Lord is upon me,
because he has anointed me
to bring good news to the poor (Luke 4:18).

Similar themes also appear in the Magnificat (Luke 1:46-55), depicting the grand eschatological reversal, in which the last are now to be first.

One can see the theology of fecundity emerging in two ways in the New Testament, first implicitly, then explicitly. A case can be made, for example, that prophetic and apocalyptic texts such as Isa. 25:6-9, which depict the coming of the nations in the end times in pilgrimage to Zion, surrounded by the fecundity of a new creation, lie behind the witness of Matthew to Jesus. Matthew sees Jesus "on the mountain" (such as the Mountain of Transfiguration) at key points throughout his Gospel, culminating in the "mountain-experience" of the commissioning of the disciples to go to all the nations.[42]

It is not too far from this christological Zion theology in Matthew to the wisdom theology of the great christological hymn of Col. 1:15f., in which the ancient themes of *shalom* and fecundity are again announced, only this time with a christological focus. The Pauline author of Colossians apparently took over that hymn and added accents regarding the cross of Christ and the mission of the church, which gave the hymn its present form. But those additions by no means were intended to have the effect that the hymn's original wisdom Christology should be left behind.[43] On the contrary, the Christ who is confessed in Col. 1:15f. is precisely the Christ *who makes peace with all things*, through the blood of his cross, and the Christ in whom all things consist.

Nor is it far from the christological Zion theology of Matthew and the christological wisdom theology of Colossians to the christological apocalyptic of Paul in Romans 8. Here Paul tells us that the whole creation is groaning in travail as it awaits the time of its liberation, along with the children of God. Here the universal themes of deliverance and blessing, justice and fecundity coalesce.[44]

All of this can be seen to come to its conclusion in the apocalyptic visions of Revelation 21, with the proclamation of the New Jerusalem and the New Heavens and the New Earth. The *omega* of God's history with the creation is thus not the same as the *alpha*, but the ending is commensurate with the beginning: it is *universal*. The story of the whole creation that was told in the beginning turns out to be the story that is concluded at the ending—now, through Christ Jesus, the lamb upon the throne. The future and the fullness thereof, envisioned in the first chapter of the Bible, the dawning of universal *shalom* on the day of God's final Sabbath rest, is thus seen to have been realized. In Paul's words now, Christ turns over his dominion to the Father, so that God might be all in all (1 Cor. 15:28).

These brief considerations concerning the New Testament show how it might be possible for us to reaffirm the hermeneutic of Luther—*was Christum treibt*—for the whole Bible, but to do this now in terms of our universal hermeneutic of the future and the fullness thereof—*was ta eschata und ta panta treibt*. A christological concentration of that universal hermeneutic seems to be more than possible.[45]

Some Thematic Guidelines

Explorations of Genesis 1 and 2 and reflections about a consonant approach to the New Testament witness obviously cannot tell us the whole biblical truth. But these explorations and reflections do suggest a framework for a biblically informed theological approach to the global issues of environmental justice and cosmic meaning that are confronting us in these times. To this end, consider the following to be some preliminary thematic guidelines for further reflection, based on the foregoing reading of Genesis 1 and 2, and consonant with projected New Testament interpretations.

1. God has a universal history with all things: with many communities of being. God is not just interested in human being and human well-being.[46]

2. God places the human creature within a world of living creatures, all of whom have their divinely allotted and protected places and vocations.

3. Humans are called by God to care for the earth, not only for the sake of their own being and well-being, so that they might find sustenance for their bodies and establish a rich and just communal life, but also as caretakers of the garden, so that the whole garden might more fully flourish, for its own sake. Amassing of wealth from the earth for the sake of self-aggrandizement is thereby excluded. Any attempt to dominate the earth is likewise excluded.

4. Humans are also called by God to live within divinely mandated limits. Since humans are earth-creatures, not gods, they must live with, and indeed can only flourish within, limits of knowledge, capacity, and environmental niche. Hence humility and restraint before all the creatures of the earth are divinely mandated virtues.

5. God places the human creature in a world within a world, the human community, for a unique life of praise and self-giving. In this particular community of being, the blessings of the earth are to be regarded as a commonwealth given by God in abundance for the sake of constant sufficiency

and seasonal festivity, and to be shared justly with all other members of the human family. As humans commune with God and with one another, moreover, they are also blessed with a certain communion with all the other creatures of the earth, since humans are very much "of the earth." In this respect, indeed, humans are free to take the lead, in solidarity with all other creatures, in giving praise to God the Creator.

6. As the divinely covenanted, universal goal for all things is *shalom*, so the divinely mandated life for humans in this world is a life of *shalom*, with God, with each other, and with all creatures, in anticipation of the dawning of the great and glorious seventh day, the eternal Sabbath of God, when all the hungry shall finally be fed and all relationships of domination shall finally be overcome, when the lamb will lie down with the lion, when death shall be no more, and all things shall be made new.

7. Since humans have in fact turned away from God, self-conscious violence has become the *de facto* norm of their relationships with one another and with other creatures. The fatal flaw in human history is located in the human heart, not in the finitude of the earth, nor in some imagined fallenness of the earth. This is the crisis that lies at the root of the desolations of human history. This is the crisis, also, that God has long struggled to resolve, beginning with the promise to Abraham concerning the land and coming to a glorious conclusion in the mission of the Christ of God, who died on the cross to make peace with all things and to inaugurate the coming of the New Heavens and the New Earth, and who will finally hand over his rule to the Father, so that God may be all in all.

Chapter 4

Retelling the Story Narratively

Beyond Evolutionary Anthropocentrism

"For he has made known to us in all wisdom and insight the mystery of his will, according to the purpose which he set forth in Christ, a plan for the fullness of time, to unite all things in him, things in heaven and things on earth." (Eph. 1:9-10)

Albert Gore writes in his remarkably comprehensive book *Earth in the Balance,*

> The old story of God's covenant with both the earth and humankind and its assignment to human beings of the role of good stewards and faithful servants, was—before it was interpreted and twisted in the service of the Cartesian worldview—a powerful, noble, and just explanation of who we are in relationship to God's earth. What we need today is a fresh telling of our story with the distortions removed.[1]

In response to this challenge, Gore endorses "a renewed investigation of the wisdom distilled by all faiths."[2] From this kind of "panreligious perspective,"[3] he himself suggestively summarizes some of the rich and diverse religious insights that are available to the human community today. He points to the teachings of Native American religions, archaic earth-goddess religions, Islam, Hinduism, Sikhism, Baha'i, and "the Judeo-Christian tradition," along with the spiritual insights suggested by "the Gaia hypothesis."[4]

Whether the "fresh telling of our story" from a "panreligious perspective" that Gore envisions is possible can be debated, given the vast diversity of religious perspectives in our global civilization. But if that is to be our ultimate goal, it will surely not be achievable apart from the penultimate revision of traditional religious perspectives, all of which, by definition, were construed by their adherents long before the global environmental crisis that Gore has described so vividly became such an urgent challenge for our species.

It is something of an embarrassment, in this respect, that Gore's own Christian tradition has not given him the theological tools he clearly needs to respond to the global environmental crisis, notwithstanding his own eagerness to learn and his own impressive gifts of understanding. "Why does it feel faintly heretical to a Christian," he asks, "to suppose that God is in us as human beings? Why do our children believe that the Kingdom of God is *up*, somewhere in the ethereal reaches of space, far removed from this planet?"[5] Nor is Gore alone in this respect, by any means. As we have had occasion to observe, not a few thoughtful Christians, championed by critics like Matthew Fox, have found their own religious tradition ecologically restrictive in these times of global environmental crisis, even bankrupt.

One of the urgent challenges Gore's argument bequeaths to his Christian readers, therefore, is this: to respond to his call for a "fresh telling of our story, with the distortions removed." In this respect, the thought of one twentieth-century Christian theologian commends itself for our attention, with great if not unique promise.

The cosmic vision of Pierre Teilhard de Chardin, which Gore himself[6] and many others from a variety of religious traditions have celebrated, well illustrates "the ambiguous ecological promise" of Christian theology, past and present.[7] Teilhard's thought is both identifiably Christian and cosmic in scope. And it *is* promising—as well as ambiguous. It takes us to the threshold of a genuinely Christian ecological and cosmic vision, if not yet fully into the inner sanctum of such a theologically shaped vision. It reflects earlier universalizing theological visions, such as the mature Augustine's, and behind them the biblical vision itself, of the future and the fullness thereof. Teilhard's whole theology, indeed, can be read as a theology of *genesis*. In this respect, moreover, Teilhard's thought is also strikingly contemporary and publicly accessible, since genesis, for him, means evolution.[8]

This is the immediate project before us, then, in response to Gore's challenge and in conversation with Teilhard: the search for a Christian vision of reality that is both critically and constructively ecological and cosmic in scope. This is a particularistic quest for a viable theology of nature: *to tell not just the human side of the story, but the whole cosmic story.*[9] This is a quest for a vision of reality that is no longer anthropocentric, even in evolutionary terms, that is holistic, that construes all things symmetrically in relationship with each other—a vision of reality that understands human being and becoming as essentially embedded in the universal history of the cosmos and that attributes eternal value to the entire universe in its fullness, not just to human life alone. It is, more particularly, an adventure of soul and mind and heart to interpret the ancient cosmic Christology of the Letter to the Ephesians: "With all wisdom and insight he has made known to us the mystery of his will, according to his good pleasure that he set forth in Christ, as a plan for the fullness of time, to gather up all things in him, things in heaven and things on earth" (Eph. 1:8-10).[10]

Whether this penultimate intra-Christian project will then serve the ultimate quest for a new cosmic story told from a panreligious perspective is a question that others will have to address.[11] But the penultimate project itself is surely worthwhile, for the sake of serious-minded Christian citizens such as Gore, if not yet for the faithful adherents of every other religious tradition that is also seeking to respond to today's global environmental crisis.

Teilhard's Cosmic Vision

Pierre Teilhard de Chardin (1881–1955) was a solitary theological visionary. An outstanding paleontologist in his own right, he was also a mystical thinker, whose insights rank with the most eminent philosophers and theologians in the classical Western tradition, beginning with Origen and Plotinus.[12] Teilhard explored the way of solitude and the inner journey. Pursuing that way, however, his inner eye knew no bounds. He sought to bring the whole of human knowing—from the meticulous rigors of the natural sciences to the soaring insights of speculative cosmology and theology—into one grand vision. A lifelong Roman Catholic, Teilhard saw many of his most insightful works banned by his own church for much of his life, precisely (one can judge with the wisdom of hindsight) because those works were so visionary, and so different from the pedestrian, textbook theology that lesser minds in the hierarchy of the church tended to prefer.

Teilhard's thought unfolds in what he himself thought of as two stages, first, what he called the "phenomenological" or the descriptive-scientific stage, then in what he thought of as his explicitly "theological" stage. He held that, in principle, *any* observer who has eyes to see can identify the validity and the coherence of his phenomenological description of the universe.[13] Only well into the course of his thought, Teilhard maintained, when he explicitly begins to talk about God, Christ, and the church, is knowledge of what traditional theology has called "revelation" a prerequisite.

The integrating theme of Teilhard's vision is the revolutionary construct of *evolution*, associated in modern times, of course, with the name of Charles Darwin, but deeply rooted in the traditions of speculative philosophy and theology in the West, and mediated to Teilhard through the seventeenth-century German philosopher G. F. Leibnitz. Teilhard sought to see and to understand the whole of reality, from the primordial energies studied by physics to the complexities of human culture and community, under the rubric of this one construct. He characteristically thought of the whole of reality, then, in terms of *genesis*, as a universal process of becoming.

Although the philosophy of mechanism was much in vogue when he began to write at the turn of the twentieth century, and although the mechanical view of nature, championed most notably by Isaac Newton, dominated the thought-world of most natural scientists in those days, Teilhard himself always felt much more at home with a more organic, process-view of nature. Indeed, a dynamic, metaphysical construct of *energy*—akin to motifs that would much later become commonplace in post-Einsteinian physics—shaped his every thought about material and spiritual realities, from his earliest days. This is reflected in his conceptuality of "the without" and "the within."

For Teilhard, all entities and all communities of entities and indeed the cosmic whole have both a without and a within. The former he identified with the traditional construct of "matter," the latter with the traditional construct of "spirit." Again following Leibnitz, Teilhard projected a certain kind of panpsychism. Even the most material of realities, in his view, have some consciousness, however diffuse. A pebble, for example, has a "within," however inert it might appear.

If Teilhard's universalizing vision scandalized the church of his time, it all the more scandalized many natural scientists of his day and subsequently. The schoolmen of the church were unhappy with Teilhard's enthusiastic adoption of the construct of evolution. The schoolmen of the academy were offended by how he shaped the construct of evolution. Teilhard envisioned a universal process of genesis, a cosmos in which all things were evolving. But he also maintained that this universal process of genesis is at once a highly focused process of *orthogenesis*. That construct, which literally suggests things coming into being in a straight line, was decisively rejected by Darwin and has been as derisively rejected by most post-Darwinian biologists. The idea of orthogenesis suggests an underlying purpose in the universal unfolding of cosmic evolution.

With Darwin and the neo-Darwinians, Teilhard did accept the anti-orthogenetic notion of natural selection. The process of evolution, for Teilhard, is not simply a straight line, by any means. The whole process of evolution, he believed, "proceeds step by step by dint of billionfold trial and error."[14] It is an infinite process of groping or "cosmic drift." That explains why the whole process has taken such an extended time in realizing the underlying purpose given with its very being and eliciting its universal becoming.

That some otherwise secular cosmologists in our day are now speaking of an "anthropic principle" as the driving, underlying reality of the entire universe, from the first moments of its birth, and that some contemporary mathematicians and other scientists are now exploring the dimensions of an underlying order in, with, and under the ostensible chaos of perceived biophysical reality, was of course unknown to Teilhard. He was very much the solitary explorer in his time, and he scandalized many in both church and academy with strange ideas—above all what for him were the universal themes of genesis and orthogenesis.

What is the underlying purpose of the cosmos? What is that universal *telos* that moves and shapes all things through a vast and infinite process of cosmic drift? Teilhard thought of this purpose unfolding in terms of what he calls "the ascending axis of hominization."[15] Cosmic evolution has always had one goal, he believed. From the rudimentary beginnings of the universe, evolution has followed a line—drifting and turning back on itself and then drifting a billionfold more, but a line nevertheless—leading to *the emergence of human life*. This has been the inner drive, the one main axis of evolution, according to Teilhard, however random its morphology.

In this connection, Teilhard introduced the concept of a universal law, which for him was as fundamental to nature as the law of gravity, the second law of thermodynamics, or the law of conservation of energy. This is the law of "complexity-consciousness." This law describes the universal process of cosmic evolution as an ever-increasing development toward higher organization and more intense and unified forms of consciousness. There are, then, Teilhard pointed out, two axial lines in the universe. The first is the impressive *quantitative* one that runs from the subatomic world to the galactic world, the axis of physical infinity. This material aspect of the universe, Teilhard granted, is ultimately tending toward death, according to the second law of thermodynamics. The second is the often obscured, *qualitative* line: the evolutionary axis of complexity-consciousness. According to this law, in the midst of the dying physical cosmos, life and consciousness are gradually emerging and intensifying. This is the axis—complexity and consciousness—that Teilhard saw as the key to understanding the purpose and meaning of the whole universe and the history of evolution in particular. This is the orthogenetic line of evolution.

The law of complexity-consciousness, Teilhard maintained, applies everywhere, even where it cannot be observed. Since all entities have both a without and a within, both a certain state of material organization and a certain state of consciousness, when and where the one increases, the other will increase, too. A larger and more organized brain, for example, will sooner or later be the occasion for the development of a more intense form of consciousness. All this reveals Teilhard's underlying assumptions about *the primacy of the personal* in the history of cosmic evolution.

But Teilhard's personalism is more than just a passive phenomenological description of a universal process that has its final goal in the emergence of self-conscious, rationally communicating human creatures. Teilhard's personalistic vision of reality also has an activist thrust, not unlike the thought of Karl Marx. According to Teilhard, the human species is now in a position to bring *the whole universe* to its originally intended fulfillment, to realize its underlying purpose, *by actions initiated and consummated by humans.* In this sense, the future of the whole universe hinges on the proper exercise of human freedom. Humankind, Teilhard suggested, is "evolution conscious of itself." Evolution, therefore, will ascend to its next level only through the proper use of human consciousness. In theological terms, the reign of God will not arrive unless humans consciously work to make it arrive.

In projecting his cosmic vision with this anthropocentric focus, Teilhard also traced the unfolding of the main axis of evolution through a series of stages or dimensions of *genesis*. The whole universal process begins with *cosmogenesis,* the coming into being and the increasing organization of physical matter. After many billions of years, by apparent accident, he suggested, a habitable place finally came into being—the earth. This set the stage for another random process of cosmic drift, *biogenesis*, the emergence of life. Through a similarly lengthy process, life covered the earth; henceforth this could be called the biosphere. In this sphere, complexification then proceeded on a vast scale. In retrospect, we can see that life's greatest density passed through those creatures possessing a central nervous system. Teilhard called that facet of evolution *cephalization*. With cephalization, he pointed out, one can see the first signs of emergent consciousness.

Then came a step in the history of evolution comparable only to the birth of life: the emergence of mind or self-consciousness in the human creature, the most cephalized of all living creatures. This, Teilhard called noogenesis or *homogenesis*. Quantitatively speaking, the appearance of humanity was almost totally without significance. Here Teilhard agreed with Darwin and Darwin's twentieth-century disciples. In almost all respects the human creature was dwarfed by other creatures; it appeared as one weak product of a billionfold cosmic drift. As Teilhard said with his characteristic sense of drama, the human creature "came silently into the world." Nevertheless, here was a phenomenon expressing the flow of the universe itself: "However solitary his advent, man emerged from a general groping of the world. He was born a direct lineal descendant from a total effort of life, so that the species has an axial value and a preeminent dignity."[16] With the emergence of the human creature, moreover, the interiority of matter, the within, finally becomes the primary factor. Here, finally, spirit rules over matter, or it can. Humans are self-conscious beings. They know themselves and are free to shape their lives rationally and spiritually.

But evolution does not stop with the emergence of human life, according to Teilhard. It continues to press forward and upward in two partially overlapping phases. The first phase is expansion or planetization. The human creature multiplies and fills the earth. Concomitantly, the quality of human life—that is, culture—develops and intensifies. This is the second phase, the phase of compression or convergence. The noosphere begins to close in upon itself and to encircle the earth.

In the noosphere, Teilhard maintained, evolution is now approaching its limits. It is ready for another major step forward. He saw signs of this impending new development in the increasing growth and complexity of social organization in our century. Teilhard acknowledged evils in the emergence of some kinds of twentieth-century totalitarian social organizations, but he preferred to highlight the promise of these globalizing institutions. Now that evolution has become conscious of itself, he held, and now that global human society has taken on a soul of its own, according to the principle that the whole is greater than the sum of the parts, we humans are beginning to realize that the whole universal process of evolution is passing through us and to that extent that *everything depends on us for its further development.*

This conception of a humanity that has reached the limits of its terrestrial expansion and is fast approaching the limits of its spiritual and cultural compression led Teilhard further: to pose the question of an Omega Point. He asked: Is it not reasonable to assume that the whole universal evolutionary process has a final cone, which is the end-goal of the efficacy of the law of complexity-consciousness? This took Teilhard's phenomenology explicitly to the boundary of his theology, since he had discerned that the whole process is tending toward the production of purer and purer forms of personalized spirit, through the emergence and the cultural compression of the human creature. So Teilhard postulated this possibility: as human life is progressively integrated and spiritualized, is it not conceivable that evolution will pass through one final stage of cosmic involution into the reality of sheer personalized spirit? That would mean that evil—which, for Teilhard, is the disintegration and the disunion of reality—will have been abolished. Perfect union of spiritualized personal reality, an ultrasynthesized humankind, will have come into being.

At this point in setting forth his universal vision of cosmic evolution, Teilhard explicitly crossed the line between what he understood as phenomenology and what he understood as theology. Self-consciously, on the basis of divine revelation, Teilhard affirmed that the exalted Jesus Christ is the central point and purpose of the whole universe, of all things visible and invisible, of the whole realm of matter and the whole realm of spirit. Which is to say: the whole universal process of genesis is finally to be seen as a process of *christogenesis*, the emergence of the living, cosmically fulfilled Christ. The exalted, resurrected Christ, and the body of believers united to him, is the Omega Point of the whole universe. In this context, Teilhard frequently alluded to the "cosmic christology" of some New Testament writings, especially Ephesians and Colossians, and in particular Eph. 1:8-10, where the universal divine purpose is affirmed as a plan to unite all things in Christ.

In metaphysical terms, Teilhard saw the exalted Christ functioning as the Prime Mover of the universe; not as its efficient cause, as the "God way back there" who set all things in motion. No, God is not way back at the beginning, in isolation as the efficient cause, the watchmaker. Rather God is the ever-present final cause. The "Prime Mover," Teilhard said characteristically, "is ahead."[17] Christ, in other words, is a kind of universal, spiritual magnet that touches the within of entities and, in that process of eliciting, draws the whole universe to itself, organizing and ordering the universe in, with, and under its virtually infinite meanderings of cosmic drift, to find its fulfillment one day, united in him.

More specifically, Teilhard taught, the ultimate spiritual energy that radiates from Christ and draws all things to him and orders all things for him is—*divine love*. Ultimate reality is thus charity—the spiritual force that draws all things toward final union with God in Christ. This is the primal energy that was working from the beginning of all things on the within of primordial matter, drawing it forward and upward along the axis of complexity-consciousness.

Teilhard suggested that the mystics of all ages have unconsciously and proleptically intuited that spiritual consummation of all things in Christ that is yet to come. More glorious, for Teilhard, is the Christian community's self-conscious, proleptic participation in the mysteries of the exalted Christ in the Sacrament of the Altar, the Eucharist, which is a present experience of the exalted Christ who is the Omega Point of all things.

But in the end, for Teilhard, the mystical gives way to the practical, the *vita contemplativa* to the *vita activa*. For it is only by the action of self-conscious participants in the life of the exalted Christ that the final reign of God will be ushered in, the glorious day of the universal involution of the whole process of cosmic evolution. Teilhard held that the logical-existential result of the universal evolutionary process is that Christians are called to join with all people of goodwill in building up a world society of peace and justice; that is at once the building up of the body of Christ. As Teilhard suggested in a note in 1918, Christ needs the results of human labor so that he can reach his plenitude, his own fullness.

When Christ does reach his own fullness, his highly intensified, infinitely spiritualized body will be the only surviving reality, according to Teilhard. Biophysical reality generally will die and disintegrate toward nothingness. But human reality will be transfigured into the white spiritual heat of ultimate charity, united in the fullness of Jesus Christ. That will be the final cephalization of the universe, which Teilhard referred to as an act of spiritual ecstasy in God. Then the vast universal process of genesis—cosmogenesis, biogenesis, homogenesis, and christogenesis—will come to its conclusion. The cosmic ascent of humanity will have reached its final goal, union with the universal Christ, and through him union with God, who will then be all in all.

The Liabilities and the Promise of Teilhard's Cosmic Vision

Teilhard's cosmic vision surely represents what Gore has called for, "a fresh telling" of the Christian story. This is a vision that self-consciously comprehends the whole cosmos. It reflects the grand theological schema of premodern theologians such as Augustine and it is fully commensurate, in particular, christologically commensurate, with the biblical vision itself: of the future and the fullness thereof. Further, Teilhard's vision is construed with a breathtaking comprehensiveness, a striking coherence, and a zealous attention to detail that sets it apart from many other contemporary narratives of the Christian story. In addition, while forging a solid theological substance, Teilhard shapes his thought thoroughly in evolutionary terms, which give it a deep resonance with modern cultural and scientific sensibilities.

Teilhard's thought, in every respect, is suggestively and tenaciously ecological and cosmic in scope. It depicts the evolutionary interrelatedness of all things with rigor and passion. But whether Teilhard has also fully moved beyond the distortions of the past, as Gore has also rightfully called contemporary Christian thinkers to do, is another question. To probe this question, it is necessary not only to see Teilhard's thought over against the Enlightenment and modernity, which is Gore's primary frame of reference when he points to some of the distortions of the classical Christian story, but much more deeply to see Teilhard's cosmic vision as an expression of classical Western thought more generally, especially the worldview shaped by the metaphysical and metapoetic imagery of what Arthur Lovejoy called the Great Chain of Being.[18]

The conceptuality of the Great Chain of Being is, at root, a vision of a metaphorical mountain (Teilhard himself uses the image of the cone). The whole of reality is construed as an ontological hierarchy, with the One at the apex and the Many at the nadir. Somewhere in the middle of the hierarchy there is a gradated break, between matter and spirit. The One—or God—at the apex is pure spirit. The Many at the nadir are purely material, something almost nothing, fading into nonbeing. As one surveys the hierarchy of being from its lowest to its uppermost levels, one sees that matter, as it ascends from the sheer material elements to rocks, for example, then to living creatures, begins to approach the spiritual dimension of the hierarchy. These dimensions meet in the human creature, who is partially material and partially spiritual. The remainder of the hierarchy is populated by a variety of spiritual creatures, angels, for example, until the hierarchy reaches its apex in the purely spiritual One, called God.

Arthur Lovejoy observed that historically this hierarchy was construed in two radically different ways. The first, the otherworldly construal, envisioned the movement of the whole of reality to be properly from the nadir to the apex. The dialectics of reality, then, had a purely spiritual goal (*telos*). Matter was viewed as something to be overcome and left behind. The goal for the whole process was for spiritual reality, insofar as it was embedded in matter—some construals would say "imprisoned" in matter—to ascend toward and ultimately to be absorbed by, the purely spiritual One. The second, the this-worldly construal of the hierarchy, envisioned the movement of the whole of reality to be properly from the apex to the nadir. The dialectics of reality, seen in this way, had the goal of the unification of spirit with matter. The imagery was typically the vision of the One *overflowing* throughout the hierarchy and embracing all things.

It seems clear that Teilhard's cosmic vision was a captive of the first, the world-denying construal of the hierarchy of being, however much he celebrates physical reality and life as stages along the way of cosmic evolution.[19] Teilhard bequeathed to us an instrumental view of biophysical reality, one that suggests that the raison d'être of biophysical reality is that it is to be used for the emergence and the purposes of spiritual reality, which is to say, for the sake of human beings and their evolutionary destiny.

In this connection, Teilhard characteristically accents human *dominion over* nature, even domination, rather than contemplation or respect for nature. Which makes perfect sense, according to his schema, since that is the raison d'être of the cosmos in the first place. Further, Teilhard states in so many words that the biophysical world is to be *destroyed,* appropriately so in his view, so that the proper end of the cosmos, intensified, purely spiritual matter, can emerge and remain for all eternity. The legacy of his thought, then, as he construes it is, in effect, the continual domination and the final abrogation of nature.

This is the legacy of a certain kind of theological anthropocentrism, which holds that persons—embodied spirits—are what is truly real and valuable in God's good creation. The corollary of this view is that matter, biophysical reality, is in itself valueless. Matter is valuable only instrumentally. It gains its value as a mere means that makes the life of persons with a personal God possible. Teilhard's thought exemplifies this kind of narrow personalism with a remarkable consistency and a relentless passion, even to the point of explicitly teaching that nonpersonal matter will one day be totally annihilated. It will sink into nothingness, since its instrumental purpose—making possible the history of persons with God—will have been achieved.

This, needless to say, is not the kind of theological vision that one can readily think of as ecological and cosmic: a symmetrical vision of the holistic interrelatedness of all things that attributes eternal value to all things. Rather, after all has been said and done, it is a highly anthropocentric vision. Orthogenesis for Teilhard is most essentially, both ontologically and ethically, homogenesis. That is the end-result of Teilhard's own kind of evolutionary construal of the classical chain of being conceptuality. That is also the liability of his thought.

But everything changes when we recontextualize his thought: when we move beyond his particular kind of theological anthropocentrism into the context of a world-affirming—and also evolutionary—construal of the hierarchy of being. Then a radically different vision emerges, one that is thoroughly Teilhardian, yet at the same time thoroughly ecological and also cosmic in scope. One begins with the image of a hierarchy of being that is *overflowing,* whose *telos* from the very beginning is the total and perfect union of spirit and matter, *not* the total and perfect unification of spirit apart from matter.

This is how the cosmic, ecological vision for which we are searching can begin to come into focus.[20] One can think of God, in whom spirit and matter are perfectly united, at the very beginning of cosmic history calling into being a vast cosmic sea of scattered and undifferentiated material entities, each with its own interiority, its within, each with its own exteriority, its without, each with a certain state of consciousness, each with a certain kind of physical organization. The purpose of God in so calling the cosmos into being is to give of God's own eternal life, love, and glory by invoking and shepherding a universal history with all things, so as to mirror God's own infinite life in a vast diversity and gradation of finite creatures, and also to bring that world to its final fulfillment in communion with God's own eternal life.

Further, following the witness of biblical texts like John 1:1, which announces that "in the beginning was the Word," and Genesis 1:1, which can be read as alluding to the Spirit "hovering" over the primeval waters, and informed by classical theological interpretations of these texts, on which Teilhard was also dependent, we can say that *the agency of God* in this divine eliciting of the universe from nothing into the course of a universal history with God is the very voice of God, the eternal Word or Logos of God, who is the firstborn of all creation. All things are thus created in him and through him and for him. Concomitantly, we can affirm that this universal history is at once enlivened from within by the breath of God, which accompanies the Word. The eternal Spirit of God, whom the Nicene Creed calls "the Lifegiver," is the *actualizing matrix* of God. In more dramatically metaphorical terms, we can say with the early Christian theologian Irenaeus: the Word and the Spirit are the "hands of God."[21]

Then, with Teilhard, we can think of the entire universe as being elicited by the Word and Spirit of God through a succession of stages or phases of *genesis:* cosmogenesis, biogenesis, and noogenesis. And we can recapitulate his description of the law of complexity-consciousness. But according to *this* construal of cosmic history, each stage or phase of the cosmos has its own integrity. Each is an end in itself, as well as a stage along the way. What the German historian Leopold von Ranke once said about "world history," we can now say about cosmic history: "Every epoch is immediate to God" (*Jede Epoch ist unmittelbar zu Gott*). Orthogenesis, we must contend, is a pluralistic, universalistic construct, not a singular, particularistic construct. For each stage of cosmic evolutionary history has its own divinely established, eternal value throughout the course of its history: since every creature, and indeed all creatures together, are one day to be consummated in God, not just the so-called spiritual creatures. One can think, then, of an *Omega World*, not, as Teilhard would say, an Omega Point, as the final future of all things.

Further, with a view to the divine eliciting of all things from the very beginning, we can think of the world as charged with the love of God, both with respect to every entity and with respect to the cosmic whole. The creative divine speaking is in fact a voice of intimacy and immediacy, through the vitalizing breath of God that energizes the within of every creature. There is no vision of domination here, rather nurturing. The very being of the divine is in, with, and under all things, calling them to new realizations of being, befriending them, caring for them. Love, indeed, as Teilhard holds in this respect, is what "makes the world go round"—divine love. Self-giving love is ultimate reality, not domineering, arbitrary power. The whole universe pulsates with that divine energy.

That eliciting, nurturing character of the divine love is the ultimate energy of the universe also helps to explain the nearly infinite extent of cosmic drift. The Prime Mover, who is ahead, as Teilhard says, moves all things by the loving power of persuasion, as it were, rather than by the arbitrary power of domination. Love is patient, as Paul insists in 1 Corinthians 13—in this case infinitely patient. Love does not insist on its own way. Love does not "lord it over" anyone or anything. Love elicits. Love persuades. Love embraces.

This whole universal process is given being and becoming by God, it is important to observe, as a process that is *good, but not perfect*. Called forth by the Word and energized by the Spirit, the whole universe is *imperfect* from the very beginning. The world as created is both good—and mortal. The world as created good is at once a world where creatures come into being and pass out of being. All things will die. All things must die. That is how they are called into being. That is how they are given their becoming.

A certain unconscious violence, accordingly, is also given with the goodness of creation, the "natural" violence of transiency, destruction, and death. And this unconscious violence as a matter of course will baffle and even alienate the sensibilities of finite human minds and hearts. God has purposes with the whole universe, with the galaxies, with the black holes, with the supernovas, with the ichthyosaurs and the dinosaurs, with the viruses and the quarks and the neutrinos and all the rest, that we do not and will never understand until the day when all things are made new and God is all in all. So death and suffering and violence and the infinite magnitudes and dialectics of the whole universe, although created good, are for us clothed in mystery, and, sometimes, profoundly repulsive.[22]

Further, through a nearly infinitely extended cosmic process, God wills the human creature into being in order to have personal communion with humankind. This infinitely circuitous and spiraling line of cosmic emergence—*homogenesis*—which finally came to fruition on planet Earth after eons of cosmic drift, is a line that was at the center of God's purposes (*prima inter pares*) from the very beginning, because God, as the perfect unity of matter and spirit, is personal, and hence originally willed to mirror God's infinite being in a world where God could enter into communion with other similarly personal beings. But the emergence of humankind is not the sole purpose of the cosmos, by any means. God wills to bring into being an infinitely variegated, multidimensional cosmos, in order to mirror His infinite being in that finite cosmos and to enter into a history with that cosmos in a myriad of appropriate ways, one of these being God's particular history with humankind.

From the very beginning, moreover, it was in the mind and will of God that the divine creative Word should take on flesh in the life of a single human being. This was for two reasons, we may say, in response to the traditional Christian question concerning the rationale of the Incarnation, "Why the God-Man?" (*Cur Deus Homo?*)[23]

The first eternal intentionality for the Incarnation of the Word of God had to do with the culmination and consummation of the entire cosmic history of God with the universe. It was fitting that the universal Word or Logos should be incarnate in the being of one who, among all finite creatures, most reflected the fullness of the divine personhood, as the perfect unity of matter and spirit. The one who himself is the mirror of God, the eternal Logos, fittingly becomes embodied in the creature, who, under the conditions of finitude, most fully images forth the qualities of divine life, that is, the human creature. This divine unfolding may appropriately be called, with Teilhard, *christogenesis.*

The Incarnation of the Word thus signaled the beginning of the ending of all things, the first day of the final unfolding of the consummation of the entire cosmos—the day when God will finally be universally incarnate, when God will be all in all. This is one of the accents of what may appropriately be called a cosmic Christology, building with Teilhard on the testimony of New Testament writings such as Ephesians and Colossians.

There was also a second reason for the Incarnation of the Word. It appears that *this* intentionality of the divine Incarnation was not really taken with full seriousness by Teilhard. This, as we saw, was also Matthew Fox's propensity.[24] The second intentionality of the Incarnation has to do with the *restoration* of the human creature to humanity's proper place in the unfolding history of God with the entire cosmos. This aspect of the Incarnation is, in a certain sense, accidental. God, we may believe, was eternally *prepared* for this possibility, but only actualized it when it became necessary to do so.

Here we can helpfully invoke the traditional Christian testimony to the fall and redemption. While death and suffering are given with the created goodness of the cosmos, self-conscious rebellion against God, the arrogance of humanity's will-to-power, is not. And that is precisely the existentially congenital condition of humankind: to exist, by its own doing, in a state of radical alienation from God.

This broken relationship with the Creator then has destructive implications for human relationships with other humans and with other creatures. Bereft of God, the human creature turns to the ways of self-seeking violence and power over other humans and over other creatures.

When indeed we survey the sometimes awesome scope of violence that is given with nature's goodness—the threat of a large comet crashing into the earth, for example—together with the will-to-power of human conglomerates such as National Socialism, we come face to face with a stark but unavoidable mystery: *radical evil.* Teilhard, for all his testimony to death in nature, nevertheless tended to domesticate mortality in this respect. He also tended to minimize the evils of human history—the pogroms and the mass executions, the fratricide and the genocide—as if they did not exist, or as if they "naturally" were part of the dynamics of cosmic drift. Teilhard was a child of Enlightenment optimism in this respect, much more than a student of classical Christian interpretations of history, such as Augustine's. But we who live in the aftermath of Hiroshima and Dresden, of Dachau and Buchenwald, of apartheid and the killing fields, can no longer allow ourselves to do that. Augustine called human history a "mass of perdition." We know what he meant. Teilhard, apparently, did not.

This means, in turn, that our understanding of *christogenesis* must be commensurate with the breadth and depth of the radical evil that we know we confront. The classical theology of redemption addressed itself to precisely these realities, as we have earlier had occasion to observe. It envisioned the coming of the Christ not merely as a forcordained sending by God—which it was—but also as a sending by God predicated on the enormity of radical evil, with its accidental but horrible destructive power, above all as that evil is generated individually and collectively by the human will-to-power. Christ therefore must die, as the Letter to the Colossians affirms, in order to make peace with all things by the blood of his cross (Col. 1:20). Christ therefore must rise victorious over death, in order to claim all things for the power of his majestic life (cf. 1 Cor. 15:20-28). Otherwise the ontic fragility and the existential brokenness of human life would not allow the human creature to participate in the forward thrust of cosmic evolution.

The Incarnation of the Word is thus a response to the human condition of alienation from God and rebellion against God, as well as a divine cosmic unfolding intended to move the whole of cosmic history into its final stage. United with the Word made flesh, human creatures are *restored* to their proper place in the unfolding history of God with the cosmos. Thus united, they are free to live in peace with one another and with all other creatures, according to the imperfect canons of creation's goodness. Now they may live as an exemplary human community, as a city set upon a hill, whose light cannot be hidden.

Teilhard was right, then, in projecting the idea that the reign of God cannot come without human effort. But he was wrong in leaving the impression that this construct pertains to the species at large. No, in light of the twofold purpose for the Incarnation, particularly now the second, it is clear that *one* human only, the God incarnate, can and does inaugurate and build the reign of God, and that other humans are able to participate in the building of that reign on earth only in union with and in dependence on the new relationship with God that Christ has forged for them.

Still, participate they can and participate they must. The Christian vision of the real calls for a life that embodies that vision in the real. We will return to this theme—the question of ethics—in the concluding chapter of this study. But first it is necessary for us to explore how this recontextualized Teilhardian telling of the classical Christian story can be envisioned interpersonally, enacted ritually, and experienced spiritually. These are the concerns of the next three chapters.

Chapter 5

Reenvisioning the Story Interpersonally

Beyond Anthropocentric Personalism

"Out of the ground the LORD God made to grow every tree that is pleasant to the sight and good for food, the tree of life also in the midst of the garden . . . " (Gen. 2:9)

One day in the middle of the Garden of Eden, the second chapter of Genesis tells us, the Lord God walked about in the cool of the evening. Finding the two earth creatures, who had been trying to hide, because of their disobedience, God spoke to them (Gen. 3:8-9).

In a certain sense, the image of the Deity walking is easy to interpret. This is obviously a marvelous poetic image. But the image of the Deity speaking is something else. That God spoke with Adam and Eve signals, for the biblical mind, that the Lord God had entered into a personal relationship with them. This was already highlighted in the first chapter of Genesis, when, in a sequence of creative acts of speaking, the Creator first spoke in the first person to the human creatures (Gen. 1:28).

The striking poetic image of God speaking as we see it in Genesis 2 is therefore more than an image. It gives expression to an underlying theological conviction, that *God is personal and that humans likewise are personal.* Paul Tillich called this "biblical personalism."[1]

The Christian story, as it has classically presupposed the substance of biblical faith, has taken that kind of theological personalism for granted, as we saw in the case of Teilhard. But it now appears that that very personalism, that ancient and venerable theological conviction of the classical tradition, has become a deep-seated liability in this era of ecological crisis and cosmic anxieties. Even if we retell the Christian story in a way that recontextualizes the anthropocentrism of Teilhard, even if we can then envision a universal, cosmic history in which all creatures, not just humans, have eternal value, can we even think in a way that allows us to attribute real significance to personal relationships with the impersonal world of nature? Given the high value we Christians place on personal relationships, with God and with one another, what could it possibly mean for us to befriend the creatures of nature?

Consider the tree of life (Gen. 2:9). What kind of relationship did the Lord God have with that tree and what kind of relationship to the tree did the Lord expect Adam and Eve to have? A personal relationship with a tree?

Such questions point to a major challenge for Christian theology in these times of global crisis: to develop a comprehensive conceptuality so that the classical Christian story, once retold ecologically and cosmically, can then be reenvisioned interpersonally. Biblical personalism and its Christian theological heir seem well equipped to give expression to the heights and depths of God's relationship with us humans, and of our relationship to God, but where does that leave the tree? Is the tree only part of the "scenery" of God's history with humanity, as theologian Emil Brunner confidently announced in the first part of the last century? Or is the tree something else? How should I relate to the great and glorious maple tree in my own front yard?

It is a matter of theological urgency for us to consider in depth the legacy and the liability of theological personalism in its anthropocentric expression and then to determine how a genuine ecological and cosmic conceptuality can be defined within the parameters of the selfsame personalism. This I propose to do, in conversation with a great twentieth-century Jewish thinker, Martin Buber, who himself pondered descriptively—or phenomenologically—what it can mean to relate oneself to a tree.

The Legacy and the Liability of Anthropocentric Personalism

The Christian tradition, of course, has had no monopoly on a personalistic approach to the life of faith. Among other places, a profound theological personalism was kept alive and indeed richly nurtured in numerous communities of Hasidic Jews in Europe, during the Middle Ages and beyond. From those Hasidic traditions emerged one work, written by a modern Jewish theologian, that had a profound influence on Christian theology in ensuing decades: Martin's Buber's short but moving poetic meditations on personal relationships, *I and Thou*.[2]

Protestant theologians, for their own reasons, were especially attracted to the kind of theological personalism that came to expression in *I and Thou*. In a variety of ways, thinkers such as Karl Barth, Emil Brunner, Karl Heim, and Friedrich Gogarten employed the kind of conceptuality suggested by Buber's work—and by others with similar interests, such as Ferdinand Ebner[3]—as a key methodological construct.[4] That personalistic way of thinking served them well in their varying attempts to develop their theology as what they thought of as the-anthropology, a description of the history between God and humankind. It also served them well—this was especially true in Brunner's case—in the task that some of them undertook to differentiate theological language from the language of the natural sciences, and to validate theological discourse alongside the natural sciences, disciplines that deal with "impersonal nature."

Whereas, however, that kind of personalism may have served theologians like Barth and Brunner well in their theological work in their day, it clearly presupposes what I have elsewhere called the eclipse of nature in modern Christian thought.[5] After all, the I-Thou conceptuality, as it has been employed in modern theology, brings with it a fateful double, the construct of the I-It relationship. That relationship, as Buber and others have described it, is manipulative and potentially, if not always actually, exploitative. The It is a mere object, a thing. The It has no raison d'être other than its availability for manipulation. The It can only be a slave to a master. Is the whole world of nature, therefore, to be understood to be merely a collection of objects, awaiting mastery and probably exploitation?

This is a question that probably never forcefully dawned on theologians like Barth and Brunner a half century ago. But it is a question that must surely stop us in our tracks, given our ecological sensibilities and our environmental predicament. When you see one tree, have you seen them all? Has our faith tradition, as we have received it, not equipped us, truly, to see a tree? Has our faith tradition, also in this conceptual sense, been anthropocentric to the point of debilitating the faith itself?

Must it be either/or? Must we choose either to hold on to the profound personalism of the theological tradition or to relinquish it, on the grounds that that conceptuality is incapable of allowing us to describe and to advocate relationships with nature that are anything but exploitative?

Paul Tillich, for one, understood the force of that question already in the first half of the twentieth century, as he indicated in his little book *Biblical Religion and the Search for Ultimate Reality*.[6] And he made his choice, self-consciously and with much soul-searching, for he knew how important theological personalism had been for the Christian tradition, since its very beginnings and down to his own day.

Tillich chose to bracket or to move beyond personalism. He chose to interpret "God" as a symbol for Being Itself. He decided to argue that, while "the personal" is rooted in God, God as Being Itself is "more than personal." This is what some Tillich scholars have called his "hyperpersonalism." Which is to say: For Tillich, while the personal is rooted in God, God is beyond the personal.

That fundamental choice is surely a direction for Christian theologians to ponder today, as we explore what it means to think ecologically and cosmically. Hyperpersonalism clearly makes possible a conceptuality that gives equal voice to nature, alongside humanity. Both nature and humanity, according to this way of thinking, have their ontological ground in Being Itself, in their own ways undoubtedly, but neither one has what might readily be thought of otherwise as a privileged relationship to God. That is to say, according to the perspective of hyperpersonalism, no longer are God and humanity in the same ontic class, while nature is in another, lesser class. According to the hyperpersonalistic way of thinking, both nature and humanity are in the same ontic class, while God is in another. God is the "Ground of Being," as Tillich often said, of every finite creature.

That the hyperpersonalistic approach to theology may well bring with it a rich theological potential in this ecological era has already been suggested by the kind of nature-mysticism and the kind of ecological wisdom that came to expression in Tillich's works, in an era when the theme of nature was more or less a theological taboo.[7] In his preaching, in particular, Tillich was hermeneutically equipped to make a strong plea for the salvation of nature, as his 1948 sermon "Nature, Also, Mourns for a Lost God" shows.

In that sermon, Tillich recounts a conversation he once had with a great biologist, as they were sitting together underneath a tree. The biologist told Tillich: "I want to know what this tree means for itself. It is so strange, so unapproachable." Tillich observed in his sermon that although that biologist had had extensive knowledge about the tree, what the man really had wanted was to be able to commune with the tree. Then Tillich commented, incisively:

> Is such communion possible in our period of history? Is nature not completely subjected to the will and willfulness of man? This technical civilization, the pride of mankind, has brought about a tremendous devastation of original nature, of the land, of animals, of plants. It has

kept genuine nature in small reservations and occupied everything for domination and ruthless exploitation. And worse: many of us have lost the ability to live with nature. We fill it with the noise of empty talk, instead of listening to its many voices, and through them, to the voiceless music of the universe. Separated from the soil by a machine, we speed through nature, catching glimpses of it, but never comprehending its greatness or feeling its power. Who is still able to penetrate, meditating and contemplating, the creative ground of nature?[8]

That is the kind of sensitivity for our life in nature that Tillich's hyper-personalist theological perspective allows and, indeed, encourages.

Can we commune with the tree? Is friendship divine in this respect also? While some will undoubtedly want to explore the potential of hyper-personalism in theology, following the example of Tillich, I do not think that that direction is the only viable spiritual alternative, by any means, however promising it might appear. I believe that it is possible to imagine what it might mean to commune with a tree, while thinking within the parameters of the personalistic theological tradition of the classical Christian story that we have inherited and that we have contemplated in recontextualized, Teilhardian terms. I believe that it is possible in this respect to have a theology of both/and, both a profound theological personalism and a rich experience of nature: to be able to conceptualize a viable ecological and cosmic relationality within the matrix of theological personalism.

On the other hand, to choose *not* to be concerned with such issues, to assume that the received tradition of theological personalism provides us with everything the community of faith needs to proclaim and embody the biblical message in these times, I also believe, is to choose the way of folly. That kind of choice may well satisfy those who have decided to station themselves at the theological gates today, as defenders of the confessional status quo, as protectors of the church's "deposit of faith." But I am convinced that kind of response will only have the effect of finally demonstrating to everyone what critics like Matthew Fox have claimed vociferously for some time, that in this respect no deposit can be found, that Christian theology is ecologically bankrupt.

Whatever judgment one may wish to render about Matthew Fox's proposed "creation spirituality," and we have had occasion to raise some serious questions about his proposals, there can be no doubt that his work has filled a spiritual vacuum in our time. Can there in fact be a way for those of us who choose to remain fully the self-conscious heirs of the classical Christian story to envision what it means to commune with a tree?

Buber's Idiosyncratic Rendering of I-Thou and I-It

The richness of Buber's description of the I-Thou relationship was neglected by Christian theologians who drew on the kind of thinking that came to expression in his classic explorations. Buber envisioned the I-Thou relationship as including certain relationships to the physical-vital world of nature. A case in point is the I-Thou relation Buber understood to be possible between a person and *a tree.*

"It can ... come about," Buber writes, "if I have both will and grace, that in considering the tree I become bound up in relation to it. The tree is now no longer It. I have been seized by the power of exclusiveness."[9] Contrast this to Karl Barth's assertion that the only place in the cosmos where we no longer say It and I, but Thou, is before the human countenance.[10] For Barth, there can be no I-Thou relationship with a tree, in any sense, an assumption he shares with most other well-known Christian theologians who have employed the I-Thou, I-It conceptuality.

This means that in general theological usage, all relationships between humans and nature are assumed to be I-It relationships. This is to assume that all relationships between humans and nature are distant, manipulative, and instrumental, if not exploitative—the main characteristics of the I-It relationship, as Buber depicts it. But this then brings with it certain theological tensions, not to say contradictions, of which theologians like Barth did not even appear to have been aware.

Consider the human body. Is the human body always merely an It? Should one relate oneself to the body of another person, the Thou, in order to have that body at one's disposal, to use it, to manipulate it at will? One would consistently have to relate oneself to the body of the Thou in such a manner if one assumed, first, that the human body is part of the material-vital world more generally (no one will want to question this assumption) and, second, that the only possible relation between humans and nature is the I-It relation (as this way of thinking leads one to assume).

Given the psychosomatic unity of the self, which the Bible takes for granted and which modern medical research consistently confirms, one could not truly relate oneself to the Thou as a whole person without in some respects turning the Thou into an It. To cite a particular case: no one can be a "sex object," without being an object in some sense, and without therefore having his or her personhood or Thou-ness that much diminished. It will be necessary, therefore, to find a way to relate to the body of the Thou so that that body is an end in itself, not merely a means or an instrument for other ends.[11]

Buber can envision a relationship to the body as an end in itself, on his own terms, because for him relationships to material-vital entities can be comprehended as an aspect of the I-Thou relation. Indeed, Buber was even able to write a paean for "brother body," after the fashion of St. Francis.[12] That way of vibrant articulation, however, has not been readily open to those who have neglected Buber's extensive conception of the I-Thou relationship.

The case is much the same when we consider the general relationship that can obtain between humans and the larger world of nature. Surely the idea of the I-It relation is an accurate rendering of some human relations with nature, but not all. One need only think of the psalmist's praise of the glories of nature. The psalmist is obviously at this point not involved in an I-It relationship. Still more obvious is the case of St. Francis, who lived with the creatures of nature as brothers and sisters. Those relationships were clearly not I-It relationships. Barth's statement that one can say "Thou" only before the human countenance leaves him with no way to account for, or to adopt, the testimony of the psalmist or St. Francis.

Then there is the somewhat more subtle problem of our relationship with God. Theologians such as Barth and Tillich, taking a cue from modern biblical research, emphatically claim that God is the living God, that is, a God not only of spirit, but also of power. Barth has made the point explicitly: "If God has no nature, if He is that chemically distilled absolute spirit, He does nothing, and in fact he can do nothing. . . . Acts happen only in the unity of spirit and nature. If such a unity is to be denied to God, then . . . there is no true, real history of his doing things in any genuine sense of the term."[13] Buber likewise wants to emphasize the divine power and vitality, but at the same time—with Barth and over against Tillich—he wants to say that God is personal.[14]

Buber is in a position to do this consistently, since his basic notion of the I-Thou relationship explicitly includes a relationship to the vitality of the human body and since, for him more generally, an I-Thou relationship to all natural entities is conceivable. Hence, problematic as predication of the term "Thou" to a God of infinite power and vitality may be, in Buber's case at least, the fundamental analogical terms permit the predication.[15]

Anyone who in this respect would follow Barth, in contrast, will face a problem. If God is both spirit and nature, as Barth says, God must also in some sense be an It, and that would imply that God is in some sense at our disposal. Which, of course, any true disciple of Barth would never want to suggest.

Buber's conceptuality for the I-Thou relationship, exemplified by his description of a particular relationship between a human being and a tree, is therefore much to be preferred over the more coherent interpretations of the relationship by thinkers such as Barth. On the other hand, Buber's vision of the I-Thou relationship has its own problems, on his own terms. This is because, for him, the chief characteristic of the I-Thou relationship is mutuality.[16] In a word, in what sense can a tree be responsive? Further, according to Buber's own schema, *speech* is of the essence of an I-Thou relation between humans: "Speech in its ontological sense was at all times present wherever men regarded one another in the mutuality of I and Thou."[17] But obviously a tree cannot speak. In what sense, then, can it possibly be meaningful to talk about an I-Thou relationship with a tree?[18]

Buber recognized the problem at this point. In a postscript to his final edition of *I and Thou*, he considered the matter directly.[19] A certain kind of reciprocity in the I-Thou relation to the tree is conceivable, he suggests. The natural world generally is characterized by spontaneity. This is particularly true of the animal world. With animals, he says, we are at the "threshold of mutuality." Buber grants willingly, however, that he has not said the last word regarding this problem. "Clearly," he comments, "there is no unified answer to this question."[20]

In the balance, it appears that Buber has chosen the better way, even if it does appear to be idiosyncratic. Not to think of the I-Thou relation as extending to nature in some respect creates the three significant difficulties mentioned above, regarding our relationship with other humans as embodied, our relationship with nature more generally, and our relationship with God. On the other hand, it is permissible to state that with regard to the I-Thou relationship with the tree we have come to the limits of our knowing—but that it is nevertheless necessary to say something in this respect in order not to say nothing at all.[21]

An Ecological and Cosmic Conceptuality: I-Thou, I-It, and I-Ens

There is a better way. It is possible, and therefore surely desirable under the circumstances, to modify Buber's rendering of the I-Thou, I-It conceptuality so that it is more coherent, not quite so idiosyncratic.[22] It is possible to speak of *a third type of relation,* a construct that will make available a truly ecological and cosmic conceptuality, one that accounts for rich relationships between persons and nature that are not I-It relationships.

Interestingly enough, Buber himself came close to suggesting this kind of modification of his own position explicitly in his early "mystical" writings, prior to his "existential" and "dialogic" periods.[23] Those writings are the basis for his later interest in depicting the I-Thou relation inclusively, as comprehending certain encounters with nature as well as with persons.[24]

I propose to call this third type of relationship an "I-Ens relation," from the Latin participle for "being." And I want to identify this third kind of relationship by offering a phenomenological description of the personal experience, throughout which I will draw on the testimony of a number of witnesses, from traditional interpreters of the Scriptures such as Luther and Calvin to latter-day witnesses inspired by the same Scriptures, such as John Muir, whenever their testimony rings true.

I will leave it to others to address certain "systematic" questions that this kind of phenomenological approach does not answer.[25] In particular, I will assume that I-Ens relationships between persons and entities in the world of "fabricated nature"—nature taken up into or stamped by the world of human spirit, such as chairs, buildings, molten steel, even whole cities—are just as authentic and just as meaningful as are I-Ens relationships between persons and the entities of cultivated or wild nature.[26]

The I-Ens relation is characterized by the existence of both terms of the relation in a present moment. Both poles of the relation have a certain fluidity, an openness to new possibilities. The Ens, in particular, is a presenting reality, not circumscribed by the detached inspection of the human eye. To employ Buber's terminology, the Ens is primarily presence (*Gegenwart*), rather than object (*Gegenstand*).[27] There is a certain immediacy to the I-Ens relation. The objectifying mode of human consciousness does not come between a person and a tree in this respect, as it does come between the two in an I-It relationship.[28] In this sense the I-Ens relation is not a juxtaposition of a mere subject over against a mere object. It refers to a subjective pole and an objective pole bound together in an intimate community.

If one remembers that the I-Ens relation is intimate, fluid, and present, and that the poles of the relation cannot be drawn apart without transforming it into I and It, it is then possible to describe each pole of the relation in turn.

The Ens is characterized by its givenness. An Ens does not fit into a utilitarian description of the world. Like a two-dimensional painting, it confronts me directly with an exclusive claim, a claim that will not allow me to pass beyond it, in order to set it in a larger schema of means and ends. Insofar as it remains an Ens, it stands in the middle of my path. I do not pass it by with a fleeting glance, as I do an It—however long I may engage myself with the It.[29] I come to a halt and I contemplate the maple tree in my front yard, for example, and rejoice in all its glories, especially in the fall, when its leaves glow with a glorious brightness. I do not immediately think that the tree may need pruning or spraying or even removal. As an Ens, that tree stands before me in its own right, a beautiful entity posited there for its own sake. I contemplate it and am captivated by it.[30] I do not penetrate behind its sheer givenness.

Along with its givenness, the Ens also exhibits a certain mysterious activity or spontaneity, born from what Teilhard would call its "within." I cannot fully predict how the Ens will behave from moment to moment. Insofar as it is an Ens, its activity and passivity will not always match my expectations. It will grow, decay, develop, stand silently still, or disappear in a way that I cannot fully understand. This will remain the case even when whatever scientific knowledge I have of any particular Ens is integrated into my encounter with that Ens.[31]

The Ens has still another characteristic that deserves comment here. It has beauty, a quality that as a matter of course has already come to our attention. In a certain sense, the idea of beauty unites the other characteristics of the Ens that we have considered to this point—its givenness and its mysterious activity or spontaneity. What makes an entity beautiful, of course, cannot easily be defined in one paragraph or even a whole volume.[32]

One might say tentatively that the Ens is beautiful, whether in a simple or a profound way—whether beautiful in the strict sense or sublime[33]—because it is an integrated whole. It displays unity and diversity in harmony with each other. Every Ens is thereby like a beautiful symphony. The symphony's unity is one with its diversity, although the one or the other may predominate at any given moment. Also, the symphony never loses its givenness, its claim for its own unique place, its mysterious activity, and its movement, which can appear so unpredictable.

John Muir was suggesting much the same idea when he said that "music is one of the attributes of matter, into whatever forms it may be organized." As a case in point, Muir referred to a certain valley of his acquaintance: "Fancy the waving, pulsing melody of the vast flower-congregations of the Hollow flowing from myriad voices of tuned petal and pistil, and heaps of sculptured pollen."[34] John Calvin—who in many ways was the teacher of Muir in this respect—expressed the same idea: "all things above and below" are "beautifully arranged" so that they may "respond to each other in the most harmonious concert."[35]

Among the characteristics of the subjective pole of the I-Ens relation the mood of wonder is perhaps the most important. Wonder includes, first, a person's total attention. This is part of the significance of Martin Luther's remark, "If you really examined a kernel of grain thoroughly, you would die of wonder."[36] One does not enter into wonder, in other words, if one's attention is divided. If such were the case, the Ens would become an It.

Wonder includes, second, a person's openness to the Ens, his or her willingness to forget preconceptions of what the Ens is or should be. As Muir once reported about a walk through a grove of tillandsia-draped oaks in the southern United States: "I gazed awestricken as one newly arrived from another world."[37] That is to say, to enter into wonder, one must be predisposed to encounter the unexpected. One must put away the guide-book or the textbook and look at the world with one's own eyes.

Wonder also includes, third, the willingness to become small and lowly, the willingness to humble oneself, especially before objects that are other-wise insignificant—the blade of grass, the broken piece of colored glass at the side of the road, the ant making its way across the picnic cloth. One must know how to allot the Ens a space of its own. One must not automat-ically pass by it or manipulate it or dispose of it or kill it.[38]

Wonder further includes, fourth, a profound sense of gratitude. The I stands before the Ens always with gratitude, never with greed. The Ens can never be property. The Ens always belongs, without any qualification, to the Creator and to the Creator alone. The Ens is never "mine." The Ens is always "Thine." Once it is mine, greed begins to take over. Greed breeds mindless manipulation and finally ruthless exploitation. But when the other creature is Thine, the I of the I-Ens relation always stands before the Ens in grati-tude. Gratitude, in contrast to greed, brings with it contemplation and cel-ebration, sometimes with joyful abandon.

The mood of wonder is closely related to two others, repulsion on the one hand, delight on the other.[39] The first is the mood appropriate for beings, Entia, which comes from what the literature of romanticism some-times calls the dark side of the world and what some American writers, more particularly, think of as the wilderness. The dark side of the world is perhaps best symbolized by Melville's white whale, Moby Dick. The whale comes from the ocean—"which is the dark side of this earth, and which is two thirds of the earth."[40] On gazing at the whale, one feels "the Deity and the dread powers more forcibly than in beholding any other object in liv-ing nature."[41] With the whale and the ocean in mind, one can say: "Though in many of its aspects this visible world seems formed in love, the invisible spheres were formed in fright."[42]

If wonder is sometimes and to varying degrees complemented by repul-sion, at other times and also to varying degrees it is complemented by delight. Here the music changes from Mahler to Mozart. One sees the earth not so much as covered except for a third by the dark ocean, but as being framed, in Calvin's words, as a "magnificent theater."[43] One senses that "God has stretched out his hand to us to give us the splendor of the sun and the moon to enjoy."[44] Hence Calvin can also say: "Let us not be ashamed to take pious delight in the works of God open and manifest in this most beautiful theater."[45] John Muir, following Calvin's admonition, thereby could write of the chain of islands off the western coast of Canada: "There the eye easily takes in and revels in their beauty with ever fresh delight."[46] In the context of urban life, one can recall the similar experience of many visitors to New York City whose eyes take in and revel in the beauty of the skyline as they approach from the sea. Still within an urban context and still within the mood of delight, but closer to the microcosmic, Paul Tillich once told how as a young boy he had been enthralled and captivated at the sight of molten steel in a factory in Berlin. "*That* is God," he said to himself, with boyish abandon.[47]

The mood of the subject that is perhaps most difficult to describe—we have already met it in the words of Melville, Calvin, and Tillich—can be called the sense for the divine presence.[48] This could also be called, in Tillich's terminology, an awareness of a "dimension of depth" in the I-Ens relation. As Calvin writes of the whole creation: "For to everyone who approaches this heavenly building with a pure mind, the effect cannot but be that he is plunged into amazed adoration at the sight of the Wisdom, the Goodness, and the Power of God."[49] Elsewhere Calvin treats the same basic theme:

> We see, indeed, the world with our eyes, we tread the earth with our feet, we touch innumerable kinds of God's works with our hands, we inhale a sweet and pleasant fragrance from herbs and flowers, we enjoy boundless benefits, but in those very things of which we attain some knowledge, there dwells such an immensity of divine power, goodness, and wisdom, as absorbs all our senses.[50]

This passage is not unlike the Hasidic saying that Buber chose as a dedication for one of his books. For Hasidism, "there is no rung of being on which we cannot find the Holiness of God everywhere and at all times."[51] So Buber himself comments, "Because God is immanent in the world, the world becomes—in a general religious sense—a sacrament."[52]

The fundamental idea before us can be summarized as follows. In encountering the Ens, I am captivated by its openness to the infinite, by its openness to a dimension that lies behind and permeates its givenness, its spontaneity, and its beauty.[53] Muir once expressed this in his own characteristic way by saying of a group of California redwoods, "Every tree seemed religious and conscious of the presence of God."[54] Of a certain Alaskan glacier, he wrote: "Every feature glowed with intention, reflecting the plans of God."[55] One might recapitulate all this with the words of the psalmist, "The heavens are telling the glory of God, and the firmament proclaims his handiwork" (Ps. 19:1).

With the construct of the I-Ens relationship thus before us, we now have access to the construct of a genuine ecological and cosmic conceptuality. The distinctiveness of interpersonal relationships is preserved. The Christian can still celebrate the God revealed in and through Jesus Christ as a personal God, indeed as the Person in whose light all other personhood is established and sustained. This is the I-Thou relationship.

Furthermore, factual, although not always desirable, human relationships to nature that are manipulative are accounted for by this conceptuality. We humans *do* intervene in nature in numerous ways, often manipulatively, sometimes for the sake of our survival, unavoidably. We also appropriately intervene in the earth for the purposes of building up human community, above all by the construction and conservation of cities. And we intervene, appropriately, especially in our era, by caring for the earth, by setting aside wilderness areas, for example, or by restoring areas previously devastated by a variety of human uses and abuse. All this, to one degree or another, falls under the rubric of the I-It relationship.

Most important, for our purposes here, we now can account for, and then in appropriate ways become advocates for, increasingly desirable relationships of mutuality and cooperation between persons and other creatures of nature. This is the I-Ens relationship. With the availability of this kind of holistic thinking, theological personalism need no longer be anthropocentric. Now it can be ecological and cosmic, conceptually as well as narratively.

I can salute the maple tree in my front yard as a member of my own extended family.

Chapter 6

Reenacting the Story Ritually

Beyond the Milieu of the Gothic Spirit

"Am I a God near, says the Lord, *and not a God afar off? . . . Do I not fill heaven and earth? says the* Lord.*" (Jer. 23:23-24)*

In his short but incisive ethical study *Moral Fragments and Moral Community,* Larry Rasmussen analyzes the trends of the modern world that have brought us all to the brink of widespread political and social upheaval, environmental degradation, individual isolation and despair, and moral anomie.[1] What this situation of global crisis requires, he argues, is the emergence of a large variety of "communal enclaves" around the world that will socialize their members into distinctive, observable ways of life that publicly demonstrate creative new possibilities of the moral life. These exemplary moral communities will, in turn, shape larger social, political, cultural, and religious institutions in a way that will have a global impact for the better on the destructive trends that now seem to be so intractable and so pernicious everywhere.

One of these exemplary moral communities, Rasmussen pleads, must be the church of Jesus Christ. Indeed, the church, in his view, may be situated to respond creatively to the current global crisis like few others, if not uniquely situated. "For a community whose very first article of faith is a confession of God as the Creator of a good creation, and whose vision has been that of all creation redeemed to its fullest possible flourishing, this moment is a reply to an extraordinary invitation and an ancient hope."[2]

Pursuant to that thought, Rasmussen characterizes four communal moral qualities that must characterize the church in these times of crisis. He wants the church to be a "people of the way," a servant community: (1) that has an inclusive, egalitarian membership; (2) that shows a pioneering creative lifestyle; (3) that serves as a way station or a haven of rest and renewal for all its members and for countless strangers; and (4) that takes on the role of moral critic of the whole society.[3] We will return to consider similar thoughts in the concluding chapter of this book.

At the very end of his discussion, Rasmussen turns to the thought of worship. "What remains to be said about the four roles is only that they, like the life of the community itself, come together focally in worship. Worship for a people of the way was and is 'the communal cultivation of an alternative construction of society and of history.'"[4] While Rasmussen is well aware of the formative power of ritual in human life generally and in the life of the Christian community in particular, the whole subject sounds like something of an afterthought, as he develops his argument in *Moral Fragments and Moral Community*.

This kind of relegation of worship to the end, intended or not, must be corrected in the context of our discussion here, emphatically. Because, it appears, anthropocentric traditions in worship in the Christian West have left the Christian community ill-equipped to be the kind of exemplary moral community that Rasmussen so appropriately calls it to be. In fact, it could be argued that one of the main reasons that the church has found itself so ill equipped in so many ways to respond to the environmental—and other—dimensions of today's global crisis is precisely those anthropocentric traditions of worship.

Worship, in fact, is not an afterthought that gives expression to other, more fundamental commitments of the church's life. It is much closer to the truth to say that worship constitutes the church's life, for better or for worse. Worship can be called the mode of identity-formation of the church's life.

Theologians and other church leaders in pragmatic, practical, bottom-line America do not readily find themselves attuned to theological reflections about worship, especially insofar as such reflections come to focus on the sacramental life of the church. Theologically informed American Christians may wistfully refer to the cosmic insights of Eastern Christianity, which they know are rooted in a rich liturgical life. They may express admiration for the "creation spirituality" of a Matthew Fox, which Fox himself regularly and often dramatically ties to the establishment of new, nontraditional rituals. But the wistfulness and the admiration typically soon give way to the pragmatism.

The real theological business of the day, for many thoughtful American Christians, is ethics or evangelism or perhaps both. Which, in turn, characteristically means attending to the communal inculcation of values (character ethics), lifting up a call for social justice and good stewardship (political and social ethics), or mandating the church to take the witness of the gospel to all nations, at home and abroad (evangelization).

What those who follow the pragmatic way characteristically miss, however, is that neither the communal inculcation of values, nor the proclamation of social justice and good stewardship, nor again the kerygmatic call to evangelization emerges *ex nihilo.* Nor can these activities be sustained *ex nihilo.* This is because the mission of the church is not first and foremost doing. The mission of the church is first and foremost being, a case that I argued more than three decades ago and that still needs to be argued resolutely, perhaps all the more vigorously, in view of the dissonances of our increasingly postmodern situation.[5] The doing of the church flows from the being of the church. The works of the church flow from the grace given to the church. The life of faithful discipleship grows from the rich soil of faithful communal ritual. The church at work is totally dependent on the church at worship.

This kind of observation has been delineated by many phenomenologists of religion, past and present, with regard to the formative power of ritual in human experience more generally. Erik H. Erikson, for one, argued from the perspective of developmental psychology that ritual generally is the mode of identity-formation. The parent, for example, who enters the room where the infant has just awakened and who smiles at the infant, morning after morning, day after day, is engaging in a ritual that inculcates what Erikson called "basic trust." The infant does not develop basic trust, and so does not appropriately enter into the processes of psychological maturization, according to Erikson, apart from such rituals.

Likewise for the worship of the church: this is the way the church inculcates values such as the four highlighted by Rasmussen, in particular those that are of most interest to us here, which shape the church's ethos of cosmic awareness and ecological responsibility. Every Christian environmental ethic, in this sense, presupposes the generative matrix of the worship of the church, for better or for worse.

It is sobering, then, to observe that much of the church's traditional worship, as I have suggested, has been shaped by a sometimes acosmic theological anthropocentrism, to the disservice of the church's ecological and cosmic witness. This is the ambiguity of the Gothic Spirit.

The Ambiguity of the Gothic Spirit

Few have ever walked into a great Gothic cathedral without at first stand-ing still, awestruck by the vision: the narrative richness of the towering west façade and its entrances, the effulgence of light everywhere inside, the soar-ing heights, the sometimes subtle, sometimes brilliant colors of the stained glass, the simple but often elegant contours of the high altar, and much more. To walk into a great Gothic cathedral is to walk into a world apart, a world of dazzling and overpowering beauty and sanctity.

The cathedrals were designed, indeed, to be a world apart: a world that luminously, harmoniously, and powerfully proclaims the mystery of divine truth, insofar as that truth can be grasped by sinful mortals. Erwin Panofsky has instructively juxtaposed the high Gothic cathedrals with the great systematic and synthetic works of philosophy and theology pro-duced by the leading theologians of the medieval era, the *summae* con-structed by geniuses such as Thomas Aquinas.[6] "In its imagery," Panofsky explains, "the high Gothic cathedral sought to embody the whole of Christian knowledge, theological, moral, natural, and historical, with everything in its place and that which no longer found its place, sup-pressed."[7] Further, and again like the *summa*, Panofsky argues, the high Gothic cathedral represented a vast, harmonious, and hierarchical arrangement according to a system of homologous parts and parts of parts.[8]

We know what that system of harmonious arrangement was. We have already encountered it in our discussion of Teilhard de Chardin. It was the metaphysical and metapoetic vision of the Great Chain of Being. This can be illustrated with reference to the story of what was perhaps the single most influential Gothic structure of the medieval era, the abbey church of St. Denis in France, which was envisioned in the twelfth century by the emi-nent Abbot Suger of St. Denis.[9] Suger was a champion of the metaphysics and the metapoetics of the Great Chain of Being.

As Otto von Simson tells us, the abbey of St. Denis itself owed its influ-ential ecclesiastical position to the fact that "it preserved the relics of the saint and martyr who, in the third century, had converted France to Chris-tianity and was hence revered as the patron of the royal house and of the realm. But this St. Denis was held to be identical with an Eastern theologian who was one of the great mystical writers of the early Christian era and, in fact, of the Christian tradition."[10] This Denis has come to be called Pseudo-Areopagite or, more simply, Dionysius the Areopagite. With reference to the thought of this Dionysius, George Duby comments, "Suger designed St. Denis as a monument of applied theology."[11]

The works of Dionysius, available to Suger in translation and beloved by him, above all the *Celestial Hierarchy*, depicted the vision of the Great Chain of Being in all its fullness. In those writings Suger found a majestic testimony to the effulgence of light and to both of the principles we saw Panofsky identify, a comprehensive representation of the rich and manifold fullness of created reality and an arrangement that was harmonious and hierarchical.

For our purposes here, what is important is not any of the details of this story or any particular Gothic cathedral, but what can be called the Gothic spirit, which enshrined the metaphysics and the metapoetics of the Great Chain of Being. That was a vision of reality that extended from sheer matter or nonbeing at the nadir, through gradations of being—mineral, biological, human, and angelic—to pure spirit or God or "the One" at the apex.

Fatefully, in this hierarchical vision, the line that divided matter from spirit was believed to run through the human creature, who, as body, is matter and who, as soul, is spirit. Some scholars have talked about a "spirit-matter dualism," in this connection. In one respect, the human creature is on the side of the angels; in the other the human creature is on the side of the animals. But what is critical for the unfolding of the vision is this: within the whole biophysical world, the human creature is the only creature with spirit. Herein lies the grounds for this vision's anthropocentrism, over against the whole material creation. For, in effect, as we saw in our review of Teilhard's employment of the same conceptuality, the only material creature that is finally important in the greater scheme of things is the human creature. In biblical imagery, according to this way of thinking, only Adam and Eve in the garden, no other earthly creatures, have an eternal destiny.

Here we touch on the ambiguity of the Gothic vision. In my study *The Travail of Nature*, I identified two fundamental metaphors that this hierarchical conceptuality presupposes, the metaphor of ascent and the metaphor of fecundity.[12] When this hierarchy is viewed from below, as if one were standing at the base of a great mountain, the metaphor of ascent dominates. Here the spirituality drives the soul to ascend up to the spiritual One, high above, and to leave the world of matter behind, as if one were climbing a mountain to contemplate the sun. In contrast, when the hierarchy is viewed from above, as if one were standing at the peak of a great mountain surveying the surrounding valleys below, the metaphor of fecundity dominates. Here the spirituality drives the soul to contemplate and to identify itself with the descending of God or the One, the overflowing of the Divine, to encompass and embrace the whole of the spiritual and material universe.

As Dionysius depicted the Great Chain of Being, more particularly, there were two major ontological movements in the hierarchy: first, the overflowing movement from God extending to the fullness of created beings below, second, the movement of return of the Many to the One, toward union with the eternal world of pure spirit above. The theme of light dominated Dionysius' two-movement vision, as Duby eloquently explains:

> At the core of the treatise was one idea: God is light. Every creature stems from that initial, uncreated, creative light. Every creature receives and transmits the divine illumination according to its capacity, that is, according to its rank in the scale of beings, according to the level at which God's intentions situated it hierarchically. The universe, born of an irradiance, was a downward-spilling burst of luminosity, and the light emanating from the primal Being established every created being in its immutable place. But it united all beings, linking them with love, irrigating the entire world, establishing order and coherence within it. And because every object reflected light to a greater or lesser degree, the initial irradiance brought forth from the depths of the shadow, by means of a continuous chain of reflections, a contrary movement, a movement of reflection back toward the source of its effulgence. In this way the luminous act of creation brought about of itself a gradual ascension leading backward, step by step, to the invisible and ineffable Being from which all proceeds.[13]

This vision, Duby concludes, was to be the key to Gothic art, "an art of light, clarity, and dazzling radiance. . . . and Suger's abbey church was its prototype."[14]

It was the metaphor of ascent that drove the Gothic spirit. That is indicated dramatically by the Gothic heights themselves, pointing to salvation above. The Gothic cathedral surely offered representations of the world of nature below, and sometimes richly. But it was the second movement of the great hierarchical flow of reality that most fascinated the theologians and the mystics of that era: the ascent to heaven, leaving the world of nature behind. The great Thomas Aquinas would leave no doubt about this ascent: salvation, the return of the Many to the One, the ascent of souls to God, meant that nature as we know it, the world of trees and mountains, animals and oceans, would be abrogated.[15] On the last day, there will be no new creation of all things, according to Thomas, only spiritual beings.

In this kind of Gothic setting, the meaning of *worship* could move only in one direction finally, to accent the ascent of the soul to God, and the abandonment of the material world. Yes, preachers and teachers could on occasion talk about the glories of the material-vital creation, and poets such as Dante could celebrate them.[16] And both the mystics and the common folk of faith could see the glories of the creation illustrated in the cathedrals, as worshipers were bathed in the descending light. But the Gothic spirit brought with it the fascination with the light of heaven, the eternal light of God, and of the return of the soul to union with the self-same eternal light above. So when in the eucharistic liturgy the celebrant uttered phrases to the people such as "lift up your hearts," we may imagine both he and they knew exactly what he meant, as he stood at the high altar, dwarfed by the immense heights of the cathedral and defined by the effulgence of the light coming in from above: salvation is above, removed from this world of matter.

That there were a variety of other trends in medieval worship, in addition to the theme of ascent, can be taken for granted. Above all, the church moved emphatically to safeguard and indeed to celebrate the idea of the real presence of Christ in the eucharistic elements on the altar, the descent of the Savior into "the flesh" of the bread and the wine.[17] But such emphases by no means undercut the dominant theology and spirituality of the Gothic spirit. The Eucharist in that epoch was nothing if it was not a means of grace by which people of faith could be freed for their heavenly ascent, above and beyond the world of created matter.

If matter was thus left behind—or below—by the dynamics of the Gothic spirit, that should not be taken to mean that it was of no interest to the powers that be of the Gothic era. On the contrary, the anthropocentrism of the Gothic spirit brought with it, and probably was also fostered by, a burgeoning new kind of cultural engagement with nature, in terms of scientific empiricism and technological mastery. This was reflected in the art of Gothic era. Historian Lynn White Jr. explains: "The emergence of Gothic art reflects a fundamental change in the European attitude toward the natural environment. Things ceased to be merely symbols, rebuses, *Dei vestigia*, and became objects interesting and important in themselves, quite apart from man's spiritual needs."[18] The great cathedrals themselves were dramatic expressions of this new confidence in understanding and mastering nature.

The two trends actually appear to have been one: the spiritual rising above and the mundane quest for mastery. The more the faithful aspired to transcend matter in order to be with God above the heavens, the more they also, in this era, engaged themselves with the earth below as mere matter, as a world at their disposal, as an It. This was not yet the spirit of domination of the modern era, by any means, but it undoubtedly set in motion cultural and economic forces that would prepare the way for the aggressive scientific and technological trends of modernity.

How much has the Gothic spirit in worship persisted in later eras? It surely seems to have persisted forcefully in those traditions whose theology and spirituality have taken the metaphysics and the metapoetics of the Great Chain of Being as a datum of life and thought. Teilhard de Chardin stood in this tradition. He projected the same kind of spiritualizing vision of the end times as did Thomas Aquinas. Teilhard's spirituality, likewise, was predicated on a vision of the soul's ascent to God.

The Gothic spirit also appears to have persisted more generally in a variety of Christian traditions, in subsequent eras, above all in the form of the architectural and spiritual emphases on the experience of *the heights* in worship. In many forms of Christian worship, the language that God is *high above* is taken for granted and reinforced continually with hymns, preaching, and prayers, even in the midst of church buildings that, externally, have little resemblance to historic Gothic styles.

However pervasive the Gothic spirit may or may not be in our time, we must be on our guard against it, wherever signs of it appear, lest this spiritualizing, anthropocentric liturgical milieu continue to inculcate in the faithful habits of thought and action that presuppose the inferiority and the final annihilation of the material world and that, in turn, validate the this-worldly fittingness of the aggressive mastery of nature.

The Promise of "God with Us"

Given the influence of the Gothic spirit both directly and indirectly on the practice of worship in the Christian churches, it will be instructive to turn to a very different kind of theological thinker, who took issue with the Great Chain of Being conceptuality, Martin Luther. Luther also took passionate issue with the whole idea of the ascent of the soul to God. Rather, for Luther, God is always "God with us," immanent in our world, immediately active in the world of creation where we live, on our level. More particularly, for Luther, God is always "God with us"—the biblical name is "Immanuel"—in the person of the Savior, the Word of God incarnate, Jesus Christ. The whole of Luther's theology, in this respect, might well be read as a commentary on the words of the prophet Jeremiah: "Am I a God near, says the Lord, and not a God afar off? . . . Do I not fill heaven and earth? says the Lord" (23:23-24).

Luther, in effect, canceled the second movement depicted by the Great Chain of Being conceptuality in its Dionysian form, the return of the spiritual creatures to God. For Luther, in contrast, the Creator is continually overflowing into the created world: the Creator is "in, with, and under" all things, immediately present, not high and lifted up at the apex of some grand hierarchy, far removed from this world:

It is God who creates, effects and preserves all things through his almighty power and right hand, as our Creed confesses. For he dispatches no officials or angels when he creates or preserves something, but all this is the work of the Divine power itself. If He is to create it or preserve it, however, he must be present and must make and preserve His creation both in its innermost and outermost aspects.[19]

For Luther, likewise, the Redeemer is continually overflowing, as the risen and ascended Lord, into the whole created world. In this respect, as in every other for Luther, the Creator and the Redeemer are one.

Yet in Luther's view, how much the Creator is known, and how much the Redeemer is known, in, with, and under all things, is another matter. Luther sometimes offered differing responses to that epistemological question. That God *is* with us, however, immediately and intimately and overpoweringly with us, as both Creator and Redeemer, for Luther, of that there can be no doubt. This is a typical utterance:

God is substantially present everywhere, in and through all creatures, in all their parts and places, so that the world is full of God and He fills all, but without His being encompassed and surrounded by it. He is at the same time outside and above all creatures. These are all exceedingly incomprehensible matters; yet they are articles of our faith and are attended clearly and mightily in Holy Writ.[20]

Luther's approach to worship can be described in similar terms. One might call it the liturgy of Immanuel, "God with us." In this respect, Luther's understanding of the sacraments of the church, Baptism and Eucharist, is most revealing and therefore most helpful for our own explorations.

To this end, two historical clarifications are necessary. First, since the time of Augustine, a variety of theologians adopted his affirmation that the sacraments are "visible words." These theologians did so for typically sound theological reasons, particularly in the context of post-Augustinian Reformation theology. To think of the sacraments this way appealed to many, since it appeared to be a congenial way to support Luther's approach to the sacraments, which was shaped by his theology of the Word. The contemporary Lutheran theologian Robert W. Jenson has therefore titled his highly regarded study of the sacraments, *Visible Words*, with substantive as well as historical appropriateness.[21]

But when we speak this way, it is important to recall which "Word" we are identifying. This is the Word of "God with us," God in the flesh in Jesus Christ. This, further, is the selfsame Christ proclaimed by the Pauline writer of Colossians, the One in whom "all things hold together" (Col. 1:17) and the One who makes peace with all things by the blood of his cross (Col. 1:20). This is the cosmic Christ, whom we have envisioned in these explorations as the inaugurator of the new creation, as the One who draws all things to himself, and as the One who restores every sinner to his or her rightful relationship to the plan of the Father to unite all things in him.

All too often, however, the idea that the sacraments are visible words has been taken, by default if not consciously, in a different sense: to mean the proclamation of the word of doctrine, rather than the mediation of the Word made flesh. That critical shift of nuance already was under way in the sixteenth century in the appropriation of Martin Luther's sacramental theology by his ardent champion, Philipp Melanchthon. As a result, for some Christian traditions, the sacraments have tended to become illustrations of an idea, dispensations announcing the unmerited grace of God perhaps, but basically understood as rites that have been instituted by God for the sake of simple, even illiterate souls in order to teach them about what God has revealed more directly in the written or proclaimed Word, in immediate revelations to the soul, or by the dogmatic authority of the church. So we must state resolutely and affirmatively that the sacraments of Baptism and Eucharist, as "visible words," are indeed sacraments of the real presence of the cosmic Word made flesh.

The second clarification has to do with what might sound like an obscure point in sacramental theology, but is not. It goes to the heart of the matter. We must question those theologians who minimize Luther's theology of the ubiquity of the risen and ascended Christ. This teaching has been something of an embarrassment to even the most enthusiastic of Luther's followers; it has scandalized many others

To those theologians who pass by Luther's teaching about the ubiquity of the risen and ascended Christ with a respectful silence, as well as to those who reject this teaching out of hand, we must say: Do you understand Luther's theology of the immanence of God in the creation in the first place? Luther has a highly sophisticated rendering of the divine immanence in the whole creation, in dialectical terms, by means of his maximization of spatial pronouns—as evidenced, for example, in the often cited phrase about God's presence being "in, with, and under."

Further, Luther understands space, paradoxically: first and foremost as God's space, a theological fundamental that Karl Barth may well have learned from Luther even as Barth was at the same time rejecting Luther's sacramental theology in other ways. Luther's theological depiction of space is primarily a description of *God's* space, then the world's. So Luther can readily suggest that the whole of the godhead is present in the baby on Mary's lap. He can make the same affirmation about a grain of wheat!

God's space is not limited by the space of this world. On the contrary, God's space dwarfs, indwells, overwhelms, and embraces the space of this world:

> For how can reason tolerate it that the Divine majesty is so small that it can be substantially present in a grain, on a grain, over a grain, through a grain, within and without, and that, although it is a single Majesty, it nevertheless is entirely in each grain separately, no matter how immeasurably numerous these grains may be? . . . And that the same Majesty is so large that neither this world nor a thousand worlds can encompass it and say: "Behold, there it is!" . . . . His own divine essence can be in all creatures collectively and in each one individually more profoundly, more intimately, more present than the creature is in itself; yet it can be encompassed nowhere and by no one. It encompasses all things and dwells in all, but not one thing encompasses it and dwells in it.[22]

Luther's sense of God's immediate presence in the creation has been given dramatic expression in our time by Jürgen Moltmann, in his statement that God creates the cosmos within the divine being.[23] For Moltmann, God's presence envelops and permeates the world. On the other hand, Luther was more dialectical than Moltmann. Luther would *also* have said "outside." For Luther, no single spatial preposition, including "within," can describe the power and the mystery and the radical immediacy of the divine presence. For similar reasons, Luther would have rejected as not sufficiently dialectical the assertion by theologians such Sallie McFague in our time, that the cosmos *is* God's body.[24] For Luther, God's glory is too great and God's immediacy in all things too mysterious to allow such a one-dimensional, literalizing theological predication.

Further, when Luther states, concerning the ascension of the risen Lord to the right hand of the Father, that "the right hand of God is everywhere" (*dextera dei ubique est*), the reformer is merely giving his rich theology of the divine immanence what is for him an appropriate christological concreteness. Since, for Luther, God the Father is "in, with, and under" all things, so is the ascended Son of God. This christological qualification of the divine immanence then makes it possible for Luther to carry through his program of accenting the descent of the God who is our Immanuel, with specific reference to sacramental theology. For Luther, the same God who was and is in, with, and under all things—*finitum capax infinitum*—is also fully present in the child on the lap of Mary, and therefore also fully present in the waters of Baptism and in the bread and the wine of the Eucharist, and so known by the faithful, whenever those sacraments are administered according to the selfsame cosmic Word.

Why, then, we must ask theologians who back away from this cosmic theology of Luther, are you so embarrassed or even scandalized by the doctrine of the ubiquity of the risen Christ? Is not the risen Christ, who, as St. Paul teaches, reigns throughout the cosmos (1 Corinthians 15, Colossians 1), really present at any time and any place in Baptism and Eucharist? Is he not really present, as he promised, wherever two or three are gathered in his name? And is this not the same Christ who appeared visibly to Mary at the tomb and to Thomas behind closed doors?

In light of these considerations, the theological burden of the proof would seem to rest squarely on the shoulders of those who would minimize or reject Luther's theology of the ubiquity of the risen and ascended Christ. In this respect, as in many others, Luther's theological affirmations seem to have been not only appropriate but commendable interpretations of the witness of Holy Scripture.

In so doing, Luther in effect transvalued the Gothic spirit. For Luther, both with respect to creation and redemption, and in particular with regard to worship, descent, not ascent, is the image that shapes every theological affirmation.

It remains, then, to explore the rich and deep connections between this theology of the cosmic Word made flesh, the ascended Son of God, and the liturgical praxis of Baptism and Eucharist.

The Cosmic Meanings of Baptism and Eucharist

The ancient church testified to the cosmic meanings of Baptism in numerous ways, especially in the architecture of baptisteries. Often those free-standing structures were designed to image-forth the whole cosmos, with domed ceilings, for example, representing the heavens. Their octagonal shapes, moreover, told the story of the universal history of salvation, for all who had eyes to see. For the ancient Christian mind, the eighth day of creation was the day of the resurrection, the restoration and the perfection of the whole creation. Recent church architecture has tended to move in the direction of restoring that kind of cosmic symbolism for the baptismal font, through the introduction of living waters in some magnitude, by the incorporation of cosmic imagery on the font and its setting, and by the placement of fonts near or at the center of the public liturgical action. But generally, it would appear, those suggestive architectural expressions have not been maximized as they might have been in any architecturally consistent fashion.

But what cannot be accomplished in structures that cannot be rebuilt, or instituted in new structures, for all manner of architectural and financial reasons, can surely be accomplished in the baptismal rite itself, with the ample use of water, with a baptismal prayer of cosmic amplitude, and with other appropriate liturgical enactments, such as enhanced musical settings.

The celebratory baptismal prayer offered in the *Lutheran Book of Worship* offers us one good verbal expression of these ritual meanings.[25] Notwithstanding certain limitations, in particular its muted eschatological witness, this is a powerfully suggestive cosmic prayer:

> Holy God, mighty Lord, gracious Father: We give you thanks, for in the beginning your Spirit moved over the waters and you created heaven and earth. By the gift of water you nourish and sustain us and all living things.
>
> By the waters of the flood you condemned the wicked and saved those whom you had chosen, Noah and his family. You led Israel by the pillar of cloud and fire through the sea, out of slavery into the freedom of the promised land. In the waters of the Jordan your Son was baptized by John and anointed with the Spirit. By the baptism of his own death and resurrection your beloved Son has set us free from bondage to sin and death, and has opened the way to the joy and freedom of everlasting life. He made water a sign of the kingdom and of cleansing and rebirth. In obedience to his command, we make disciples of all nations, baptizing them in the name of the Father, and of the Son, and of the Holy Spirit.
>
> Pour out your Holy Spirit, so that those who are here baptized may be given new life. Wash away the sin of all those who are cleansed by this water and bring them forth as inheritors of your glorious kingdom.
>
> To you be given praise and honor and worship through your Son, Jesus Christ our Lord, in the unity of the Holy Spirit, now and forever. Amen.

This prayer tells "the mighty acts of God" in cosmic history, with impressive trinitarian terms. Unfortunately it understates the eschatological promise for the renewal of all things, given with Baptism, that the baptized is united with the death and resurrection of the One who will come again to make all things new. Reference could easily have been made in this prayer to the river of the City of God, set in the midst of the New Heavens and the New Earth, proclaimed by Revelation (22:1-2). Still, this prayer forcefully professes the fullness of the mighty acts of God in creation, redemption, and consummation, culminating with its—muted, but evident—witness to the gloriously universal reign of God that is yet to be fully realized.

Anecdotal evidence suggests, sadly, that even in congregations that have access to baptismal prayers of such cosmic plenitude, the use of those prayers is minimized—often for reasons of saving time. Thereby the salvation of the

One who has saved all of time is minimized and marginalized, in favor of other atheological and mundane concerns. Would that the church of our time could hearken back to the days of the great bronze-based pools of water placed centrally in the ancient temple of the Hebrew people, where issues of chaos and cosmos, nonbeing and being, death and life, were evidently at stake. Would that the church could set aside creatively envisioned architectural baptismal spaces, akin to the freestanding baptisteries of old that were shaped and permeated by cosmic symbolism. Would that church musicians today could be encouraged to create dramatic works for the sake of baptismal liturgies, giving expression to the cosmic plenitude of the death and resurrection of Christ: works that tell of cacophonic thunder and lightning, reminiscent of Psalm 29, and also of the halcyon harmonies of the whole creation, reminiscent of Psalm 104. Would that priests and pastors could have the liturgical imagination to find ways to draw on such creations in order to enhance baptismal liturgies, precisely for the sake of—saving time.

A similar, expansive use of the classical Christian imagination, in the name of the cosmic Word of God, should be brought to bear on the church's eucharistic celebrations in these times of environmental and existential crisis. As Robert Jenson and others have convincingly argued, when our Lord said "do this" with reference to the institution of the Eucharist, he meant what he said, which was: *to give thanks*. Some congregations have opted, in contrast, merely to repeat the eucharistic words of institution as the essence of the spoken eucharistic rite. However much that liturgical truncation may have been motivated by a commitment to evangelical simplicity, it has also been sustained, in all likelihood, by the drive to "save time"—because "time is money"—that has dominated bourgeois Christianity in the modern West. On the contrary, our time requires something countercultural and much more biblical: taking the time to give thanks as our Lord commanded us to do.

The Great Prayer of Thanksgiving, given a place of prominence in numerous ecumenical liturgies in our time, is therefore an appropriate and urgently needed liturgical matrix, especially since, as a prayer of praise for the mighty acts of God, as it has come to be understood generally in our day, it includes as a matter of course a number of vivid "creation-themes."[26] Like the celebratory baptismal prayer we have already considered, the Great Prayer of Thanksgiving is a narration of the mighty acts of God, beginning with creation, focusing on redemption—where "the words of institution" have their fitting and indispensable place—and coming to rest in the vision of the consummation of all things that is yet to come. So, for example, the Great Prayer of Thanksgiving in the *Lutheran Book of Worship* begins: "Holy God, mighty Lord, gracious Father: Endless is your mercy and eternal is your reign. You have filled all creation with light and life; heaven and earth are full of your glory."[27] This recapitulates the witness of Genesis 1, which is further adumbrated in Psalm 104, and brought to christological completion in Col. 1:15ff. and Revelation 21: that the God of this holy meal is the One who, from the very beginning, had a purpose for all things, not just humankind, and that this God is indeed in, with, and under all things, and will one day bring all things to fulfillment in the day of the New Heavens and the New Earth.

Then follows the narration of the history of salvation, beginning with Abraham and coming to fulfillment "at this the end of all the ages," in the Son sent by the Father, who proclaimed the reign of God and instituted his holy meal. This Son is further identified, eschatologically, as the One who will come in power "to share with us the great and promised feast," when he comes again "as victorious Lord of all." These liturgical meanings reflect the testimony of the Book of Revelation, that the Lord who is host at this banquet is the very Lord who, as Lord of lords and King of kings, will come again to judge the world in righteousness and will inaugurate the great and eternal cosmic day of shalom, when God will finally be all in all. The Lord who is host at this eucharistic feast is the Lord of all, then, the *Pantokrater,* in whom, and by whom all things consist.

Seen from this angle of vision, traditional reflection about the real presence of Christ in the sacramental elements can both be reaffirmed and transvalued, cosmically. Of course, according to the Catholic faith, the crucified and risen Lord is *truly and really present*, in, with, and under the eucharistic elements. But that is not all, by any means.

At this point we can learn from some of the early testimonies of Huldrych Zwingli, one of the great theological opponents of Luther. In rejecting what Zwingli then had received as the normative Catholic doctrine of transubstantiation of the eucharistic elements, Zwingli said, in effect: no, it is not the elements, it is the people gathered who are transubstantiated into the body of Christ. While holding to the witness of the church catholic about the real presence of Christ in the eucharistic elements, it is certainly possible and indeed mandatory, biblically speaking, also to learn from Zwingli in this respect: that the crucified and risen Christ is truly present, embodied, in the company of the faithful who gather around the eucharistic table in order to lift up the bread and the wine in thanksgiving and to receive those elements in return as the true and real body and blood of Christ. St. Paul's theology of the church as the veritable and visible body of Christ mandates that we say at least this much about the real presence of Christ in the people of Christ, so that we might fittingly "discern [. . .] the body" (cf. 1 Cor. 11:29).[28]

With eyes of faith thus illuminated, one can further see the figure of the crucified and risen Christ in, with, and under *the liturgical actions of the priestly celebrant* in particular, the one who is called by God to offer the Great Prayer of Thanksgiving and to administer the bread and the wine with Christlike love to the faithful gathered around the table.

Inspired by this vision of the fullness of the cosmic Christ, really present in bread and wine, offered and distributed, and really present in people singing and praying and in priestly ministrations, it is also possible to envision, in faith and hope, a kind of pervasively overflowing revelation of the glory of the ubiquitous Christ: beginning with the sacramental elements at the center of ever-expanding concentric circles of divine energy—like ripples in a smooth pond, driven by a single, centric entrance of a new reality into the whole interrelated universal system—flowing from the elements to the people, then encompassing the whole house or the cathedral where the people have gathered, and, still more, ever expanding to the whole earth and thence to the entire cosmos: so that the faithful participants in this eucharistic feast in some small measure, in this revelatory moment, experience the great cosmic banquet that is yet to come, when God will indeed be all in all.[29]

As we witness this vision of the cosmic Word embodied in the sacramental praxis of the church, we may take it for granted that the architectural and artistic setting of these sacraments will enhance rather than inhibit the liturgical celebration. We have already had occasion to observe how important the right kind of architectural setting is for the celebration of Baptism in accord with the cosmic Word. This is all the more the case for that sacrament that is the culminating center of the church's sacramental ministries, the Eucharist.

Great liturgical music that lifts up the cosmic universality of the Eucharist is readily available, even in the smallest of parish settings. Great liturgical iconography and architecture that serve and elaborate the cosmic universality of the Eucharist are often more difficult to put in place, for a variety of typically pragmatic reasons. But this should be the goal: for a congregation to live in a church house or a cathedral that attests the multicultural dimensions of the human family and the multidimensional aspects of the cosmos, wild nature, cultivated nature, and fabricated nature, and that does not mask those rich diversities by artificial or so-called supernatural aesthetic elaborations. Artists who serve the church should therefore be encouraged to find ways to give testimony to the terrors and the glories of our multigalactic universe, as well as to the desecrations and the beauties of the good earth, nearer at hand. Icons of urban elegance, moreover, perchance a large polished brass crucifix in the simple but transfixing style of a Brancusi, should also be given liturgical prominence, as an affirmation of the renewal of all things through the mission of the cosmic Christ, a renewal that will include the world of fabricated nature as well as cultivated and wild nature. The introduction of the freestanding central table as the focal point of eucharistic celebration in our time has, furthermore, done much to accent the presence of God with God's people, as distinct from the high altar against the east wall, removed from the people, which suggests that the way of salvation is the way of ascent.

In this respect, the move away from the hierarchical motifs of Gothic architecture in our era probably needs to be sustained, at least until the time when the cosmic liturgy of the church catholic has been much more extensively ritualized in practice than it is at the present. For all their beauties and their visual celebrations of the creation, the motifs of the Gothic typically prompt the souls of the faithful to rise *above* the rich diversities and also the pervasive degradations of this material and cultural world, in the direction of union with the purely undifferentiated, absolutely transcendent spiritual One.

A post-Gothic structure such as the Crystal Cathedral in California is, in this respect, worthy of discussion, if not emulation. On the one hand, its transparent glass walls allow visions of a polluted earth and a cosmos groaning in travail as the faithful contemplate visible signs of the earth's pollution and occasional storms of lightning and thunder. On the other hand, such a structure also can give glimpses of the whole creation transfigured in glory, attested beautifully, in the case of the Crystal Cathedral, by the near gardens and the distant mountains.

That the eucharistic life of the church should not only afford visions of the creation but also overflow beyond the bounds of the house or the cathedral space, also needs to be emphasized: not only in terms of the ministries of the people in their weekday callings, but also in terms of the witness of the house or the cathedral and the adjacent grounds. Liturgical processions, wherever possible, should take the form of walking through the yard or processing in the streets or fields. Inner-city churches, in particular, should seek to find ways to demonstrate the promise of the gospel by the cultivation of flowers, trees, and gardens, and, wherever possible, by the introduction of fountains and hidden, shaded walkways, where the homeless and the disenfranchised can find some secure moments of rest, and the birds of the air can find some safe places to nest.[30] All this can serve as testimony to the renewal of the whole cosmos celebrated by the sacramental ministry of the church.

This should be the vision: the bread and the wine on the table are, for those eucharistic moments, positioned at the center of the cosmos, and the revelation of the divine energies of the crucified and risen cosmic Christ, in whom all things consist, radiates from that center to reach out to peoples of every nation, male and female, Jew and Greek, slave and free, and indeed to every dimension of the cosmos as a universal, multi-galactic whole.

Is there at this point a distant but suggestively analogous consonance with some of the images bequeathed to us by cosmological physics?[31] If I can imagine an originating creative moment of all things, when the totality of universal matter was no larger than a ball that I could hold in my hand, just prior to some universal explosion (the much-discussed Big Bang), is it not also possible to imagine, similarly, a redemptive moment of all things, wrought first in the particularity of the Word made flesh, and then re-presented and extended around the planet, in the power of the Holy Spirit, whenever priestly hands take bread and lift up the cup, according to the same cosmic Word of God?

Further explorations along this line of thought might then disclose that what was once called by theologians such as Brunner "the scandal of particularity" is no scandal at all. Rather, *that* is the characteristic *modus operandi* of the cosmic Word, both in creation and redemption. Is it not the case that the gospel truth is always in the particulars? With such thoughts before us, we might then choose to say: the hands that hold bread and cup are the hands that hold the center of the universe, as that center now is moving through time and space, from the Alpha of the universe to its Omega. William Blake's words could then be taken with a new seriousness, in a way that he more than likely never intended them to be taken, in his poem "Auguries of Innocence," "Hold infinity in the palm of your hand/And eternity in an hour."

This universal vision must be narrated throughout the entire course of the liturgy. This narration takes the concrete form of the proclamation of the cosmic Word of God, in, with, and under those ritual actions that are the formative sacramental ministrations of the church's life, Baptism and Eucharist, as well as in those focal moments that are given over to preaching the selfsame Word. In most classical expressions of the church's liturgy, indeed, virtually every word in the ritual is a word from Holy Scripture. Hence the whole liturgy is one grand proclamation of the Word of God.

In these times of ecological and cosmic alienation, however, the classic narrative flow of the liturgy should not simply be allowed to "take care of itself," as it is handed down from generation to generation, however replete it might be, and is, with testimonies from the Word of God. There is ample evidence, indeed, that the Scripture texts that have been traditionally read as part of the church's yearly liturgical cycle have typically *not* been chosen to give voice to the universality of the creation-faith celebrated by theologians such as the mature Augustine and, behind those testimonies, to the creation-faith of the Scriptures themselves: to the God who is always "God with us," in creation as well as in redemption. Today's church requires imaginative interventions on the part of its liturgical leaders. Some have already experimented, for example, with the introduction of a "creation-cycle" of lectionary readings during the Pentecost season, typically during the fall, overlapping the feast day of St. Francis.[32]

Further, unless the preachers of the church persistently, imaginatively, and forcefully tell the revised classical story in their sermons and in their teaching, the whole case for a liturgy that is ecologically and cosmically formative, according to the cosmic Word of God, could easily be lost. The faithful need to hear the whole classical story retold in this manner so that they can see with new eyes the ministrations of the cosmic Word of God in their midst, especially in the sacraments of Baptism and Eucharist; and then, there is some hope, they might realize also that that very Word of God is addressing them in the particular proclamations of the Word that the liturgy offers them.[33]

The sacramental ministrations of the church, thus enacted, interpreted, and made complete by the proclamation of the Word, in this way become the mode of the church's identity-formation, ecologically and cosmically, with a scope that is commensurate with the ecological and cosmic crisis that we are facing today.

The Letter to the Ephesians takes this kind of ritualized cosmic experience for granted. It assumes that God the Father is the One who is "above all and through all and in all" (4:6) and that the Son of this cosmic Father is the One in whom "all things," things on heaven and things on earth, are gathered up (1:10). It further assumes that this cosmic ministry of God the Father and the Son is magnified and celebrated by the strangers and sojourners called together from every nation (2:19) and inspired by the Spirit of the same God, in one exuberant moment of thanksgiving: "Be filled with the Spirit, as you sing psalms and hymns and spiritual songs among yourselves, singing and making melody to the Lord in your hearts, giving thanks to God the Father at all times and for everything in the name of our Lord Jesus Christ" (5:18-20). That, in broad biblical compass, is what it can mean to reenact the classical Christian story ritually in our time, as we move beyond the milieu of the Gothic spirit.

Chapter 7

Reexperiencing the Story Spiritually

Beyond the Ecology of Death

"So they left the tomb quickly with fear and great joy, and ran to tell his disciples. Suddenly Jesus met them. . . . And they came to him, took hold of his feet, and worshiped him. Then Jesus said to them, 'Do not be afraid; go and tell my brothers to go to Galilee; there they will see me.'" (Matt. 28:8-10)

It is still possible and illuminating to claim the major theme of Ernest Becker's classic, *The Denial of Death*,[1] as a contemporary cultural truth in its own right. Notwithstanding all the horror movies and all the fascination with violence and death in our media, we Americans do tend to soft-pedal the realities of death and dying, if not deny them outright. Nowhere is this more apparent than in our patterns of behavior and our attitudes toward nature.[2]

Americans tend to think of encountering raw nature as driving through Yellowstone National Park in an air-conditioned sports utility vehicle or roughing it at a backyard barbecue. Many of the more affluent in our society get close to nature by taking refuge in gated communities, surrounded by the manufactured serenity of forested exurban developments. Across the land, Americans' passions for their natural surroundings are extensively and expensively—some $40 billion a year—invested in lawn care. No other crop grown in America occupies more land. Some forty thousand square miles are under cultivation, roughly the size of the whole state of Pennsylvania. The nature that many Americans seem to know best, and the nature that many Americans surely love, is a nature that has been tamed, pacified, and refracted through the lenses of Disney, a nature where one can be *at home:* "where the buffalo roam, and the deer and the antelope play, where never is heard a discouraging word, and the skies are not cloudy all day." Nary a word about death or violence here.

Even the eminent Henry David Thoreau, celebrated today for his passion for wildness and his life apart from civilization in the primal naturalness of Walden Pond, typically managed to leave his retreat in the wilds once a week in order to go home, where, among other things, his mother did his laundry. Thoreau's comfortable passion for the wilds did change, when he made his memorable trip to Maine's Mount Katahdin, on the slopes of which he encountered Maine's horrendous blackflies. Thereafter his romance with the wilderness was considerably muted.

The truth of nature, as a matter of fact, is more nearly expressed by those blackflies than by our backyard barbecues. The truth of nature is suffering and death. People die. The birds of the air and the lilies of the field die. The extraordinarily beautiful garden planet on which we humans live will one day die. Our solar system and our local galaxy will, in due course, surely perish. Likewise for the whole universe, whether with a bang or a whimper: the last destiny of the entire cosmos, by any thoughtful contemporary reckoning, is unquestionably death. As everything is related to everything else in nature, so nature is a vast nexus of violence and death. Let us call this nexus *the ecology of death.* This ecology is sometimes etched with wrenching individual pain, sometimes with catastrophic cosmic upheavals.

Articulated variously in our time by poets and novelists, philosophers and filmmakers, this truth about nature has been given a compelling scientific currency in the modern era—however domesticated or otherwise denied in our popular culture—by evolutionary biologists, beginning with Charles Darwin himself. Some scholars, to be sure, have more recently sought to highlight evidences of altruism and cooperation in nature. But the final word of evolutionary biology always seems to come to this: death is the engine of nature. Living things overpopulate their territories: large numbers of any species typically perish; a few, normally the best adapted, survive. The commanding metaphor of life on this planet, the "survival of the fittest," is therefore really a metaphor of blood and gore. Nature, if we see it with our eyes wide open, is the world of death par excellence.

No one has given expression to this truth more forcefully than the contemporary American essayist and poet, Annie Dillard. This is her classic description of her encounter with a frog in a pond—a setting that a William Wordsworth or a Thoreau or any one of their less gifted heirs might well have romanticized, in terms of peace and life. Dillard tells the unvarnished, unromantic truth of warfare and death in nature:

> He was a very small frog with wide, dull eyes. And just as I looked at him, he slowly crumpled and began to sag. . . . His skin emptied and drooped; his very skull seemed to collapse and settle like a kicked tent. . . . Soon, part of his skin, formless as a pricked balloon, lay in floating folds like bright scum on the top of the water: it was a monstrous and terrifying thing. I gaped bewildered, appalled. An oval shadow hung in the water behind the drained frog; then the shadow glided away. The frog skin bag started to sink.

What had happened? The frog had been attacked by a giant brown beetle:

> It eats insects, tadpoles, fish, and frogs. Its grasping forelegs are mighty and hook inward. It seizes a victim with these legs, hugs it tight, and paralyzes it with enzymes injected during a vicious bite. The one bite is the only bite it ever takes. Through the puncture shoot the poisons that dissolve the victim's muscles and bones and organs—all but the skin—and through it the giant water bug sucks out the victim's body, reduced to a juice.[3]

The Grim Reaper, in this case the beetle, is the truth of nature, as far as Dillard is concerned, a truth she expounds with breathtaking perspicacity in her most famous work, *Pilgrim at Tinker Creek*, and all the more starkly in her more recent study *For the Time Being*.[4]

Now, Christians who take their faith seriously are unable to deny death. A religion that has a crucified Messiah as its fulcrum hardly permits that. It is no wonder that many Christians past and present have instead opted for a spirituality that takes the soul away from it all, "the flight of the alone to the Alone":[5] the quest to rise above the painful and death-ridden biophysical world toward unity with an eternal and all-transcending spiritual deity above.

Can we in fact do otherwise, spiritually? Is it really possible for us to embrace the ecology of death? Is it spiritually realistic to aspire to encounter nature untamed, unpacified, and unromanticized, with all its ambiguities and its death-driven violence, as a gift from the giver of every good and perfect gift, as a tabernacle of the most high, and thereby to be able to embrace nature spiritually, as a world charged with the glory of God, overflowing with blessings, beauty, and goodness?

That is what the classical Celtic saints did. And that is why we need them as our mentors today: so that, having confronted the stark reality of death in nature, our spirituality will sustain, not undermine, our theology of nature. It will finally do us no good to reclaim the classical Christian story historically, biblically, narratively, interpersonally, and ritually for the sake of a fresh theology of nature, if we do not also reexperience that story spiritually, to the same end. In this world of death and violence, a nature-affirming theology requires a nature-affirming spirituality. The cosmic discipline of the church's Sunday liturgy, in particular, requires a consonant cosmic discipline of weekday piety. Otherwise the soul of the believer will be divided, even at war with itself.

The Celtic saints' apperceptions of nature have frequently been celebrated. But too often the Celtic saints have been romanticized, as if they were the predecessors of Wordsworth in his peaceful Lake District or Thoreau in the safe and serene milieu of Walden. On the contrary, *death* was their daily bread—and still they embraced nature as the gracious gift of God, their creator and redeemer. How were they able to do that?

That is the question I took with me to the isles of the Celtic saints in July of 1996. Along the way on that spiritual journey I learned a spirituality of nature, beyond the ecology of death.

To the World of the Celtic Saints

Such thoughts, along with other more conventional intentions, drove me to join my spouse of thirty years for an anniversary holiday. But my first memorable experience on the Emerald Isle was raw shock. I stood stunned on the sidewalk of a little village reading the lead story of the tabloid *Evening News:* "229 Die on U.S. Flight to Paris." Two days earlier, we also had flown out of Kennedy Airport in New York at the same time, 8:30 P.M. That huge explosion twenty miles off Moriches Inlet, at the east end of Long Island, at 8:45 P.M., could easily have been us.

I had come to the regions of historic Celtic Christianity for a holiday. But what had I come to see? Churches in ruins? Ancient abbeys with panoramic vistas? Rugged landscapes and sublime seascapes? Elegant gardens and gracious castles? Images of artistic greatness, like those in the Book of Kells? I kept thinking about the passengers on that doomed TWA flight. Much as I tried to concentrate on other things, images of human bodies in free-fall, at twenty thousand feet, kept flooding my mind.

Death surely was the constant companion of the Celtic saints, who flourished spiritually in Ireland, Wales, and Scotland, from about the fifth to the tenth centuries C.E.[6] The impression that I had consistently gleaned from my readings about these luminaries is that they had not tried to avoid the subject. Rather, they had lived to die. They had self-consciously, even eagerly, sought to prepare for the world to come with the passing of each day. St. Patrick himself had apparently hoped for martyrdom, an ending that the relatively peaceful Irish society of his time denied him. The lives of the Celtic saints, in that sense, were sacraments of death. Their followers could set aside their very bones, and venerate those bones long after the saints had departed this world, because, for the followers, those bones partook of the power of the saints' public pilgrimage to eternity.

Reveries in the Rain

The lives of the Celtic saints, and the daily experience of most of their monastic brothers and sisters, were in all likelihood cold and damp much of the time. To sleep in their dank, musty, and smoky hide-covered huts must have been like lying down in a swamp. Never mind the wood pillows, the winter winds, and the nocturnal hours for prayers. Never mind the long and arduous labors of the brothers and the sisters in the bogs and the rocky fields during the day, or the endless hours fishing in the rivers or the seas. Never mind the insects. Never mind the pneumonia and the never-ending hacking coughs. The cold and the damp of their beds must have been distressing and depressing enough for any mortal.

Thoughts like these went through my mind as I stood in the rain, at the shore of Lake Gill in Northwestern Ireland contemplating the island that William Butler Yeats celebrated in one of his early poems, "The Lake Isle of Innisfree." The world he saw then was quite different. It was akin to Wordsworth's beloved Lake District:

> I will arise and go now, and go to Innisfree,
> And a small cabin build there, of clay and wattles made:
> Nine bean-rows will I have there, a hive for the honeybee,
> And live alone in the bee-loud glade.
>
> And I shall have some peace there, for peace comes dropping slow,
> Dropping from the veils of the morning to where the cricket sings;
> There midnight's all a glimmer, and noon a purple glow,
> And evening full of linnet's wings.
>
> I will arise and go now, for always night and day
> I hear lake water lapping with low sounds by the shore;
> While I stand in the roadway, or on the pavement grey,
> I hear it in the deep heart's core.[7]

At peace with such a vision at the edge of the lake on a sunny day, were it to have rained, Yeats could always have retreated to the spacious comforts of his father's warm, dry Victorian home, all the more to savor his romantic reveries. In contrast, the historic saints had only their damp, mossy beds in their dark huts. How different their reveries must have been!

Encountering the Captain of Our Salvation

Little is known about the culture and history of the neolithic peoples in Ireland, who built their dwellings and their tombs in some of the very areas where the Celtic saints were later to establish their communities.[8] What death meant to the common folk who labored so massively to build tombs like the one whose ruins we visited at Creevykeel, along the midwestern coast of Ireland, no one knows. Some scholars and a number of popularizing writers have speculated about the spirituality of those peoples on the basis of what is known about later, pre-Christian Celtic tribes.

The ruins of the vast tomb at Creevykeel were mute. Only in retrospect did it dawn on me that the outline of that whole megalithic edifice, almost as long and as wide as a football field, when seen from the air, seemed to suggest the form of a ship. That would make sense, I thought, since in the history of religions many peoples envisioned death as a voyage to some other land, whether bright or shadowy, blissful or damned.

The thought of a ship, some 3,700 years later, was taken for granted by the Celtic saints. They were well-acquainted with the seas—like St. Patrick who was captured by pirates and made a slave early in his life. The coastal waters around Ireland, Wales, and Scotland and the rivers that flowed into those waters were as much the spiritual milieu of the Celtic saints as the monastic communities they so laboriously constructed at the edge of the sea or in secluded settings inland. On the Dingle Peninsula, the Gallarus Oratory, dating from about the sixth century, was a case in point. Imagine a small, deep-hulled fishing ship overturned along the beach, projecting a kind of tentlike image against the sky. That's how this tiny but elegant chapel appeared to me.

The building itself pulsated with energy. It was built brilliantly with countless discus-shaped stones, most of which I imagined I could have lifted. Its stones were cantilevered and held together without mortar. I supposed that that minuscule nave could have held eleven or twelve worshipers, no more. But its testimony was as powerful as any Gothic cathedral I had ever seen. It called forth deep longings in my soul. Had I been there alone with my wife, freed from the social conventions presupposed by most tourists, I would have eagerly fallen to my knees on the cold stone floor.

The energy emanating from the building was enhanced by its spectacular natural setting, on a rising coastal plain, halfway between the nearby mountain heights and the sea. That setting suggested biblical motifs, undoubtedly intentionally so: the vision of the chaotic waters below, with the image of the creative Spirit of God hovering over them all, and the sight of the timeless mountain peaks above, to which we lift up our eyes.

That kind of elegantly modest tentlike structure, in that majestic cosmic setting, not some megalithic tomb of gargantuan proportions that dominated everything else, was the most revealing monument that the Celtic saints and their coworkers bequeathed to the church of ensuing centuries. Life for them was a precarious journey toward death, toward the "place of my resurrection," as St. Columba said. And the saints consistently enacted that vision. They regularly uprooted themselves and their followers, and set off fearlessly for the foreboding unknown, on land or sea, to establish yet another community, where they would await the reign of God, at the place of their resurrection.

But for the Celtic saints and their followers life was also much more. It was surely a journey toward death. But it was also a journey led by, and empowered by, the crucified and risen Lord. Their eschatological journey was self-consciously a christological and, therefore, also a profoundly sacramental journey. Theirs was a pilgrimage to death in the midst of which the One who was to come had already arrived and had taken to the road with them, akin to the experience of the disciples with the risen Lord on the way to Emmaus. Like the women who had just come from the empty tomb of the crucified Jesus, the Celtic saints encountered the risen Christ on the road, and heard him tell them, along the way, to go still further, to yet another Galilee, to meet him there.

Their spirituality came to its most characteristic public expression as they stood inside those dark stone "ships" like the Gallarus Oratory, with the altar candles illuminating the body and the blood of the One they surely knew as the captain of their salvation—an image that is not anachronistic, even though we may know it best as it was voiced so powerfully in the twentieth century by the composer Ralph Vaughan Williams.[9] That image was deeply rooted in their spiritual sensibility, as we can hear in the words of the captivating "Lorca" or "Breastplate" prayer attributed to St. Patrick (in all probability this magnificent hymn was composed some three centuries after his death). Invoking first the Trinity, then the power of Christ's life, from birth and baptism to resurrection and ascension, and also the powers of the hosts of heaven, angels and archangels, prophets and apostles, the writer calls upon God "to pilot me." He or she prays for Christ to protect him or her "against poison and burning, against drowning and wounding" so that he or she might be safe and saved in Christ's presence: "Christ with me, Christ before me, behind me; Christ within me, Christ beneath me, Christ above me."[10] The image of the Savior who is the captain of our salvation would easily have come to the minds of many of the Celtic saints, beginning at least as early as Patrick's time, familiar as most of them were with the perils of seafaring and assured as all of them were of the ever-present, personal care of the living Christ.

Voyaging came to be one of the primary, perhaps the single most important, Celtic Christian metaphors for the spiritual life. This is impressively illustrated in the ninth-century Christian epic *The Voyage of St. Brendan*.[11] Drawing on the cultural riches of the voyage motif in archaic Irish oral poetry, this epic narrates a search for the promised land or the new Paradise witnessed to by the Bible. Brendan's journey takes seven years. It is a spiritual voyage that could readily have been imagined from within the shiplike structure of a Gallarus Oratory. This is how Thomas Finan describes it:

> The [seven] years are cycles marked by the Christian seasons and the great feasts of the liturgical year, for which the voyagers always return to the same islands. And ever investing everything, even at sea, the aura of the monastic ritual of the daily Hours, link hours, days, seasons and years in a rosary of prayer.[12]

During the course of this voyage narrative, as in the "Breastplate of St. Patrick," we hear how Brendan always depends on the vital and personal presence of the Savior. The risen Lord is constantly, actively, and caringly present for and with the saint, which, in turn, makes it possible for Brendan to experience the whole range of Divine glories in the created world around him, along the way. "The Lord Jesus Christ," the voyager is told, "did not allow you to find [the promised land] immediately because first He wished to show you the richness of His wonders in the deep."[13]

In this sense, the Celtic saints set one of the church's most popular traditional spiritualities on its head. Spirituality no longer meant for them the flight of the alone to the Alone, rising above it all to commune with the spiritual One above, but rather encountering the enfleshed One from above, who had overcome the powers of death, the risen Lord, in, with, and under the world of nature: "Christ within me, Christ beneath me, Christ above me." The Celtic saints could embrace the ecology of death in nature, not because they were embracing nature as such, but because, when they embraced nature, they were there embracing the risen Christ. That encounter then took away "the sting of death" for them, however wrenching that sting might actually have been, and freed them to rest their souls contemplatively in the beauties of earth, sky, and water, and to love all the creatures, large and small, they encountered there.

Contemplating the Specter of Death

Questions to ponder: When at the beginning of the twentieth century Yeats dreamed of building a small cabin on the island of Innisfree in Lake Gill, was he somehow attempting to enter into the mind of the neolithic peoples of that region? Was that cabin, where he dreamed that he might have discovered peace, in fact his imagined tomb, whence he could journey on into some other world? Was he drinking deeply, knowingly or not, in the spirits of Creevykeel?

We know from Yeats's own notes that, at the time when he wrote about Innisfree, Henry David Thoreau's example was very much on Yeats's mind; and Thoreau was one who had imagined himself as having embarked on a kind of neolithic spiritual journey. How much was Yeats's earliest vision shaped by the quest for some "primal" experience of death?

Whether Yeats ever visited the Gallarus Oratory, or any comparable structure in Ireland, would be another interesting question to explore. If he had entered into the dark interior of one of those stone oratories, however, would he have understood where he was?

Later in his life, far away from his youthfully innocent encounters at Innisfree, the experience of death was still on his mind, but no longer as a peaceful journey, nor surely as the door to salvation, in communion with the crucified and risen Savior, as it was for the Celtic saints. Death came to represent something profoundly sinister for Yeats, as we can see in the apocalyptic imagery of his most famous poem, "The Second Coming":

> Things fall apart; the centre cannot hold;
> Mere anarchy is loosed upon the world,
> The blood-dimmed tide is loosed, and everywhere
> The ceremony of innocence is drowned.[14]

It sounds to me as if not even the powerful, cantilevered walls of a Gallarus Oratory, in Yeats's view, would withstand such a tide. *Götterdämmerung* is the final word of this life, it appears. All things, for the older Yeats, end forever in the apocalypse: death, which is now, dramatically, no longer a peaceful prospect.

Discovering the Communion of Saints

One of the dead who was much on my mind, as we careened through the one-lane roads of the beautiful Irish countryside, heading toward Wales and Scotland, was another traveler, most dear to me, one of the commonplace saints of this world, my younger sister, Mary, who had died of brain cancer in 1993 at the relatively young age of fifty-one.

In her adult years, Mary had been a consummate and passionate traveler. She had traveled abroad extensively and robustly, from dawn to dusk and on into the night. Her question at the end of every day of travel had always been, "Where are we going tomorrow?"

This was the way my wife and I traveled, as a matter of fact, rushing here and there in order to have time to rest and to contemplate. We must have been truly a comical sight, constantly hurrying up in order to slow down, driving at breakneck speeds in order to search out and explore the ruins of yet one more abbey or one more breathtaking coastal vista or one more garden of historic renown. So typically American, it must have appeared. But I kept thinking about Mary. Now and again, as we drove, I felt her presence.

As a pastor, I had learned that the experience of encountering departed loved ones is still strong for some, in our own day. People will gladly talk about that kind of experience with someone they trust. Hence my sense of my sister Mary's presence with me on the road was not that unusual. But the spiritual experience of the whole company of the saints, with whom we are one, had escaped me much of my life. As I thought about Mary, however, I began to imagine afresh what the experience of the fellowship of all the saints might be like. I knew the words and the music by heart: "Oh, blest communion, fellowship divine, we feebly struggle, they in glory shine; yet all are one within your great design."[15]

But as I reflected about that experience along the road, I began to back off. What was going on? With many others, I had long before observed that our mostly hyperactive and overly consumptive American culture is profoundly impoverished spiritually. That hunger has driven countless thousands into the arms of often naive and historically ill-informed New Age prophets and pundits. Witness the hundreds of books on the "inspiration" shelves of the mall bookstores, beginning with *The Celestine Prophecy* and *A Book of Angels* and extending to testaments about healing by crystals, near-death experiences, encounters with aliens, paranormal voyages to the neolithic age, and much more—or much less. It all called to mind Paul Tillich's pointed response years ago, quoted by the *New York Times*, to a portrait of the crucifixion by the then immensely popular twentieth-century surrealist painter, Salvador Dali: "That's junk."

Was I now about to start encountering angels and other spiritual apparitions, too, along with the presence of the saints? I had the urge to wheel the car around and to rush somewhere—perchance to the grave of David Hume—in order to confess all my irrationalities. On the other hand, had not the Creator fashioned all things visible and invisible, as I had confessed with my lips in the words of the Nicene Creed all my life? And why, by the way, had the preeminent Protestant theologian of the twentieth century, Karl Barth, who so forcefully had rejected everything that was "religious" in this world, especially popular religiosity or "culture religion," devoted a whole volume of his monumental *Church Dogmatics* to angels?

For Celtic Christians, the invisible hosts of the heavens, the saints and the angels, were as real as the visible hosts of this world. The saints who had departed this life were as accessible for many of the Celtic faithful as your next-door neighbor or, in my case, my own deceased sister. More accessible, as a matter of fact: especially the presence of "the founders," saints such as Patrick or Columba. To understand *Life of St. Columba* by Adomnan of Iona, we have to understand that Columba was a living presence for Adomnan, not only a subject of historical memory, surely not merely an object of historical scrutiny.[16] Philip Sheldrake has instructively described the rich world of that spirituality this way:

> What was normally invisible could break through into human perception. The invocation of saints and angels was not a matter of calling down strange powers from outside human experience. Rather it concerned a bringing into explicit consciousness a dimension of the created world. . . . The blessed dead were in some sense already risen yet still part of the Church and therefore living presences among the human community on earth.[17]

Hesitant, but unable to resist, I felt my own soul being touched and taken captive by that spirituality.

On the other hand, saintly presence or not, I missed my sister enormously. I wanted her back the way she was. She had held my extended family together. She had understood me like few others. I loved her smile. I hated the brain tumor that killed her. Her absence was a wound in my soul that would not heal.

Maybe that's why I secretly wanted to touch the bones of one of the Irish saints. That was the tomb I really wanted to visit: to see if I could feel the power of eternal life in this world and be healed. In conversation with the Scriptures, I had long before concluded that spirituality, to be real, must also be *tangibility*—what we have heard and seen and touched with our hands (1 John 1:1).

Touching "Dem Bones"

As a schoolboy, I used to throw myself into singing the great spiritual "Dem Bones" with great abandon. I never knew quite why. I was not given to such public displays of participation. Nor, for all the obstreperous youthful questions I drilled at my Sunday-school teachers—above all, various expressions of the theodicy question—do I remember ever once raising any questions about the resurrection of the body. Which is surprising, because that doctrine is perhaps the most preposterous of orthodox Christian beliefs.

Nor did the coarseness of the traditional confession in the Apostles' Creed ever befuddle me as a theology student—resurrection of the flesh (*resurrectio carnis*). I just took it for granted.

I remember one homiletical experience that might otherwise have thrown a young preacher into a deep depression. An eminent Harvard New Testament scholar, at the time a member of my congregation, instructed me one Sunday morning in response to my sermon, that, to understand the meaning of the resurrection, I would be well advised to try to understand the Gospel of John a little more deeply and explore John's sophisticated theology of "the body" more extensively, and not be so influenced by what he called the "crass" terminology of the Apostles' Creed. All this talk about the resurrection of the flesh, he said, made me sound like some kind of theological butcher! I wondered at the time what his problem was.

Still, relics had never been part of my spiritual experience—real bones, holy bones. On the contrary, like most heirs of the Lutheran Reformation I grew up theologically with deeply rooted suspicions about relics. But as we visited one abbey after another, and as I read more and more about the story of the historic Celtic saints, I began to wonder. I began to consider "Dem Bones" all over again, or maybe for the first time. (Never mind centuries of experience with relics and centuries of spiritual reflection about relics on the Roman Catholic side of the aisle.[18] It was all new to me.)

Consider the logic of the Incarnation. The Word became flesh and dwelt among us, and He has now been glorified. Henceforth the very bones of the Savior are charged with divine glory.

Then consider the work of the Lifegiver, the Holy Spirit. As Luther taught us, the spirit communicates the real presence of the crucified and risen Christ to us, in word and sacrament, which we receive and internalize, in and by faith. Luther espoused a "Christ-mysticism" in this respect. By the power of the Holy Spirit, we are one with Christ—the ubiquitous, enfleshed Christ—and then Christ also dwells in us.

Luther did not sufficiently emphasize, however—and this is no surprise, given his struggle with the so-called enthusiasts—the New Testament teaching about the gifts of the Spirit. The indwelling of the Holy Spirit, by Whom Christ himself dwells in us, is a differentiated indwelling, according to Holy Scripture.

One of these differentiations is the physical halo—or spiritual aura—given to some. This is what I concluded along the way in Ireland. Some of the saints positively glow with the divine glory, in virtue of the indwelling Christ. Their very bones, accordingly, reveal glimmers of the resurrected body of the eternal reign of God. The bones of these saints emanate holiness. Whether waking or sleeping, whether alive or dead, "Dem Bones" participate in the power of the life everlasting that they herewith reveal, for those who have been given eyes to see by the selfsame Spirit, in the midst of this world of death and darkness.

Some evidence suggests that the faithful in Ireland in the earliest centuries of Christian experience in that land would go to the entombed resting places of such saints to touch their bones. That was a viable spiritual impulse, a consistent expression of the logic of the Incarnation, I decided, an experience that had largely escaped Christians such as myself, who had been raised theologically in opposition to indulgences and magic.

The Mystery amid the Absurdity

At Crianlarich, Scotland, in a small but elegant mountain hotel, the service for dinner for the dozen or so guests was family-style. The young man sitting across from me, it turned out, was an American Joyce scholar who had come to Scotland to deliver an academic paper. He enthusiastically described himself as a Joycean. Son of a Methodist minister, he had lost both parents at age eighteen and then lost his faith, too, in college. Somehow, he explained, twenty years later he found his way to psychic stability, away from the wracking episodes of depression that had constantly debilitated him since his college days, by devoting his mind and heart to Joyce.

Did Joyce "consent to being"? I asked, invoking the question of H. Richard Niebuhr. Did Joyce make that fundamental, pre-rational decision that life is good, that there *is* meaning, that somehow the center holds, notwithstanding all the death and all the violence?

I posed the question not as an intense reader of Joyce, but as a fascinated observer of one so devoted to Joyce. While in Ireland, I had read Umberto Eco's essay, *The Aesthetics of Chaosmos.*[19] As far as I understood Eco, Joyce projected a world in which the center does not hold, for which the last word is not *cosmos* but *chaos*.

"No," said the effervescent, self-assured young scholar, Joyce believed that it all did have meaning. For Joyce, he said, "life is a journey from mystery through absurdity to mystery." Well, I thought, and so I said: "methinks the young scholar doth protest too much." This was Joyce's vision, as described by Eco:

> The world is actually the total horizon of insignificant events which bind themselves in continuous constellations, each one the beginning and the end of a vital relation, center, and periphery, first cause and last effect of a chain of meetings and oppositions, parenthoods, and contradictions. Good or bad, this is the world with which contemporary man must deal, be it through abstract science or concrete everyday experience. This is the world he is learning to accept, acknowledging it as his country of origin.[20]

Contrast the world of the Celtic saints: Columba, for example, the man who founded the monastic community on the small Scottish island of Iona, to which we had made a long and soulful pilgrimage the day before. For Columba, life is a journey surrounded and engulfed by sin and death and the violence of sin. Yes, life is a journey from mystery to mystery through absurdity. But for Columba, and for all the Celtic saints, the center holds, because the mystery has spoken. It is thereby *the* mystery. "In the beginning was the Word" (John 1:1). And the mystery has disclosed itself on the cross in the agony of self-giving love. For God so loved the world that he gave his only Son" (John 3:16). And the mystery has drawn near to us lost and condemned creatures and tented among us (John 1:14). The mystery has kept sacramental company—*cum panis*—with us in the Gallarus Oratories of this world (Luke 24:13-35). And the mystery is going before us to Galilee (Matt. 28:7), to be revealed fully to us one great and glorious day on the other side of this vale of tears and absurdity (Rev. 21:1f.).

For this reason Columba and all the Celtic saints knew and loved the mystery. They consented with enthusiasm to being. Hence, notwithstanding all the pain, all the suffering, and all the hacking coughs in the night, their world was profoundly cosmos, not chaos. So Columba knew, as he set out from Ireland to establish a new Christian community at Iona, that he was heading toward "the place of his resurrection."

Walking Together

After dinner, my wife, Laurel, and I walked around the elegant grounds of that small hotel in the moors, which we had discovered as if by accident. What beautiful surprises we found! The sun had decided to bless us at the end of that day with unambiguous light and reassuring warmth. The vistas of the moors, and the heavy evening shadows gradually covering them, were charged with the glory of the Lord. The imaginatively designed and well cared-for flower beds around us spoke their own poetry.

It is permissible, now and again, to walk in the cool of the day in the garden of God, reminiscent of Adam and Eve in their earliest days, notwithstanding the violence and the poverty of the world "outside the garden," precisely because the center does hold. Walking around, or "sauntering," as Thoreau liked to say—he happily albeit mistakenly traced the derivation of "saunter" to the French *Sainte Terre,* for Holy Land—must surely be part of any saintly pilgrimage. Sauntering gives time to ponder the journey prayerfully. And so I did.

Why is travel so alluring? Never mind an Odysseus or an Abraham. What about everyman and everywoman?

An op-ed essay I once read described how traveling can be anti-entropic for all of us. The writer observed that our mundane experience, especially the experience of those of us older than fifty, is inevitably a trek toward death. Limitations are our daily bread in these years, along with an ever-increasing number of painful losses. Travel, the author argued, can be a salutary interruption, even a timeless moment, in the story of our trek toward death that is so deeply embedded in our routine experience.

The essayist did not say this, but in light of the journeys of the Celtic saints, we can see that the whole of life in this world *is* travel, anti-entropic travel indeed, however much the timeless moments may be regularly obscured by the absurdities.

Being with my dear spouse on this Celtic journey gave it a timeless quality. The great Karl Barth read holy matrimony directly from the Trinity. This is the image of God in this world, he argued: husband and wife. Much more can and should be read from the Trinity, I believe: relationships with friends, life in a variety of human communities, and, indeed, companionship with all the creatures of God. But holy matrimony will surely be one of the most important of those readings. Strikingly, Celtic monasticism had, as a matter of course, included married lay workers, and even, for some time, married clergy, in its inner circles. Which was consistent overall with its inclusive and, in that sense, catholic spirituality. I, for one, could not have imagined learning or doing anything of significance—including praying—on that Celtic holiday had I been alone, bereft of my lifelong partner in the Lord. One has to *be* before one can embark on the journey. And holy matrimony had been of my being for thirty years.

When Columba set out from Ireland to travel to Iona, interestingly enough, he did not go alone. He did not travel with a spouse, surely, but his being was apparently constituted by relationship, too, not only established in solitude. He took twelve brother-monks with him for the journey. "Wherever they went," Lisa Bitel observed suggestively, "Irish monks took their well-developed social models and their intense need to form communities with them."[21]

Communing with Earth and Sea

They also took with them a vision of *communitas* that was inclusive, holistic, even cosmic. They lived in community with the whole world of nature, with "all things visible," as well as with the angels and saints above and every human creature here below. This was the aspect of their spirituality that, as a matter of course, fascinated me the most: their embrace of nature and its ecology of death. Of Columba, Finan has written: "The aura that surrounds [him] is one of a love and tenderness and *sympathie* towards all creatures great and small, the weary songbird or the elements of earth and seas and sky."[22] The cosmic world of the Celtic saints was indeed charged with divinity, as this medieval Irish poem indicates:

> I am the wind which breathes upon the sea,
> I am the wave of the ocean,
> I am the murmur of the billows . . .
> I am a beam of the sun . . .
> I am a salmon in the water,
> I am a lake in the plain,
> I am a word of knowledge . . .
> I am the God who created the fire in the head[23]

Inspired by such apperceptions, as a longstanding student of Western theological images of nature, I had self-consciously come to the lands of the Celtic saints bringing with me a preeminent interest in matters ecological and theological. In my historical studies of classical Christian attitudes toward nature, I had self-consciously steered away from the spirituality of the mystics of the church and concentrated on the theology of its doctors.[24] That was a historical project that had to be completed, for a range of reasons. Our trip to Ireland, Wales, and Scotland therefore gave me good and welcome occasion to revisit and to ponder the insights of what might be called Celtic Christianity's exemplary spiritual ecology.

Philip Sheldrake has argued convincingly that the vision of the Celtic saints was primarily theocentric, not cosmocentric, and, more particularly, primarily trinitarian, not merely theistic. Not by accident did the writer of the "Breastplate of St. Patrick," in which he or she celebrated the glories of the creation—the sun's brightness, the moon's radiance, the fire's glory, the lightning's quickness, the wind's swiftness, the sea's depth, the earth's stability, the rock's solidity—call upon the Trinity:

> I rise today
> in power's strength, invoking the Trinity,
> believing in threeness,
> confessing the oneness,
> of creation's Creator.[25]

In this sense, the Celtic saints never encountered *nature*, as we typically understand that term in our culture. They encountered a world that was charged with overwhelming expressions of the majestic powers and the immediate presence of *the Creator*, who was working out mysterious and magnificent purposes in the lives of all creatures. What the Celtic saints encountered in nature was the beauty, power, glory, and vastness of *God's good creating*. This is Sheldrake's nuanced reading of the spiritual ecology of the Celtic saints:

The Celtic Christian attitude toward nature involved a profound sense of the immanence of God. This reminds us that it was not nature as such that concerned the Celts. Nature was a kind of second sacred book, parallel to the Scriptures, that revealed the divine. Did the contemplative Celtic ascetics really notice the natural world in our sense of a beautiful landscape? This is difficult to assess, but nature itself was not the object of contemplation. Although there was an immediacy in the way a human relationship with nature was expressed, for example in some early medieval Irish poetry, nature was not really a value in itself. What the monastic poets sought and found in the natural world was an image of the Creator God.[26]

This thought Sheldrake compellingly illustrates by quoting an anonymous ninth-century Christian poem from Ireland:

> I wish, O Son of the living God,
> O ancient, eternal King,
> For a hidden little hut in the wilderness
> That it may be my dwelling.
>
> An all-grey lithe little lark
> To be by its side,
> A clear pool to wash away sins
> Through the Grace of the Holy Spirit.

Quite near, a beautiful wood,
Around it on every side,
To nurse many-voiced birds,
Hiding it with its shelter.

And facing south for warmth;
A little brook across its floor,
A choice ground with many gracious gifts
Such as which be good for every plant. . . .

A pleasant church and with the linen altar-cloth,
A dwelling for God from Heaven;
Then, shining candles
Above the pure-white Scriptures. . . .

This is the husbandry I would take.
I would choose and will not hide it:
Fragrant leek,
Hens, salmon, trout, bees.
Raiment and food enough for me
From the King of fair fame,
And I to be sitting for a while
Praying God in every place.[27]

Did Yeats know this poem? Was it in his mind when he dreamed about his cabin of peace at Innisfree? The realism of this poem and its unself-conscious affirmation of the blessings of divine grace, in Baptism and Eucharist, set it well apart from Yeats's early romantic dreams, and surely dramatically apart from his later apocalyptic nightmares. Those who treasured these verses knew, by virtue of their encounter with the crucified and risen Lord, that the center does indeed hold. They had, in this sense, passionately consented to being. For them, as for Genesis, all things were therefore "very good."

Peter Brown has offered a markedly different picture of Latin Christianity in his study *The Cult of the Saints*. He argues that Latin Christianity desacralized nature, as the cult of the saints spread throughout the late Roman Empire. He concludes:

It seems to me that the most marked feature of the rise of the Christian Church in western Europe was the imposition of human administrative structures and of an ideal potentia linked to invisible human beings and to their visible human representatives, the bishop of the town, at the expense of traditions that had seemed to belong to the structure of the landscape itself.[28]

Be that as it may, the Celtic saints and their followers, it appears, never lost touch with the landscape or the seascape, for that matter. On the other hand, neither did they flee from either the perils or the promise of gathered, public human communities, the urban ethos of human life. On the contrary, they established and shepherded such communities: but not at the expense of, or over against, the larger natural environs. The journeys of the Celtic saints and the life of the communities that they sought to establish were intended to be lived in communion with the earth and the sea and all the more so in communion with the Creator, whom the saints encountered in the terrors and the beauties of earth and sea.

This sense of intimacy with nature and with God-in-nature then allowed the Celtic saints to call upon the whole creation, things visible as well as invisible, for life and assistance, as we can see in the moving words of the "Breastplate of St. Patrick." In this hymn, as N. D. O'Donoghue explains, "the world of nature is really invoked, called on for help, seen as in this regard no less responsive than the angels and saints. Sun and moon, fire and lightning, as well as the unchanging rocks and the ever-changing sea, are all seen as living and powerful friends and companions."[29]

In the same spirit, in their better moments and surely in their spiritual aspirations, the Celtic saints eschewed the kind of might-makes-right *potentia* over nature and humans that Latin culture seems to have carried with it everywhere and self-consciously celebrated. For the Celtic saints, the earth is the Lord's and the fullness thereof, first and foremost, not something to be owned or dominated by anyone. In that sense, for them, earth and sea were very much sacral realities.

Claimed by the Ecology of Life

Feeling like a child of five but unwilling to wail, and driven by some primitive impulse, I unobtrusively reached to feel the shape of my pectoral cross beneath my shirt, as the huge Aer Lingus airbus took off in choppy air and began to climb to a cruising altitude of thirty thousand feet. Had I seen what I had come out to see? What *had* I seen?

That particular pectoral cross was new. I had purchased it at Iona. It was a Celtic cross, the kind that I had often seen but never really understood. The distinctive mark of this cross is, of course, the circle surrounding the point where the arms of the cross intersect. But the reasons for the circle itself are historically obscure, although frequently discussed.

Some say the circle was originally put in place for practical reasons. Since those large crosses—many of them served as towering boundary makers—were originally carved from a soft kind of stone, the horizontal arms of the crosses tended to break off. So new and improved crosses had to be thus secured. Others say that the circle was first intended to represent the halo of the Christ figure.[30]

During our Celtic holiday, I developed yet another theory to supplement all the others, building on some observations of Sheldrake. Historically, he notes, those crosses may well have carried with them various kinds of cosmic meanings. The pillar or standing stone of pre-Christian Celtic religion symbolized the *axis mundi,* the pole that was understood to link heaven and earth.[31] While such historical roots are worthy of note, it appeared to me that the cosmic symbolism of the circle is much more to the fore here, and much more of an integral symbolic element in Celtic Christian spirituality.

The Celtic saints and their followers characteristically built their monastic communities, wherever possible, according to a circular design. And that, apparently, was because those communities were intended to represent the Creator's embrace of all things and the Creator's purpose to unify all things in the eschatological reign of God, by the mission of the risen Lord. So Sheldrake comments that the circular design of the monastic communities "undoubtedly suggested that such places were replicas of the cosmos, microcosms of the macrocosm."[32] Subliminally, then, if not self-consciously, the circles of the Celtic crosses must have functioned symbolically, it appeared to me, as testaments to the unity of all things in the crucified, according to the witness of the Letter to the Colossians:[33]

> He is the image of the invisible God, the firstborn of all creation; for in him all things in heaven and on earth were created, . . . all things have been created through him and for him. He himself is before all things, and in him all things hold together. He is the head of the body, the church; he is the beginning, the firstborn from the dead . . . . For in him all the fullness of God was pleased to dwell, and through him God was pleased to reconcile to himself all things, whether on earth or in heaven, by making peace through the blood of his cross. (1:15-20)

This christocentric cosmic interpretation made perfect historical and spiritual sense to me, since the vision of classical Celtic monasticism was inclusive, rather than exclusive. In forming their monastic cities—this is the best terminology, not *monasteries,* a term that suggests walls and separation from this world—the Celtic saints sought to explore openings to communion with the one who is the center of *this* world, in whom all things consist, who is to come again to judge all things in righteousness and to renew the face of the whole earth. And in communion with him, they experienced unity with all things. All things were, for them, included within the circle of God's grace and power: the invisible company of the saints and angels as well as the visible company of the citizens of this world, creatures of nature as well as humans, all peoples, not just their own kind, women as well as men, the married as well as the celibate, the sick and the disabled as well as the able-bodied, the poor and the oppressed as well as the rich and the powerful.

The same kind of "totalizing" vision is also evident in the Christian poetry of the period, as Finan has observed: "hymns or poems about Christ tend to tell the *whole* story, to set him in the context of the complete cosmic epic of creation, Fall, Incarnation, redemption and consummation."[34] Likewise for many of the great Celtic crosses themselves. They are replete with representations that allude to the whole history of creation and salvation, and geometric images, in addition to the circle, that suggest the fullness of the created world.[35] For this type of spirituality, Christ was self-consciously the cosmic center of all things and the foretaste of the cosmic feast in the consummated reign of God of all things yet to come.

Accordingly, the Celtic saints established their monastic "circles" not to reject the world, but to embrace it, in peace and harmony. Their expansive monastic cities were to be prefigurations of the new Edenic world of the reign to come, where the lamb would lie down with the lion and all the saints and angels would be as one body with the whole creation. The Celtic saints were surely acquainted with the brutalities of the Grim Reaper, but, all the more so, they knew themselves as claimed by the healing and life-giving powers of the gloriously enfleshed Son of God, in whom all things consist, who holds all things together.

Now, as a matter of brute historical fact, the actual lives of the Celtic monastic communities sometimes left much to be desired. The abbots were typically tied in with the ruling classes, and often got embroiled in tribal aggrandizements. Columba's celebrated spiritual pilgrimage from Ireland to Iona appears to have been occasioned, if not totally driven, by banishment from his own community, since he had sided with a losing political faction. On at least one occasion, moreover, monks from one monastic city actually waged war on another community, and several monks were killed!

But *abusus non tollit usum*—misuse does not discredit use. Compared with the social and political strife of their times, the regular patterns of waging war on both humans and nature, those monastic cities were indeed "liminal" centers, places where perhaps as nowhere else the transcendent values of inclusion, social justice, peace, and harmony with nature could be celebrated and to that degree constantly advanced, notwithstanding the ravages of death.

And numerous historical advances were indeed made. It sounds like hyperbole, but Thomas Cahill may be right when he observes in his best-selling historical entertainment *How the Irish Saved Civilization,* that Patrick was "the first human being in the history of the world to speak out unequivocally against slavery."[36] Within Patrick's lifetime, as Cahill observes, the Irish slave trade did come to a halt, and other forms of violence, such as murder and intertribal warfare, decreased.[37]

This is how Sheldrake instructively describes the exemplary monastic cities that the saintly Celtic founders sought to establish:

> Overall . . . , a religious enclosure was simply a privileged space within which a particular vision of the world could be lived out. Thus, monks in the tradition of Columbanus saw monastic settlements as anticipations of paradise in which the forces of division, violence and evil were excluded. Wild beasts were tamed and nature was regulated. . . .
>
> The Columbanian tradition, for example, believed that all people were called from birth to the experience of contemplation. So, "monastic" enclosures were places of spiritual experience and of non-violence and also places of education, wisdom and art. Within the enclosures there took place, ideally speaking, an integration of all elements of human life, as well as of all classes of human society.[38]

Those circles also included the saints and the angels, as Sheldrake explains:

> There was no real divide between this world and the "other" world of divine and spiritual beings. God was close at hand, but so were the saints and angels. The nearness of God to creation went hand in hand with a sense of the heavenly powers surrounding people day and night. It seemed natural to Celtic Christians to turn not only to God but to angels and saints for support.[39]

My new pectoral cross told me that story, I then realized. That stark cruciform center and that liminal, all-inclusive cosmic circle was what I *had* seen in the lands of the Celtic saints. Never mind what I had come out to see.

As I settled back in my seat and looked out upon the clouds below, I began to feel—as if for the first time—that the center *does* hold. With fear and great joy, it dawned on me: my wife and I were also on our way to the place of our resurrection. The ecology of death had become for me, as I pressed my pectoral cross to my heart, the ecology of life.

Chapter 8

Reliving the Story Ethically

A Personal Testament of Nature Reborn

"The LORD *God took the man and put him in the garden of Eden to care for it and to protect it." (Gen. 2:15)*

The circle of these explorations in the theology of nature is now nearly complete. At the outset, I sought to reclaim the classical Christian story from the hands of its critics historically, so that all concerned might know that we Christians have indeed a story of ecological and cosmic promise to tell. I also attempted to show how the Scriptures can legitimately be read ecologically and cosmically, beyond any narrow anthropocentrism, as an affirmation of a universal history of God. Thus inspired by the biblical witness, I ventured to retell the classical Christian story in the modern terms of evolution, by critically appropriating the cosmic and christocentric vision of Teilhard de Chardin. I further explored what it can mean for a Christian to enter into communion with the creatures of nature, as well as with God and all our human brothers and sisters, in terms of a freshly conceived "I-Ens" relationship with the creatures of nature. I then suggested that the ritual apperception of God in worship—of the God who is always "God with us," immediately and intimately with us throughout the whole creation and the fullness thereof—is existentially fundamental for all who want to understand the story and to live it. I next attempted to explore what a genuinely ecological and cosmic spirituality might look like, reflecting on the witness of the Celtic saints and contemplating their embrace of nature, beyond the ecology of death.

Now it is time to close the this circumferential argument, so that the center, the classical Christian story itself, may be seen in its biblically etched fullness. "You will know them by their fruits" (Matt. 7:16)! We Christians are called to love in deeds, not only in words. The story we tell means nothing, according to its own canons, if it does not change lives in the community of faith that treasures the story.

In these concluding explorations, I therefore want to show how the classical Christian story can be relived ethically in these times of ecological and cosmic crisis, how it can indeed change lives: for the sake of a renewed relationship with the earth and all its creatures, and indeed the whole cosmos. This is to try to tell the story of Adam and Eve all over again, whom the Lord God placed in a "garden of delights," this our earthly paradise—Eden—to care for it and to protect it (Gen. 2:15).

To this end, I want to speak concretely from the situation in which I find myself as an affluent American Christian of the early twenty-first century, one who has been struggling with the theology of nature for more than thirty years. This is a personal testament of nature reborn.[1]

The Theology of Nature in Retrospect

We American Christians have much to confess, from an ecological point of view, as well as from many other points of view. Many of us have participated "religiously" in the obsessive American drama with nature.[2] We have worshiped nature idolatrously even as we have also exploited nature selfishly, consciously or unconsciously, directly or indirectly. In this respect, as in others, we have failed to respond to our divine calling to be a light to the nations. We ourselves, or the many affluent among us, have all too often fled from the anguish of the city to seek the imagined healing balm of nature in suburbia, in farmlands, sometimes even in wilderness areas. On the other hand, very few of us have taken the time to live with the redwoods and to listen to their voices and to sense the presence of the Holy Spirit brooding over those primordial but meagerly rooted giants. We have always been in a hurry to go somewhere, it seems. Where?

The theologians in our midst have sometimes been among our worst—or best?—offenders. An idiosyncratic lot, those of us who aspire to think theologically nevertheless tend to have this in common. We come forth to speak the truth resolutely, then we retire to our studies, to let the world and the gospel go merrily on their way, along their sure and certain collision course. This is often comic beyond belief.

I remember a simple, electric conversation I had with the great Karl Barth in his study in Basel, many years ago. I had gone there to talk with him about the doctoral dissertation I was writing about his theology of creation. The encounter turned out to be an epic clash of comic obstinance, he playing the role of the elderly defender of the gospel truth, I taking the part of the eager youthful challenger. After listening to me for a short time (a very short time, it seemed to me then), this great theologian, reputed to be the Thomas Aquinas of the Reformation tradition, interrupted to scold me for my interest in nature. What, he asked, did that have to do with the faith of the Holy Bible? And, around and around the maypole of theological dialectic we then danced, each of us with some of his best brandy in our snifters. I was exhilarated at the time, because there I was, a young theology student, prancing around with a giant.

I could have done it differently, much better, much less obstinately. So could he. I could have told him how profoundly grateful I was for the stand that he had taken for the gospel over against the nature-religion of the Nazis. He could perhaps have allowed that a theological era might have been dawning elsewhere—in America of all places—in which faithfulness to the gospel would require Christian theologians to reopen discussions about the theology of nature. Actually, he ended up being less comic than I, as I recall. Had he been baiting me all along to teach me a lesson? I will never know. I do know that he closed our heated but friendly dispute with a reference to Rabbi Gamaliel from the book of Acts. Maybe, said Barth, this revival of interest in the theology of nature will be something like the birth of the early Christian movement, as the wise rabbi saw it. Don't fight it. Don't endorse it. If God is with it, nothing can stop it. If God isn't with it, nothing can help it.

I hope and trust that this book you hold, this venture in faith has indeed been called forth by God. It has taken much hope and trust, I must confess, especially at the very beginning. More than thirty years later now, with Basel far behind me, and many starts and false starts along the way, I still sometimes wonder whether the hand of the Lord has been in this struggle for a new theology of nature. Most of the time I believe it has been. This volume is one more tangible sign of that conviction.

Indeed, I believe that this is the will of the Lord: that the time for a new and compelling theology of nature is upon us today, more urgently than ever, much more so than in those relatively innocent days when I had time to go off to Europe and to sniff brandy with the likes of Barth. The time is surely at hand today, as never before, for us to find ways to move beyond the anthropocentrism of theologians like Barth himself,[3] yet without forsaking the whole heritage of the classical faith for which the likes of Barth so passionately stood, as thousands in his time imagined themselves to be marching off to the Nordic wilds, to the beat of a different drummer, *der Führer*. For those orgies of heroic self-indulgence in nature, they in fact marched along routes that sometimes took them within breathing distance of the crematoriums.

The time is at hand to search the ancient biblical documents thoroughly and passionately for a new vision of the future and the fullness thereof, yet without forgetting the one in whom "the fullness of God was pleased to dwell" (Col. 1:19). The time is at hand for us to discover new ways of relating to the multitudinous creatures of nature as God's own world—for which God has purposes and in which God takes delight, far away from the tiny niche in this immense cosmos where we live, albeit closer to us in nature than we are to ourselves—yet without forsaking the one through whom "God was pleased to reconcile to himself all things, whether on earth or in heaven, by making peace through the blood of his cross" (Col. 1:20). The time is at hand for us to address the wrenching but silent despair of these times, with a new, universal, and holistic theology of nature, yet without forgetting to contemplate the lilies of the field, for even Solomon in all his glory was not arrayed like one of these.

But even if we renew our minds and hearts in this way, reaching out for a new and more forceful theology of nature and claiming it spiritually as our own, it will all be for naught unless we also renew our lives. For by our fruits we must indeed be known.

The Ethical Fruits of a Martyr Church

Building on the kind of ethical analysis suggested by Larry Rasmussen,[4] I join with many others in sharing this hope for the church of Jesus Christ in these times: that as a "communal enclave" the church will be a beacon to the world, a light to the nations, a city set upon a hill that cannot be hidden. Wherever the faithful find themselves, whether in garden cities or urban wastelands, university laboratories or corporate boardrooms, touched by the toxins of uranium pilings or by the peace of old-growth forests, the time is at hand not just to think the theology of nature but to embody it. This is how I envision the rebirth of the church's life with nature. It is to this end that I write and for this end that I pray while I write. These are the signs.

In the life of the church, when it is faithful to its calling, I can see adumbrated the relationship with nature that God originally intended humanity to have in the garden. For, by the cross of Jesus Christ, God has intervened in our sinful history to restore us to our rightful relationship to the divine and therefore to our rightful relationship with other human beings and indeed with the whole world of nature. I can also see fragmentary signs of a communion with nature within the life of the church that is totally new, that is unprecedented, that was not given with our Edenic existence, signs of the New Heavens and the New Earth, when God will be all in all. This is because, by the resurrection of Jesus Christ, God has intervened in our mortal history to give us a foretaste of the eternal city and the eternal creation yet to come.

As a community that walks the way of the cross and is driven by the power of the resurrection, the church then lives by the grace of God as the embodied, congregated testimony of both the restoration and the foretaste God has brought forth in Christ. I want to unpack this thought now, by invoking an old word, and by drawing on both its connotations of self-sacrifice and joyful celebration of the future of God—*martyr*.

The word itself simply means "witness." But this word has been overlaid throughout the ages with rich meanings wrought by the deeds of those who themselves have become martyrs. A martyr manifests both the love of the cross and the power of the resurrection. But that overflowing of love and power is more than any single human being can carry. It can happen by the grace of God. Some individuals have carried those heavenly burdens, the love and the power. Perhaps many more will. But I am thinking here of the church as a body, as a community of witnesses. Perhaps together in our weakness, blessed by the love of God and driven by the power of God, as a body we can be a martyr church. Perhaps in our weakness we can rise to the occasion in these times, as martyrs in other eras rose to the occasions that were thrust upon them.

The challenge before this martyr church that I want to announce, among many others that must also be announced, is this: we are now free to allow the love of God in Christ Jesus so to pour into our hearts by the indwelling of the Holy Spirit that it overflows abundantly, not only to persons, especially to those in great need, but also to all the creatures of nature.

How then will this martyr church in this ecological and cosmic era love nature? Passionately and persistently and pervasively. We Christians will be a voice for the voiceless, for the sake of all the creatures of nature who have no voice in human affairs. We will listen to the plaintive cries of the great whales and hear the groaning of the rain forests, and we will be their advocates in the village square and in the courts of power, by the grace of God. All the more so we will hear the bitter wailing of the little children who live on the trash mountains of this world and who wear clothes that have been washed in streams overflowing with heinous poisons and who sometimes drink those very waters. We will cry out with those who cry from the refugee camps and the reservations for their ancestral lands, so they can return to their roots in the soil and harvest food with the love of their own hands. We will raise our voices with the desperate souls who live in impoverished city neighborhoods where children go to school with asbestos particles in the air and come home to overcrowded hovels where they grow up with lead paint in their diets. This martyr church will mount campaigns of comic beauty, in the spirit of the mythical Pied Piper, calling upon the powers that be to drive out the rats from our cities. For we know that even as rats have rights, they have no right to be crawling into the cribs of our babies in the night. With comic beauty or dead seriousness, this martyr church will also raise its voice in holy rage against the plundering of this planet's God-given bounty, in the name of all the voiceless creatures of this earth and on behalf of generations of creatures yet to be born. We will be a martyr church, witnessing in word. But not words only. We will also love nature and all the little ones of this earth in deed.

With regard to nature, I see our deeds being of four kinds, shaped in terms of four callings.[5] Three of these pertain to the restoration effected by the cross of Christ and the fourth pertains to the anticipated consummation inaugurated and proleptically given to us in Jesus Christ as our risen Lord.

The Calling to Cooperate with Nature Righteously

As restored creatures, we members of the martyr church can enter into a new life of righteous cooperation with nature. Traditionally, the words *dominion* and *stewardship* have been employed in this connection, but I now believe that it is best to retire them, for the foreseeable future, so that we do not have to explain constantly to others and to ourselves what they really mean and can instead simply say with conviction what we really mean. These terms still carry too much baggage from the anthropocentric and indeed androcentric theology of the past; they are still too fraught with the heavy images of management, control, and exploitation of persons and resources.

Righteous cooperation with nature means at least two things: intervening in the systems of nature, yes, but also doing so respectfully and creatively, attentive to nature's own God-given structures and processes, and attentive to the divinely mandated claims of social justice. Righteous cooperation with nature happens first under the rubric of the I-Ens relationship, and then only under the rubric of the I-It relationship. We contemplate nature before we seek to change it. We live with the trees before we seek to cut them. And when we do intervene, we then do so for good reasons. The burden of proof rests heavily on our own shoulders.

One middle axiom in this respect might be: never overwork the land or underpay the laborer. The land deserves its rest. The laborer is worthy of his or her hire. In this connection, it seems to me that the whole notion of private property and capital accumulation, predicated as it is on the continued exploitation of nature, is highly suspect from a theological perspective, and therefore the church should be very cautious in giving it any kind of blanket approval. The earth is the Lord's and the fullness thereof! The earth is given to us humans not as property, but—to use a term given currency in Catholic Worker circles—as *trusterty*. Righteous cooperation with nature means using the earth as God's good commonwealth in a communitarian mode, replenishing the earth at every available opportunity for the sake of further use and for the sake of future generations, and not abusing it for the sake of individual gain or class aggrandizement.

For those of us who are affluent, the mandate of righteous cooperation with nature is a particular challenge. A society of unbridled consumerism, such as our own, is an unrighteous society.[6] The toll North American and European consumers unnecessarily and perhaps unthinkingly take on nature and, by default, on the poor, is horrendous. Consider, among the numerous statistics that might be adduced here, the following: (1) Europeans and Americans spend $12 billion annually on perfumes (about this amount would provide reproductive health care for all women in developing countries); (2) Europeans and Americans spend $17 billion annually on pet food (only $13 billion would be needed to provide basic health and nutrition needs universally in the developing world).[7] This is not to begin to detail the thoughtless and greedy exhaustion of precious, nonrenewable resources, such as fossil fuels, driven by the overly consumptive economies of the developed nations. Nor is it even to touch on the polluting afterburn of that consumerism, such as global warming.

In response to this kind of unrighteous consumerism, numerous Church ethicists and Church statements have rightfully called for both socioeconomic and lifestyle changes in Western societies. One can speak, indeed, of an ecumenical consensus on these issues among the leaders—if, not yet, the members—of the churches of the world. Perhaps the two most critical of these changes for industrialized societies would be, socioeconomically, the development of an economy of sustainability and, individually, the development of a lifestyle of voluntary simplicity.[8] A martyr Church will as a matter of course be a champion for both of these causes, in the public square and among its own members. A good place to begin that advocacy, already, thankfully, the subject of much attention in some Church circles, is at that notorious symbolic center—sadly—of American consumerism, the season of Christmas. Can that festival, which celebrates the Prince of Peace born in a stable, become something more for the general populus than an orgy of consumerism?[9]

The Calling to Care for Nature Sensitively

As restored creatures, we members of the martyr church will also enter into a new life of sensitive care of the earth. This is care for nature for nature's sake, an idea that may sound odd, if not scandalous, to some who have only heard the Bible interpreted in anthropocentric or secular terms and who have not heard Gen. 2:15 correctly translated: not "to till it [the garden] and keep it," but "to serve [it] and protect it." This means serving nature as an end in itself, loving nature not for what it can do for us but for what it is and what it needs. This also means caring for the whole garden, in appropriate ways, the so-called useless plants and animals, as well as the productive ones.

It will surely be necessary to be firm in this respect, as St. Francis was said to have been firm with some of God's creatures, like the wolf. It will surely be necessary for us, from time to time, to say to brother rat and sister roach: "You do not belong here. Go live your lives in some other niche." Yes, we will defend the rights of rats and the rights of roaches to find their niche somewhere, if they can, as long as they do not stay here or in any other human homes. On the other hand, recall that Noah took all the animals with him into the ark. Presumably if his role had been only to take along certain animals for food or future investment, he might well have righteously seized upon the opportunity to leave the rats and the roaches and the blackflies behind! We are called to care sensitively for all God's creatures, as we can, in appropriate ways.

I take it, moreover, that sensitive care for nature implies three kinds of engagement with nature, pertaining to what we can think of as its three dimensions—wild, cultivated, and fabricated—with varying degrees of effective involvement.

If we think of the wilderness not just in typical American terms, as referring to the "untamed regions" where humans might easily travel and that humans might colonize for their own purposes of adventure, we have already fallen short of the biblical meanings that ought to fill this term to the overflowing. Mars is wilderness, biblically speaking. But, above all, wilderness can be taken to refer to those regions of the universe to which, we can readily imagine, humans from this planet will never travel, except at their peril—into the middle of the sun, for example, like some latter-day Icarus or to the very edges of galactic outer space and beyond into the billions of galaxies that extend through what for us is infinite space. This is wilderness par excellence, before which the command from God to us to care sensitively has only an infinitesimal meaning at most.

We can care, at least in some respects, for the wilderness areas on this planet, and so we should. We cannot do a great deal, surely, nor should we. But at least we can seek to preserve those wilderness areas that the spread of so-called civilization has not already overwhelmed, with due attention to the canons of social justice (obviously one does not rightly seek to save the whales, let us say, oblivious to the needs of hungry children). Wild nature is good, created so by God, even though in some respects we may find it repulsive. It deserves to be preserved. The efforts by many to preserve endangered species for the sake of those creatures themselves must also, in appropriate ways, be our efforts. I see no indication whatsoever in the Bible—indeed many indications to the contrary—that God would smile on an earth covered with blacktop and geodesic domes and awash in oceanic sludge, even if we humans could, in some sense, healthily live in such a world.

A poignant, illustrative case: saving the salmon in the Pacific Northwest.[10] By the end of the 1990s, what had been clear to conservationists and, in some measure, to the general public for many years, also had become clear to policy-makers: the wild Pacific salmon were nearly extinct. It appeared that a public will to save the salmon had not only emerged, but that it had solidified. "It is like being told that Mount Rainier will disappear from our skyline," said the governor of Washington state. "Life without salmon is unthinkable, but today, the unthinkable is in danger of coming true." The Puget Sound basin, all of which is to be under Endangered Species protection, contains more than three million people; 63 percent of its land is in private hands. People and institutions throughout the area will have to change their behaviors. Farms, logging operations, housing tracts, golf courses, roads and power-generating plants are likely to be affected, all to ensure that the water that is the natural habitat of the salmon will be cooler and cleaner. "Ironically," said the mayor of Seattle, "as we work to save the salmon, it may turn out that the salmon save us."

Reportedly, several church and ecumenical groups have been among the leading participants in the loose coalition of citizens' organizations and business leaders that has sparked the discussion about saving the salmon and helped solidify the public will to make the lifestyle and economic changes that will be required to carry out this vast project. We should expect no less of our churches. We Christians live with this mandate: to care sensitively for wild nature in every way we appropriately can.

We are also called to care sensitively for cultivated nature. Farmlands and other carefully managed natural reserves and parks seem to me to be a divinely intended datum of our existence together as human beings. Moreover, in view of the biblical theme that we are "of the earth," and in view of the biblical understanding of human existence as communitarian, I would argue that the burden of proof must be on the side of anyone who would advocate policies that would further turn our family farms over to agribusiness and further abrogate the family farmer's close relationship to the land in favor of massive, technological interventions with huge, computer-controlled machines and absentee owners.[11]

Our churches must be particularly attentive—proactively attentive—to the needs of those family farmers who are among the poor of the earth. One example is the rural ministry offered by the Promised Land Network, supported by the Catholic diocese of Hereford, Texas. Working with a community of more than a hundred small farmers, this ministry teaches sustainable agriculture techniques, including better grazing methods and less reliance on chemical fertilizers. The ministry also fosters community empowerment, ecological awareness, and spiritual renewal. Around the globe, experienced farmers from abroad, supported by Lutheran World Relief, help local farmers in northern Namibia to maximize traditional agricultural productivity, with organic methods and sophisticated land conservation techniques, and help to initiate cooperatives that can address communal water supply issues.

Further, Christians must again be at the forefront of those who advocate in behalf of the humane treatment of animals—both wild and cultivated—in the spirit of St. Francis and the early English Methodists, who helped to give the movement to protect animals from abuse its first historic impetus. Should we not live in a world that seeks to befriend all animals, in appropriate ways? The Church must be at the forefront of those who persistently keep raising this question.[12]

With regard to fabricated nature, sensitive care clearly entails still more human intervention. I may best be able to communicate my meaning here by this aphorism: city planning and ecological design are divine sciences. Buildings and streets should be constructed on a human scale, with attentiveness to our bodily roots in living nature and the city's organic roots in its own bioregion.[13] Wherever possible, likewise, buildings should be designed to be self-sufficient in terms of energy use and waste disposal.[14]

Can we also restore the great riverways that once gave our cities birth? Can we uncover those now-polluted streams that run under blacktop and through huge pipes to God knows where, but that once flowed through our city neighborhoods for all to see, full of wildlife, offering children secret places to play and to dream?

Moreover, the time to demythologize the automobile in this society is long overdue. The automobile in America has become a kind of god, which millions adore with virtually unquestioned devotion. But not only does this god pollute mercilessly, it has become a default planning agent, whose pervasive use has mindlessly driven the reorganization of our national life, and in the process destroyed the vitality of countless urban neighborhoods and adversely effected whole bioregions, via freeways and suburban sprawl. Many think they cannot live without the automobile. Probably it is closer to the truth to say that, unless radical social, economic, and environmental changes are made, we cannot live with it.[15] Does the Christian community have the courage to take on this highly charged but critically important issue?

Perhaps even more critical, does the Christian community have the will to take the lead, where necessary, or to work with other citizens of goodwill, wherever possible, to dream dreams and see visions of a livable future for our great metropolitan areas? Until very recently, many American churches have ridden the crest of so-called white flight from inner cities and have more or less, by default if not by conscious intention, baptized suburban sprawl. This social movement has had the effect of exacerbating the poverty of urban core areas and undermining the ecological richness of surrounding suburban and rural areas. One citizens' group in a rust-belt city, Cleveland, Ohio, is now making a difference in response to such issues. The group EcoCity Cleveland has developed what it calls an "Ohio Smart Growth Agenda" that promotes sensible development and livable communities, that maintains historic cities and towns, that preserves farmlands and open space, and that reduces tax burdens on future generations.[16]

While it is clear that this movement in Cleveland has numerous sources of support, it is also clear that it would not have nearly the public strength that it does have were it not for the visionary leadership of the Catholic archbishop of Cleveland, Anthony Pilla. In 1993 he issued a pastoral letter that outlined a new vision for Northeast Ohio and for the nation. That vision, "The Church in the City," argued that it is morally wrong for institutions or individuals to abandon old cities and the poor in favor of sprawling new development areas at the edges of metropolitan areas.[17] On the Feast of St. Francis of Assisi, October 4, 1990, Bishop Pilla had spoken directly to the theme "Christian Faith and the Environment: Reverence and

Responsibility."[18] This is the kind of leadership that we should expect from our churches everywhere, as all Christians seek to find ways to sensitively care for the earth and the poor of the earth in our urban areas.

Sensitive care means attention to the interdependence of wild, cultivated, and fabricated nature. Since we are created by God to live in the midst of all these dimensions of nature, we should make every reasonable effort to see that they overlap and interpenetrate, wherever possible. In particular, the city should have signs of cultivated nature and hints of wild nature. The farmlands should have signs of nearby or distant urban centers and hints of the wilderness. The wilderness may have hints of urban life and signs of agricultural life at its edges.

The Calling to Wonder at Nature Blessedly

As persons whose lives have been restored to our divinely intended roles in creation history, we members of the martyr church not only will lead lives of righteous cooperation and sensitive care, we also will lead lives of blessed wonder. Not for nothing does the very word *Eden* mean "delight." This means seeking opportunities to contemplate both the beautiful and the sublime aspects of the cosmos, standing in awe of both the sunset and the lion roaring for its prey, seeing the glory of God refracted in both the elegance of a Ludwig Mies van der Rohe building and in the terror of molten steel.

As guides to this wonder, perhaps Psalms 104 and 29 are among the most helpful. The first is reminiscent of the Egyptian hymn to the sun; it celebrates the gloriously harmonious diversity of the creation. The second is reminiscent of a more Babylonian-type apperception of nature, celebrating the terrible presence of Yahweh in the storm and in the pangs of birthing. To invoke a construct I introduced earlier, blessed wonder means taking time to cultivate I-Ens relationships with the creatures of nature.

It is time for all of us martyr Christians who "have trod, have trod, have trod," with everyone else, as Gerard Manley Hopkins knew so well, who have existed in a world where "all is seared with trade; bleared, smeared with toil," to hear the voice of the One to whom Hopkins devoted his life: "consider the lilies of the field, how they grow; they neither toil nor spin," and to know that "even Solomon in all his glory was not clothed like one of these" (Matt. 6:28f.). It is time for all of us martyr Christians to stand in wonder even before the specter of our wretched cities, to see their soot, their desolate parks, their crumbling bridges, and to hear their groaning in travail, yet to marvel, knowing, with Hopkins's "God's Grandeur":

And for all this, nature is never spent;
There lives the dearest freshness deep down things;
And though the last lights off the black West went
Oh, morning, at the brown brink eastward, springs—
Because the Holy Ghost over the bent
World broods with warm breast and with ah! bright wings.[19]

This vision can be ours, only if we claim the freedom we have been given to rest in the I-Ens relationship with nature, in the midst of our downtrodden world.

The Calling to Anticipate the Reign of God Joyfully

And more. Blessings overflow. Blessings abound. As members of the martyr church, we have been claimed by more than redemption, which restores us to our rightful relationship to God and therewith to our rightful relationship to other humans and to the whole world of nature. The gospel we celebrate and proclaim to the world is not only the good news of redemption established by the cross of Christ, but also the good news of the consummation of the creation inaugurated by the resurrection of Christ. So there is a fourth dimension in our renewed relationship with nature: joyful anticipation.

By hope we are in touch with the reality of God's future. We are embraced by it, in turn, through Christ. With him and through him, therefore, the church joins with choirs of angels to celebrate the new heavens, the new earth, and the new Jerusalem that is to come. And so the life of the church is transfigured, here and now, however imperfectly, by the eschatological glory of God, in and through Christ.

If I read Romans 8 correctly, I think I am right—with Oscar Cullmann—in concluding that a special kind of bodily renewal, anticipating the final resurrection, may be found in the life of the church in this world.[20] This reading of Pauline theology then has implications for our understanding of the church's ministry of healing today. I also wonder whether some kind of heightened spiritual relationship with nature more generally may not be possible in the context of the sacramental life of the church, prefiguring the kind of intimate communion with the whole earth that will be ours in those days of glory when God will be all in all. How else was it that John Calvin could have said, at the beginning of his *Institutes* that "it can be said reverently . . . that nature is God"?[21]

Perhaps as we raise such questions and think such thoughts more regularly than we have in the past, as the Spirit leads us into all truth, our eyes will be opened to gifts of God that many of us may have hitherto ignored.

At the same time, however, we know that the powers of death still reign and will continue to reign until the end times arrive, and that therefore our life as the martyr church in word and deed must always be lived, as the word *martyr* suggests, under the sign of the cross. Each of these dimensions of our restored and perfected relationship with nature—righteous cooperation, sensitive care, blessed wonder, and joyful anticipation—will regularly be contested and often undercut, in our hearts as elsewhere, by the powers of this age. This is why a balanced, holistic theology of cosmic history must always be, until the eschaton, a theology of "the Crucified God," as Jürgen Moltmann has phrased it. We see through a glass darkly. And we live with all the ambiguities and anguish of this mortal, sinful world. But we do see and we do live, with hope: for the future of the cosmos and for the continual rebirth of our own relationship with nature.

Life as a Christian has never been easy. Nor should it be any easier today. But, shaped by its ecological and cosmic ritual enactments, and buoyed by its new ecological and cosmic spirituality, this martyr church can rise to this historic occasion today, by the grace of God, to respond to what is perhaps an unprecedented calling, to love God and all God's creatures, as one great and glorious extended family, and in so doing to be a light to the nations and a city set upon a hill, whose exemplary witness cannot be hidden.

Notes

Preface

1. Erickson, Kathleen Powers. *At Eternity's Gate: The Spiritual Vision of Vincent van Gogh* (Grand Rapids: Eerdmans, 1998), 161, 162, 164, 165.

Chapter 1

1. Charles Reich, *The Greening of America* (New York: Random House, 1970). That the ecology movement was indeed a fad was stated in no uncertain terms by Richard Neuhaus, *In Defense of People: Ecology and the Seduction of Radicalism* (New York: Macmillan, 1971).

2. See Christopher Lasch, *The Culture of Narcissism: American Life in An Age of Diminishing Expectations* (New York: Norton, 1978).

3. Richard Falk, *Our Endangered Planet: Prospects and Proposals for Survival* (New York: Random House, 1971). See also Robert Heilbroner, *An Inquiry into the Human Prospect, Updated and Reconsidered for the 1980s* (New York: Norton, 1980).

4. The Worldwatch Institute's *State of the World* reports have been published annually by Norton beginning in 1984. For a stunning but sobering summary of recent trends, which suggest hopeful outcomes, notwithstanding the profundities of the crisis, see Lester R. Brown, "Threshold: Early Signs of an Environmental Awakening," *Worldwatch* 12, no. 2 (March/April 1999): 12–23.

5. See Franklin L. Jensen and Cedric W. Tilberg, eds. *The Human Crisis in Ecology* (Christian Social Responsibility Series; New York: Board of Social Ministry, Lutheran Church in America, 1972).

6. Paul Tillich, "Nature and Sacrament," *The Protestant Era*, trans. James Luther Adams (Chicago: Univ. of Chicago Press, 1957).

7. David W. Orr, *Earth in Mind: On Education, Environment, and the Human Prospect* (Washington, D.C.: Island Press, 1994), 134f.

8. This sense of cosmic alienation was already given powerful expression by Dostoyevsky, in the form of Arjkady Dolgorukov's musings on the law of entropy in *The Adolescent:* "Why must I inevitably love my neighbor or your future humanity, which I'll never see, which I'll never know, and which will eventually also disintegrate without leaving a trace. . . . when the earth will turn into an icy rock and float in airless space amidst an infinite number of other such icy rocks. . . . Why must I behave so nobly when nothing is going to last more than a moment?" Quoted by Bruce K. Ward, "Christianity and the Modern Eclipse of Nature: Two Perspectives," *Journal of the American Academy of Religion,* 63:4, 831.

9. See Philip J. Lee, *Against the Protestant Gnostics* (New York: Oxford Univ. Press, 1987); and Harold Bloom, *Omens of the Millennium: The Gnosis of Angels, Dreams, and Resurrection* (New York: G. P. Putnam, 1996).

10. It would take us too far afield here to explore how this modern alienation from nature is part of a still broader cultural problematic of fragmentation and nihilism, sometimes referred to as postmodernism. Robert Jenson has analyzed this problematic brilliantly in his essay, "How the World Lost Its Story," *First Things* 38 (October 1993): 19–24.

11. I hope that the reader new to the theology of nature will gain some awareness of the length and breadth of this relatively new theological field from the literature cited in this volume. The amount of literature in the field, little more than three decades old, is staggering. See the two book-length bibliographies: (1) most helpful because of its introduction and its careful summaries of each entry is Peter W. Bakken, Joan Gibb Engel, and J. Ronald Engel, *Ecology, Justice, and Christian Faith: A Critical Guide to the Literature* (Westport, Conn.: Greenwood Press, 1995); and (2) Joseph K. Sheldon, *Rediscovery of Creation: A Bibliographical Study of the Church's Response to the Environmental Crisis* (American Theological Library Association Bibliography Series, no. 29; Metuchen, N.J.: Scarecrow Press, 1992). The flow of this literature shows no signs of ebbing.

12. For a balanced theological evaluation of the New Age movement, see Ted Peters, *The Cosmic Self: A Penetrating Look at Today's New Age Movements* (San Francisco: Harper, 1991).

13. The impressive theology of nature by of the Catholic "geologian" Thomas Berry is mainly dependent on the findings of the natural sciences, especially scientific cosmology. See, e.g., Thomas Berry, *Befriending the Earth: A Theology of Reconciliation between Humans and the Earth* (Mystic, Conn.: Twenty-Third Publications, 1991); and, with Brian Swimme, *The Universe Story: From the Primordial Flaring Forth to the Ecozoic Era—A Celebration of the Unfolding of the Cosmos* (San Francisco: Harper-Collins, 1992). More meditative in character than the Berry and Swimme volume, but with the same kind of scientific depth, is the striking essay by Jeffrey G. Sobosan, *Romancing the Universe: Theology, Science, and Cosmology* (Grand Rapids: Eerdmans, 1999). A short but compelling essay that covers territory similar to Berry's and Sobosan's works is David S. Toolan's, "'Nature Is a Heraclitean Fire': Reflections on Cosmology in an Ecological Age," *Studies in the Spirituality of the Jesuits* 23:5 (November 1991). The prize-winning study by Larry L. Rasmussen, *Earth Community, Earth Ethics* (Maryknoll, N.Y.: Orbis Books, 1996), draws extensively from the findings of the sciences, as well as eclectically from a variety of suggestive literary and theological sources. For a general introduction to environmental ethics, written from a self-consciously reconstructionist standpoint, see James M. Gustafson, *A Sense of the Divine: The Natural Environment from a Theocentric Perspective* (Cleveland: The Pilgrim Press, 1994) [cf. my review in *dialog*, 34:4, p. 316]. Of all the scientifically oriented, reconstructionist voices during the last thirty years, however, perhaps the most forceful has been John Cobb's. For him, the findings of the natural sciences are best mediated for theological reflection through the thought patterns of Whiteheadian metaphysics. Cobb's early study, *Is It Too Late? A Theology of Ecology* (Beverly Hills, Calif.: Bruce, 1972), perhaps best exemplifies his reconstructionist perspective. See also John B. Cobb Jr., *Sustainability: Economics, Ecology, and Justice* (Maryknoll, N.Y.: Orbis Books, 1992); and, with Charles Birch, *The Liberation of Life: From the Cell to the Community* (Cambridge: Cambridge Univ. Press, 1981). For an overview of many of these issues, see Audrey R. Chapman, "Integrating Science with Eco-Theology and Eco-Ethics," *Dialog* 36 (fall 1997): 295–304.

14. Among several insightful ecofeminist volumes that might be cited here, the works by Sally McFague, *The Body of God: An Ecological Theology* (Minneapolis: Fortress Press, 1993) and Rosemary Radford Ruether, *Gaia and God: An Ecofeminist Theology of Earth Healing* (San Francisco: Harper, 1992), are perhaps the most trenchant. For an analysis of Ruether's thought, see Steven Bouma-Prediger, *The Greening of Theology: The Ecological Models of Rosemary Radford Ruether, Joseph Sittler, and Jürgen Moltmann* (Atlanta: Scholars Press, 1995). Also consult Sallie McFague's more recent monograph, which is more personally voiced: *Super, Natural Christians: How We Should Love Nature* (Minneapolis: Fortress Press, 1997).

15. See Michael Kinnamon, ed., *Signs of the Spirit: Official Report of the Seventh Assembly* (Grand Rapids, Mich.: Eerdmans, 1991). Perhaps the most forceful statements of this apologetic position by any single theologian have come from an American closely associated with the WCC, Thomas Derr. See his early study *Ecology and Human Need* (Philadelphia: Westminster, 1973). While advocates of other theological positions have been given a hearing in WCC meetings and publications, official statements by that body have mainly reflected the approach championed by Derr. Canadian theologian Douglas John Hall has also brought his considerable gifts to bear on this subject, with an approach akin to Derr's. See his study *Imaging God: Dominion as Stewardship* (Grand Rapids, Mich.: Eerdmans, 1986). Evangelical theologians have contributed to this discussion, too. See Loren Wilkenson, ed., *Earthkeeping in the Nineties: Stewardship of Creation* (Grand Rapids, Mich.: Eerdmans, 1991 [revised ed.]). A similar perspective is reflected in the impressive Presbyterian statement, *Keeping and Healing the Creation* (Louisville, Ky.: Committee on Social Witness Policy, Presbyterian Church [U.S.A.], 1989). See also the survey of the ecumenical discussion by Per Loenning, *Creation—An Ecumenical Challenge? Reflections Issuing from a Study by the Institute for Ecumenical Research, Strasbourg, France* (Macon, Ga.: Mercer Univ. Press, 1989) and the biblical discussions by Ulrich Duchrow and Gerhard Liedke, *Shalom: Biblical Perspectives on Creation, Justice, and Peace* (Geneva: WCC Publications, 1987).

While the statements of the WCC and the arguments of the theologians such as Derr and Hall have generally been thoughtful and insightful, albeit heated at times, the apologist "school" has also had its rank polemicists, who have been more interested in debunking the approaches of others, typically the reconstructionists, than in setting forth coherent and well-founded arguments of their own. Typical among these kinds of studies is Robert Royal's *The Virgin and the Dynamo: Use and Abuse of Religion in Environmental Debates* (Grand Rapids: Eerdmans, 1999). He states at the outset: "I do not think it would be wise to spend much time reading modern theology for enlightenment on environmental or other human problems" (9). Royal's book is basically downhill polemics from that point on, with a theologically sanctioned neocapitalist ideology being the silent partner of the polemics each step of the way.

16. See, for example, Wolfhart Pannenberg, *Toward a Theology of Nature: Essays on Science and Faith*, ed. Ted Peters (Louisville, Ky.: Westminster/John Knox Press, 1993); and Langdon Gilkey, *Nature, Reality, and the Sacred: The Nexus of Science and Religion* (Minneapolis: Fortress Press, 1993). For a theological analysis that focuses on the enmeshment and the meaning of *human* life in evolutionary history, see Philip Hefner, *The Human Factor: Evolution, Culture, and Religion* (Minneapolis: Fortress Press, 1993).

17. See Paul Albrecht, ed., *Faith and Science in an Unjust World: Report of the World Council of Churches' Conference on Faith, Science, and the Future* (Philadelphia: Fortress Press, 1980).

18. For an overview of this tradition, see Roderick Frazier Nash, *The Rights of Nature: A History of Environmental Ethics* (Madison: Univ. of Wisconsin Press, 1989), chap. 4: "The Greening of Religion." See also Derr, *Ecology and Human Need*, 50ff. Joseph Sittler's address, "Called to Unity," was reprinted in the *Ecumenical Review* 14 (January 1962): 177–87. For a review of Sittler's thought, see Peter Bakken, "The Ecology of Grace: Ultimacy and Environmental Ethics in Aldo Leopold and Joseph Sittler," (Ph.D. diss., Univ. of Chicago, 1991); and Steven Bouma-Prediger, *The Greening of Theology*. Sittler's influence is evident in the two major American Lutheran social statements on the environment, both revisionist projects, the first of which he helped to write (see *The Human Crisis in Ecology*, ed. Franklin L. Jensen and Cedric W. Tilberg [New York: Board of Social Ministry, Lutheran Church in America, 1972]), the second of which was shaped by theologians very much under his influence (see *Caring for Creation: Vision, Hope, and Justice* [Chicago: Commission for Church in Society, Evangelical Lutheran Church in America, 1991]).

19. James A. Nash, *Loving Nature: Ecological Integrity and Christian Responsibility* (Nashville, Tenn.: Abingdon Press, in cooperation with the Churches' Center for Theology and Public Policy, Washington, D.C., 1991). Among the "revisionists," in addition to Joseph Sittler and James Nash, I would also include one of the great contemporary German theologian, Jürgen Moltmann, whose works have been widely read in the U.S. See especially his study *The Future of Creation*, trans. Margaret Kohl (Philadelphia: Fortress Press, 1979). The best entrance to his ecological thinking is perhaps the essay he prepared for the World Council of Churches Canberra Assembly, "'. . . and Thou Renewest the Face of the Earth,'" *Ecumenical Review* 42 (1990), reprinted in *The Source of Life: The Holy Spirit and the Theology of Life*, trans. Margaret Kohl (Minneapolis: Fortress Press, 1997), chap. 10. His ecological insights, however, are so complexly woven into the fabric of the entire body of his extensive writings that they are not readily accessible to wider audiences. Many of Moltmann's readers, who have helped to keep his works on the theological best-seller lists for decades, have had other focal interests. Until very recently, the rich veins of Moltmann's ecological theology have not generally been mined. So his works have not had the kind of major impact on the discussions of ecological theology that they otherwise surely would have had. One hopes that situation will now begin to change across the theological spectrum, with the publication of the illuminating study by Steven Bouma-Prediger, *The Greening of Theology: The Ecological Models of Rosemary Radford Ruether, Joseph Sittler, and Jürgen Moltmann* (Atlanta: Scholars Press, 1995).

20. John Polkinghorne, *The Faith of a Physicist: Reflections of a Bottom-Up Thinker* (Minneapolis: Fortress Press, 1995).

21. Terrence E. Fretheim, "The Reclamation of Creation: Redemption and Law in Exodus," *Interpretation* 45 (October 1991): 354–65. For an overview of these new trends, see Theodore Hiebert, "Re-Imaging Nature: Shifts in Biblical Interpretation," *Interpretation* 50:1 (January 1996): 36–46.

22. The major pioneering work on wisdom in Old Testament studies was by the great German Old Testament scholar, Gerhard von Rad, *Wisdom in Israel* (Nashville: Abingdon, 1972). More recently, scholarly interest in the theme has intensified. See the summary article by Roland E. Murphy, "Wisdom in the Old Testament," *The Anchor Bible Dictionary*, ed. David Noel Freedman (New York: Doubleday, 1992), 6:920–31; and the monograph by Dianne Bergant, *Israel's Wisdom Literature: A Liberation-Critical Reading* (Minneapolis: Fortress Press, 1997). For an exposition of New Testament wisdom theology,

see Elizabeth A. Johnson, "Jesus the Wisdom of God: A Biblical Basis for Non-Androcentric Christology," *Ephemerides Theologicae Lovanienses*, vol. 61 (1985), 261–94; and, more generally, James D. G. Dunn, "Christology (NT)," *The Anchor Bible Dictionary*, vol. 1, 979–91.

23. Denis Edwards, *Jesus and the Wisdom of God* (Maryknoll, N.Y.: Orbis Books, 1995).

24. Thomas Derr, *Ecology and Human Need*, refers to my work as revisionist, and Claude Y. Stewart, *Nature in Grace: A Study in the Theology of Nature* (Macon, Ga.: Mercer Univ. Press, 1983), refers to me as a "neo-Reformation" thinker. To both of these characterizations I plead guilty. This was already apparent in my dissertation, "Creation and Nature: A Study of the Doctrine of Nature with Special Attention to Karl Barth's Doctrine of Creation" (Ph.D. diss., Harvard Univ., 1966), and my early programmatic monograph, *Brother Earth: Nature, God, and Ecology in a Time of Crisis* (New York: Thomas Nelson, 1970). My work in the theology of nature has been subjected to critical scrutiny by Stewart, in *Nature in Grace*, alongside the major contributions by John Cobb and Pierre Teilhard de Chardin. See also the discussion of my writings by Robert Booth Fowler in his study *The Greening of Protestant Thought* (Chapel Hill: Univ. of North Carolina Press, 1995), 92ff.

25. The reconstructionist, the apologist, and the revisionist trends in recent ecological theology can be demarcated more specifically in a number of ways. One key issue is how various thinkers approach the idea of "responsible stewardship" of the earth. Apologists like Thomas Derr tend to claim and acclaim this idea, in some form, as an ethical keystone. The revisionists and the reconstructionists, in contrast, typically reshape that idea thoroughly or reject it altogether, in view of what they discern to be the inescapable managerial and manipulative, even exploitative, implications and nuances that the idea of stewardship presupposes (human dominion over the earth, they worry, or they are convinced, tends to become domination of the earth).

26. Perhaps the most significant line of demarcation between the reconstructionists, the apologists, and the revisionists emerges in their thought about the ecological and cosmic significance of Jesus Christ. Call this the issue of cosmic christology.

A good place to see this issue framed is in the volume by apologist Thomas Derr, *Environmental Ethics and Christian Humanism* (Nashville: Abingdon Press, 1996) [Abingdon Press Studies in Christian Ethics and Economic Life, Vol. II]. The book begins with a major essay by Derr himself and then concludes with shorter critical essays by the revisionist James Nash and the apologist Richard Neuhaus. Derr is by no means embarrassed by the anthropocentrism that has shaped much Christian thinking in the modern era. On the contrary, Derr *celebrates* that anthropocentrism—and the characteristically concomitant ethical premise of theological anthropocentrism in this respect, the idea of responsible stewardship. Derr is aware that the Scriptures do have a cosmic scope; but in opposition to revisionist thinkers such as Nash and myself, Derr asserts that that cosmic dimension of biblical theology can have no theological valency (pp. 31f.).

Neuhaus, in the end, basically sides with Derr's apologist perspective, although Neuhaus displays a kind of wistful theological longing for some kind of cosmic christology that could be constructed within the flow of what he calls the Great Tradition, by which he presumably means the classical Christian theological tradition given shape by the Nicene and Chalcedonian Creeds. Neuhaus appears to be unaware not only of the recent explorations of cosmic christology within the Great Tradition by writers such as Nash and myself, he passes by, without mention, the immensely important cosmic christology of Pierre Teilhard de Chardin, the seminal ecological contributions of Jürgen Moltmann's universalizing theology of hope, and the prophetic and poetic theological explorations of Joseph Sittler's cosmic christology. That, in any case, is one clear line of demarcation between the apologists and the revisionists, their response to New Testament texts such as Colossians 1:15ff, which adumbrate the cosmic dimensions of christology.

Derr's volume also helps the reader who has eyes to see to identify christological lines of demarcation between apologist positions such as Derr's and reconstructionist theologies, particularly the contributions by ecofeminist theologians. (Regrettably, Derr does not include any reconstructionists essay in his volume, and tends to bury all the reconstructionists, above all the ecofeminists, under a heavy layer of polemics, for which he has been rightly taken to task by Nash in the latter's essay in this book. To gain a sense of what the reconstructionists are really trying to say—in many and diverse ways—one must therefore look to their own works. A good place to start, in this respect, would be the autobiographical essay by the ecofeminist theologian Sallie McFague, "An Earthly Theological Agenda," *Christian Century*, January 2–9, 1991, 12–15 [see also note 14 above].) Reconstructionists such as Sallie McFague typically play down or even reject what Emil Brunner once called "the scandal of particularity" in their christological thought: that the Word became flesh *in Jesus Christ* and dwelt among us (cf. John 1:14). For McFague, quite explicitly, Jesus Christ is *not* the body of God, surely not in any singular or unique sense: *the cosmos* is the body of God. Her cosmic christology is, in fact, a christic cosmology. As she explains, her proposal "is to consider Jesus as paradigmatic of what we find everywhere: everything that is the sacrament of God (the universe as God's body). . . ." (*The Body of God*, p. 162).

In this respect both apologists such as Derr and reconstructionists such as McFague stand apart from what might be called the universalizing particularity of New Testament thought about the Incarnation. Derr values the particularity of the Incarnation to the exclusion of the cosmic dimension. McFague claims the cosmic universality to the exclusion, it seems, of the historical particularity. Revisionists, on the other hand, as the following argument will indicate, especially chap. 4, typically attempt to give voice to both the cosmic universality of Jesus Christ and to his historical uniqueness as the Son of God, as taught first by the Gospel of John, chap. 1, and other New Testament writings, and thereafter celebrated and explicated throughout the unfolding course of the Great Tradition. For an instructive review of the early trajectory of the Great Tradition and cosmic Christology, see Russell Bradner Norris Jr., "Logos Christology as Cosmological Paradigm," *Pro Ecclesia* 5:2 (Spring 1966), 183–201.

While it is true, finally, that the New Testament does affirm, by an extension of the logic of the Incarnation, that *the church* is the body of Christ (a theme to which I will return in my discussion of the church's liturgy, chap. 6), the New Testament witness definitely draws a line at that point: the cosmos is *not* the Body of Christ. This is indicated clearly in the text of Colossians 1 itself, by what may be a redaction from a Pauline hand of what might have been an early Christian hymn that *did* affirm, or that might have been understood to have affirmed, that the cosmos is the Body of Christ. Either way, as a flat statement or a Pauline redaction, the text gives expression to that definitive line: the cosmos is *not* the Body of Christ. This is Colossians 1:17f. (italics added), speaking of the cosmic Christ: "He himself is before all things, and in him all things hold together. He is the head of the body, *the church*; he is the beginning, the first-born from the dead, so that he might come to have first place in everything."

27. I have identified these unecological elements extensively in *The Travail of Nature*.

28. Given the critical and constructive intent of the ensuing discussion, this book can be read as a project in what has come to be called explicitly, by some, "public theology." The argument of this book is predicated on both a resolve to respond to one of the great social issues of our time, the global environmental crisis and related existential issues, and on a firm and self-conscious theological commitment to the classical Christian tradition as the primary matrix of theological knowing. I have taken for granted for many years the kind of methodological assumptions that have been stated with helpful clarity by Ronald F. Thiemann. He claims rightly, I believe, that "a theology shaped by the biblical narratives and grounded in the practices of the Christian community can provide resources to enable people of faith to regain a public voice in our pluralistic culture." (*Constructing a Public Theology: The Church in a Pluralistic Culture* [Louisville, Ky.: Westminster/John Knox Press, 1991]).

29. If one reads Denis Edwards's work, *Jesus and the Wisdom of God* (see note 22) side-by-side with this study, one can speak of an ecumenical convergence of revisionist Catholic and revisionist Reformation theologies of nature. This, then, would seem to bode well for the continued flourishing of the revisionist tradition in twenty-first-century ecological theology.

30. Cf. Jenson, "How the World Lost Its Story," 19: "It is the church's constitutive task to tell the biblical *narrative* to the world in proclamation and to God in worship, and to do so in a fashion appropriate to the content of that narrative, that is, as a *promise* claimed from God and proclaimed to the world."

31. These circumferential explorations presuppose, of course, *a circumference*, a systematically coherent argument that touches all the points around the circle. For a one-volume but still comprehensive attempt to circumscribe explicitly what the whole circle looks like, with an appreciation for the kind of evolutionary and eschatological themes that the argument of this book takes for granted, see Ted Peters, *God—The World's Future: Systematic Theology for a Postmodern Era* (Minneapolis: Fortress Press, 1992).

32. Thomas S. Kuhn, *The Structure of Scientific Revolutions* (Chicago: Univ. of Chicago Press, 1962).

33. The discussion that follows draws on my essay, "The Liberation of Nature: Lynn White's Challenge Anew," *The Christian Century*, 102:18 (May 22, 1984), 530–33.

34. First published in *Science* (March 1967), 1203–7.

35. *The Environmental Handbook,* ed. Garett de Bell (New York: Ballantine, 1970).

36. See Thomas Sieger Derr, "Religion's Responsibility for the Ecological Crisis: An Argument Run Amok," *Worldview* (January 1975).

37. See my article, "The Liberation of Nature" and James Nash, *Loving Nature,* chap. 3.

38. Derr, "Religion's Responsibility . . . ," 45.

39. Derr has developed this kind of critique directed against the idea of "the rights of nature," again with a heavy emotional surcharge at various points in his more recent volume, *Environmental Ethics and Christian Humanism.* (See n. 25 above.)

40. See my study *The Travail of Nature,* chap. 7 and 8.

41. Susan Brownmiller, *Against Our Will* (New York: Simon and Schuster, 1975).

42. Krister Stendahl, *The Bible and the Role of Women: A Case Study in Hermeneutics* (Philadelphia: Fortress Press, 1966).

43. J. Christiaan Beker, *Paul the Apostle: The Triumph of God in Life and Thought* (Philadelphia: Fortress Press, 1980).

44. That many of these voices are emerging *outside* the Christian church today is sobering, but not embarrassing. When God's People fall short of the mark, when they suffer from a lack of vision, the God we know from biblical traditions is surely able to speak through other voices, just as he once called Cyrus of Persia to be his servant, in order to further the mission of his people to be a light to the nations. The causes of abolitionism and feminism were surely bolstered from outside the church, as well as from within. Why not also the cause of loving nature?

Chapter 2

1. For a review of the thought of Henry David Thoreau and John Muir, see H. Paul Santmire, *Brother Earth: Nature, God, and Ecology in a Time of Crisis* (New York: Thomas Nelson, 1970) chap. 1.

2. I explore this kind of criticism of Christianity at some length in the introduction to my book *The Travail of Nature: The Ambiguous Ecological Promise of Christian Theology* (Philadelphia: Fortress Press, 1985), chap. 1. See also James A. Nash, *Loving Nature: Ecological Integrity and Christian Responsibility* (Nashville, Tenn.: Abingdon Press, in cooperation with the Churches' Center for Theology and Public Policy, Washington, D.C., 1991), chap. 3.

3. If space permitted, a similar approach to the works of the widely read Catholic "geologian," Thomas Berry, would also be revealing. More sophisticated in his analysis and more cautious in his judgments than Matthew Fox, Berry nonetheless draws the same kind of conclusions, predicated on the same kind of analysis. See his book *The Dream of the Earth* (San Francisco: Sierra Club Books, 1988). For a thoughtful analysis of the place of such thinkers in the context of recent Catholic theology, see William C. French, "Subject-Centered and Creation-Centered Paradigms in Recent Catholic Thought," *Journal of Religion* 70 (January 1990): 48–72. Also the contributions of some Protestant process theologians would have to be considered and carefully evaluated in this context, from the same perspective. See, for example, Jay B. McDaniel, *Of God and Pelicans: A Theology of Reverence for Life* (Louisville, Ky.: Westminster/John Knox Press, 1989) and the literature he cites. Above all, the literature of theological feminism would command extensive attention, from the vantage point of the analysis we are undertaking here. Some of it is relatively superficial (see, for example, my review of *From Apocalypse to Genesis: Ecology, Feminism, and Christianity,* by Anne Primavesi, *Christian Century* 109 [April 15, 1992]: 403ff.). The works of writers such as Rosemary Radford Ruether and Sallie McFague, however, are highly sophisticated and substantive, akin in many ways to Fox's works (for Ruether, see n.13, chap. 1 above); for McFague, see especially: *The Body of God: An Ecological Theology* (Minneapolis: Fortress Press, 1993).

4. For a brief but balanced presentation and evaluation of Fox's program, see Wayne G. Boulton, "The Thoroughly Modern Mysticism of Matthew Fox," *Christian Century* 107 (April 25, 1990): 428–32. Also, see Ted Peters, *The Cosmic Self: A Penetrating Look at Today's New Age Movements* (San Francisco: Harper, 1991), chap. 3.

5. Matthew Fox, *Original Blessing: A Primer in Creation Spirituality* (Santa Fe, N.M.: Bear and Company, 1983), 54. See also, more generally, his volume *Creation Spirituality: Liberating Gifts for the Peoples of the Earth* (San Francisco: HarperCollins, 1991).

6. Fox invokes a kind of "logos Christology" at this point, reminiscent of some early Christian thinkers. In this respect, he is more concerned with the eternal Word, the *logos asarkos,* mystically understood as creatively immanent in all things (traditionally also called the *logos spermatikos*), rather than the Word made flesh, the *logos ensarkos,* redemptively and particularly present in Jesus of Nazareth. Although Fox does hold that the *logos ensarkos* is very much an expression, the clearest and most powerful for Christians, of the *logos asarkos.*

7. Matthew Fox, *The Coming of the Cosmic Christ: The Healing of Mother Earth and the Birth of a Global Renaissance* (New York: Harper and Row, 1988), 7.

8. Fox, *Original Blessing,* 123.

9. Ibid.

10. Ibid., 239.

11. Ibid., 166.

12. Ibid., 169.

13. Ibid., 235.

14. Ibid., 120f.

15. Ibid., 106f.

16. Ibid., 125.

17. Fox, *The Coming of the Cosmic Christ.* See also Fox, *Original Blessing,* 162.

18. Fox, *Original Blessing,* 275.

19. Fox, *The Coming of the Cosmic Christ,* 239.

20. Fox seems to be overreacting to the biologizing of original sin that sometimes has characterized Catholic theological manuals. He seems unaware of modern reconstructions of the doctrine, above all the influential contributions of Reinhold Niebuhr, especially his magisterial work *The Nature and Destiny of Man: A Christian Interpretation* (New York: Charles Scribner's Sons, 1955).

21. See Fox, *Original Blessing,* 151ff.

22. Charles Reich, *The Greening of America* (New York: Random House, 1970). Cf. Boulton, "The Thoroughly Modern Mysticism of Matthew Fox," 432, regarding Fox's programs for social and personal transformation: "Creation and redemption are brought so close together in Fox's work that his programs for social transformation are almost inevitably simplistic. And in his call for personal transformation ('a resurrection of the human psyche') he can sound faintly like a Robert Schuller of the left."

23. Gustav Aulen, *Christus Victor: A Historical Study of the Three Main Types of the Idea of the Atonement,* trans. A. G. Herbert (New York: Macmillan, 1967).

24. Joseph Sittler, "Called to Unity," *Ecumenical Review* 14 (January 1962): 177–87.

25. Jürgen Moltmann, *The Crucified God: The Cross of Christ as the Foundation and Criticism of Christian Theology,* trans. R. A. Wilson and John Bowden (New York: SCM Press, 1974). This work is the foundation for Moltmann's comprehensive and balanced essay, which addresses many of the themes also of concern to Matthew Fox: *God in Creation: A New Theology of Creation and the Spirit of God,* trans. Margaret Kohl (New York: SCM Press, 1985).

26. Santmire, *The Travail of Nature,* chap. 4.

27. Ibid., chap. 2.

28. See Margaret Miles, *Augustine on the Body* (Missoula, Mont.: Scholars Press, 1979).

29. Augustine, *City of God,* 22–24.

30. He never fully overcame his early androcentric bias or his patriarchal understanding of society. His theology of human history, as Langdon Gilkey has shown, though visionary in many respects, lacks a coherent infrastructure of meanings (*Reaping the Whirlwind: A Christian Interpretation of History* [New York: Seabury, 1976]). Augustine's hierarchical vision of the church and his tendency to identify it with

the reign of God also is highly problematic. In addition, his tendency to view evil in terms of privation of the good, rather than in the more active biblical terms of principalities and powers must also be challenged, along with the somewhat less-than-biblical soteriology that accompanies that understanding of evil. And he tended to biologize the theology of original sin, for which he has been appropriately criticized by many, above all by Reinhold Niebuhr (*The Nature and Destiny of Man*).

Chapter 3

1. See the discussion of Luther and Calvin in H. Paul Santmire, *The Travail of Nature: The Ambiguous Ecological Promise of Christian Theology* (Philadelphia: Fortress Press, 1985), chap. 7.

2. This is not to suggest that Luther was not concerned with the careful historical study of biblical texts. On the contrary, as an Old Testament scholar, Luther consistently and carefully struggled with exegetical questions.

3. Claus Westermann, *Blessing: In the Bible and the Life of the Church,* Overtures to Biblical Theology, trans. Keith Crim (Philadelphia: Fortress Press, 1978). While these two theologies, of deliverance and blessing, are distinct and identifiable, as Westermann has argued, the distinction should not be pushed too far, since they overlap in many ways. See the suggestive essay by George M. Landes, "Creation and Liberation," in *Creation in the Old Testament: Issues in Religion and Theology,* vol. 6, ed. Bernhard W. Anderson (Philadelphia: Fortress Press, 1984), chap. 8, and the essay by Terrence E. Fretheim, "The Reclamation of Creation: Redemption and Law in Exodus," *Interpretation* 45 (October 1991): 354–65.

4. G. Ernest Wright, *God Who Acts: Biblical Theology as Recital* (Chicago: Alec R. Allenson, 1952).

5. Cf. Landes, "Creation and Liberation," 137: "When Israel told her story of the Exodus, the wilderness wandering, and the giving of the land, Yahweh's delivering actions were depicted involving not only historical human actors and political events, but also the use of the forces and elements of nature. . . . Only the Creator-God, the One who made the sea, the animals, the heavenly bodies, and all of nature, could employ these elements in His redemptive work. But out of all her experience in liberating events, Israel did not only at some distant later date infer that the Liberator-God must be the Creator-God [the position of G. Ernest Wright], but rather, because she already knew Yahweh as the Creator of heaven and earth, she understood how it was that the wind and sea, birds and insects, sun and moon could be used as instruments supporting the divine liberating activity. From this she went on to affirm something new—something not shared by her ancient Near Eastern neighbors: the cosmic Creator was also the Liberating Creator, whose creative power was extended into history, not for the purpose of continuing or redoing cosmic creation (these ideas receive no place in biblical thinking except in an eschatological framework beyond history), but for creating a people through liberating deeds. . . ." For a comprehensive analysis of the Old Testament witness to nature, see Ronald A. Simkins, *Creator and Creation: Nature in the Worldview of Ancient Israel* (Peabody, Mass.: Hendrickson Publishers, 1994). Simkins shows, comprehensively, that the kind of approach to nature in the Old Testament championed by Wright is simply wrong.

6. Walter Brueggemann, *The Land: Place as Gift, Promise, and Challenge in Biblical Faith,* Overtures to Biblical Theology (Philadelphia: Fortress Press, 1977).

7. Ibid., 6.

8. Ibid., 49.

9. See Leviticus 25, and John Howard Yoder, *The Politics of Jesus* (Grand Rapids, Mich.: Eerdmans, 1972), chap. 3.

10. Brueggemann, 91.

11. Ibid., 100.

12. See Bernhard W. Anderson, "Introduction: Mythopoeic and Theological Dimensions of Biblical Creation Faith," in Anderson, ed., *Creation in the Old Testament,* 4–7.

13. Ibid., 8.

14. Ibid., 11.

15. Ibid.

16. Fretheim, "The Reclamation of Creation," 355.

17. Ibid., 17.

18. Ibid., 18–21.

19. This history is partially reviewed by an older study, Frank E. Robbins, *The Hexaemeral Literature* (Chicago: Univ. of Chicago Press, 1912). See, more generally, my own study *The Travail of Nature*.

20. Among the exceptions were the later commentaries of Augustine and, to some extent, the commentaries of Luther and Calvin. See my study *The Travail of Nature*, chap. 4 and 7.

21. Gregory of Nyssa, for example, depicts the cosmos as a "royal lodging" created by God for the sake of its human king, to whom God gives "all kinds of wealth . . . stored in this palace." "For this reason," says Gregory, "man was brought into the world last after the creation . . . , as one whom it behooved to be king over his subjects at his very birth" (*On the Making of Man*, 2).

22. Assessments of historical blame of this kind are risky, at best. For reflections on the argument of those who would blame Christianity for the environmental crisis, see Thomas Sieger Derr, "Religion's Responsibility for the Ecological Crisis: An Argument Run Amok," *Worldview* 18, no. 1 (January 1975): 39–45. The idea of a "rape culture" was given currency by Susan Brownmiller in her book, *Against Our Will* (New York: Simon and Schuster, 1975).

23. For a compelling reading of Genesis 1, see Phyllis Trible, *God and the Rhetoric of Sexuality*, Overtures to Biblical Theology (Philadelphia: Fortress Press, 1978), 12–23. For every detail, and for general analysis, see Claus Westermann, *Genesis 1–11: A Commentary*, trans. John J. Scullion (Minneapolis: Fortress Press, 1984), *loc. cit.*

24. See Santmire, *The Travail of Nature*, 57f.

25. Gerhard von Rad, *Genesis*, trans. John H. Marks (Philadelphia: Westminster Press, 1972), *loc. cit.*

26. Trible, *God and the Rhetoric of Sexuality*, 13.

27. Cf. S. R. Driver, *The Book of Genesis* (2d ed.; London: Methuen, 1904), 5; and von Rad, *Genesis*, 50.

28. Cf. Westermann, *Genesis*, 176: "The simple fact that the first page of the Bible speaks about heaven and earth, the sun, moon and stars, about plants and trees, about birds, fish and animals, is a certain sign that the God whom we acknowledge in the Creed as the Father of Jesus Christ is concerned with all of these creatures, and not merely with humans. A God who is understood only as the God of humankind is no longer the God of the Bible."

29. Cf. Ps. 19:3-4. In commenting on the dominion motif in Genesis 1, James Barr makes the intriguing suggestion that the most fundamental nuance of "dominion" as the Priestly author understands that motif is that the human creature is called to take a leadership role in *praising* God: "The whole framework of Genesis 1 is intended to suggest that man is man when he is in place within nature. His dominion over nature is given little definition, but in general its content is less exploitation and more leadership; a sort of primary liturgical place. ("Man and Nature: The Ecological Controversy and the Old Testament," in *Ecology and Religion in History*, ed. David Spring and Eileen Spring [New York: Harper Torchbooks, 1974], 75). On the theme of the creation's praise of God more generally, see Terrence E. Fretheim, "Nature's Praise of God in the Psalms," *Ex Auditu* 3 (1988).

30. Cf. Trible, *God and the Rhetoric of Sexuality*, 18: "Created simultaneously, male and female are not superior and subordinate. Neither has the power over the other; in fact both are given equal power."

31. See Barr, "Man and Nature: The Ecological Controversy and the Old Testament," 61–64.

32. Anderson, "Creation and Ecology," in Anderson, ed., *Creation in the Old Testament*, 159.

33. Edmund Jacob, *Theology of the Old Testament*, trans. A. W. Heathcote, P. J. Allcock (London: Hodder & Stoughton, 1955), 168.

34. For a suggestive reading of Genesis 2 and 3, see Trible, *God and the Rhetoric of Sexuality*, 72–139. More generally, see Westermann, *Genesis*, *loc. cit.*

35. Trible, *God and the Rhetoric of Sexuality*, 76.

36. Ibid., 85.

37. Cf. Westermann, *Genesis*, 228, regarding the naming of the animals: "The exercise of dominion does not begin with the use or exploitation of the animals for human ends. The meaning is not, as most interpreters think, that the man acquires power over the animals by naming them. . . . But rather that the man gives the animals their names and thereby puts them into a place in his world." In the same spirit, while "listening" to the text in a meditative monastic context, Kathleen Norris made this exegetical discovery: "God does not command Adam to name the animals; God brings them to Adam 'to see

what he will call them.' This implies that God wants to be surprised and wants Adam to play along in the continual surprise of creation." (*The Cloister Walk* [New York: Riverhead Books, 1997], 307).

38. Note that Adam names only the living things, not all things. "Names are given first to living things," Westermann comments, "because they are closest to humans" (*Genesis*, 229).

39. Trible, *God and the Rhetoric of Sexuality*, 90.

40. For a fuller exposition of this New Testament horizon, see my study *The Travail of Nature*, chap. 10.

41. See Brueggemann, *The Land*, 49.

42. Terence L. Donaldson, *Jesus on the Mountain: A Study in Matthaean Theology,* Journal for the Study of the New Testament Supplement Series 8 (Sheffield: JSOT Press, 1985).

43. So some students of Rudolf Bultmann, who had a deep-seated bias against nature, have tried to argue. For a discussion of these issues, see my study, *The Travail of Nature*, 203–7, and the literature cited there.

44. Santmire, *The Travail of Nature*, 202f.

45. I have attempted to outline such a universalistic, christocentric soteriology in my *Brother Earth: Nature, God, and Ecology in a Time of Crisis* (New York: Thomas Nelson, 1970), chap. 8. See also the sweeping affirmations of a "cosmic christology" in the works of Joseph Sittler, coming to fruition in his book, *Essays on Nature and Grace* (Philadelphia: Fortress Press, 1972).

46. Cf. Westermann, *Genesis*, 177: "P's[The Priestly writer's] account of creation does not end with the creation of human beings. The sanctification and blessing of the day of rest indicates that the story of humankind is not exhausted by the increase that comes from the blessing, not by humanity's spreading over the earth, nor even by the exercise of dominion over the rest of creation; the holy day points toward a goal. Just as in Gen[esis] 1 God's work of creation does not come to an end with the creation of humans, so too in the Bible as a whole God's work does not come to an end with the saving action by which Christ redeemed humankind. The Bible is speaking of a definitive event which concerns not only humankind but the whole of creation. . . . It is important merely to point out here that in the apocalyptic texts the Bible speaks of a goal for the whole creation, not merely for the history of humankind."

Chapter 4

1. Albert Gore, *Earth in the Balance: Ecology and the Human Spirit* (New York: Penguin Books, 1992), 218.

2. Ibid., 258.

3. Ibid., 259.

4. Ibid., 258–64.

5. Ibid., 264.

6. Ibid., 263.

7. See my study *The Travail of Nature: The Ambiguous Ecological Promise of Christian Theology* (Philadelphia: Fortress Press, 1985), especially chap. 8.

8. In an essay summarizing a more extensive argument, Georgetown University theologian John F. Haught has called upon "mainstream theology" to "examine its habit of ignoring evolution and confining its attention almost exclusively to human concerns." ("Evolution and God's Humility: How Theology Can Embrace Darwin," *Commonweal*, 127:2 [January 28, 2000], 15) He calls for "new theologies of nature genuinely responsive to the fascinating, but troubling picture of life that evolutionary science is giving us." More particularly, he highlights an understanding of God as "self-emptying love" and the "power of the future" as key constructs for such a new theology of nature. Haught also instances Teilhard de Chardin as one of the figures who creatively invoked such constructs. The argument of this book, building as it does on Teilhard's theology, is intended to celebrate and explicate those constructs, with the intention, in Haught's words, to give witness to "a God who is less Alpha than Omega[,] . . . the God of Abraham, Moses, and Jesus, the Pauline God of new creation." See further Haught's book, *God after Darwin: A Theology of Evolution* (New York: Westview Press, 1999).

9. My earliest venture to tell this story was my programmatic essay *Brother Earth: Nature, God, and Ecology in a Time of Crisis* (New York: Thomas Nelson, 1970), a work that these reflections presuppose.

These explorations build on a number of my essays, especially "Healing the Protestant Mind: Beyond the Theology of Human Dominion," in *After Nature's Revolt: Eco-Justice and Theology*, ed. Dieter T. Hessel (Minneapolis: Fortress Press, 1992), chap. 3; "The Future of the Cosmos and the Renewal of the Church's Life with Nature," in *Cosmos as Creation: Theology and Science in Consonance*, ed. Ted Peters (Nashville, Tenn.: Abingdon, 1989), chap. 9; "Toward a Christology of Nature," *dialog* 34 (fall 1995) 270–80. I also am informed by the theological discussion of "narrative theology" of the last few decades. For an introduction to that discussion, see the valuable essay by Gabriel Fackre, "Narrative Theology: An Overview," Interpretation 37 (October 1983), 340–52; and Stanley Hauerwas and L. Gregory Jones, *Why Narrative? Readings in Narrative Theology* (Grand Rapids, Mich.: Eerdmans, 1989). For a thoughtful and thought-provoking theological analysis that focuses on the meaning of human life in evolutionary history, see Philip Hefner, *The Human Factor: Evolution, Culture, and Religion* (Minneapolis: Fortress Press, 1993). For an overview of Teilhard's life and spirituality, see Ursula King, *Spirit of Fire: the Life and Vision of Teilhard de Chardin* (Maryknoll, N.Y.: Orbis Books, 1996).

10. This chapter presupposes what might be called an *accented hermeneutic* of biblical theology, particularly of the New Testament. Historically speaking, there is no such thing as *the* correct reading of the biblical materials, notwithstanding numerous interpreters who make such claims. There are various readings, with various accents, all of which, when projected by responsible scholarly interpreters, stake out claims for truthful communications of biblical meanings. This is why a community of scholarly interpreters, including those scholars who speak from the perspective of traditional readings of texts, is so critical for adequate biblical interpretation in an period of the church's life. Here the accent of the hermeneutic is quite self-conscious. As Luther accented Pauline texts from Galatians and Romans pertaining to justification by faith in his biblical interpretation, this book presupposes the centrality of world-historical and apocalyptic texts, from Genesis to Revelation, and christocentric and cosmic texts, especially those of the letters to the Colossians and the Ephesians. For a review of the promise of the world-historical and apocalyptic texts, see J. Christiaan Beker, "The Promise of Paul's Apocalyptic for Our Times," in *The Future of Christology: Essays in Honor of Leander E. Keck*, ed. Abraham J. Malherbe and Wayne Meeks (Minneapolis: Fortress Press, 1993), 152–59. For a review of the New Testament texts that highlight the cosmic vocation of Christ, see the balanced and nuanced study by Arland J. Hultgren, *Christ and His Benefits: Christology and Redemption in the New Testament* (Philadelphia: Fortress Press, 1987), chap. 7; and, in briefer compass, Robin Scroggs, "Christ the Cosmocrator and the Experience of Believers," *The Future of Christology*, 160–75. The hermeneutical wager here is that this kind of interpretive accent will speak to the mind and heart of the church circa 2000 with the kind of urgency and the kind of power that Luther's interpretation accent spoke to the mind and the heart of the church circa 1500.

11. The promise and some of the painstaking difficulties of building ties between different religions, in this respect, are illustrated in the suggestive reflections of Paul O. Ingram concerning the Christian and the Buddhist traditions in, "On the Wings of a Blue Heron," *Cross Currents*, 49:2 (Summer 1999), 206–26. An entirely different tack is taken by Max Oelschlaeger, in *Caring for Creation: An Ecumenical Approach to the Environmental Crisis* (New Haven: Yale Univ. Press, 1994). Oelschlaeger writes mainly as a philosophical pragmatist. He argues that although various religious traditions and various theologies differ markedly, many of them have this "cash value": they all can make a strong witness on behalf of an ethic of caring for creation. "Through the metaphor of caring for creation," he explains, "people of faith can reach common ground, even though the roads taken to that consensus may differ" (182). Indeed, he concludes, "at this juncture a fully ecumenical theology of nature is not necessary, for there is ample ground for solidarity in the caring for creation metaphor alone" (183). But to discuss here the relative merits of this proposal over and against Gore's call for a new pan-religious telling of our cosmic story would take us too far afield. In any case, the present study presupposes that *a retelling of the Christian story in ecological and cosmic terms is an urgent need for the church today*. On the other hand, this retelling and the theological work of the revisionist tradition that it presupposes has taken the metaphor of caring for creation as a lead metaphor may suggest that Oelschlaeger's argument could well be given more attention within the pale of our churches, as well as beyond, along with the labors of those who are committed to interreligious dialogue.

12. See Santmire, *The Travail of Nature*, chap. 3 and 8.

13. This assertion has been contested by his critics. Teilhard, in fact, tended to claim too much for his phenomenology by calling it "scientific"; that it was, in the classical sense (expressed by the German word *Wissenschaft*) of an orderly, disciplined, and logically consistent exposition of what one knows. But Teilhard's work was not "scientific" in the commonly accepted logical-empirical sense, which focuses on the process of the experimental testing and in-principle falsification of hypotheses. For our purposes here, we can cautiously bypass this problem simply by regarding Teilhard's vision of reality for what it was: a phenomenological description of the whole of reality as he saw it. As such, it stands or falls not by the canons of empirical testing and in-principle falsification, but by its power, or lack of power, to inspire us to see the whole of reality in the way that Teilhard saw it.

14. Pierre Teilhard de Chardin, *The Phenomenon of Man*, trans. Bernard Wall (New York: Harper and Row, 1959), 302.

15. Teilhard, letter, 7 October 1948. Cited by Christopher Mooney, *Teilhard de Chardin and the Mystery of Christ* (Garden City, N.Y.: Doubleday & Co., 1968), 169. For a brief review of current discussions of the anthropic principle, see Mark William Worthing, *God, Creation, and Contemporary Physics* (Minneapolis: Fortress Press, 1996), 43–55.

16. Teilhard, *Phenomenon of Man*, 188.

17. Ibid., 271.

18. See the discussion in Santmire, *The Travail of Nature*, 45ff.

19. See the discussion in ibid., chap. 8.

20. For these constructive considerations, I am drawing on the results of my programmatic essay, *Brother Earth*; my historical study *The Travail of Nature*; and several other essays detailed in n. 7 above.

21. See Santmire, *The Travail of Nature*, chap. 3.

22. For a discussion of what it can mean to relate ourselves to the repulsive aspects of nature, see below, in chap. 5, "An Ecological and Cosmic Conceptuality." I explore the spiritual encounter with death in nature in chap. 7.

23. To speak of the work of Christ this way, as having a twofold rationale, is, admittedly, to schematize the rich and diverse witness of the New Testament to this subject. On the latter, see the study by Hultgren, *Christ and His Benefits*. But some kind of theological schematization of this kind is unavoidable. The question of import in this connection is whether, or to what degree, the schematization does justice to the richness and the diversity of the New Testament witness. For a more systematic discussion of this kind of schematization, see my study *Brother Earth*, chap. 8. Cf., further, the comment by Jürgen Moltmann: "According to Paul, Christ was not merely 'delivered for our offenses' but was also 'raised for our justification' (Rom. 4:25). Reconciling sinners with God through his cross, he brings about the new righteousness, the new life, the new creature though his resurrection. The justification of the sinner is more than merely the forgiveness of sins. It leads to new life. 'Where sin increased, grace abounded all the more' (Rom. 5:20). This is the way Paul expresses the imbalance between sin and grace, and the *added value* of grace. The surplus of grace over and above the forgiveness of sins and the reconciliation of sinners represents the power of the new creation which consummates creation-in-the-beginning. It follows that the Son of God did not become man simply because of the sin of men and women, but rather for the sake of perfecting creation" (*The Trinity and the Kingdom: The Doctrine of God* [New York: Harper & Row, 1981], 116).

24. See the discussion of Matthew Fox in chap. 2.

Chapter 5

1. Paul Tillich, *Biblical Religion and the Search for Ultimate Reality* (Chicago: Univ. of Chicago Press, 1955).

2. Martin Buber, *I and Thou*, trans. Ronald Smith (2d ed.; New York: Charles Scribner's Sons, 1958).

3. Ferdinand Ebner, *Das Wort und die geistigen Realitäten: Pneumatologische Fragmente* (Vienna: Thomas Morus Presse, 1952). Gogarten alone was adamant in maintaining that he developed the distinction independently of Buber.

4. See Emil Brunner, *The Divine Human Encounter,* trans. Olive Wyon (Philadelphia: Westminster Press, 1952).

5. See my study *The Travail of Nature: The Ambiguous Ecological Promise of Christian Theology* (Philadelphia: Fortress Press, 1985), chap. 7.

6. Tillich, *Biblical Religion and the Search for Ultimate Reality.*

7. See especially his essay "Nature and Sacrament," in *The Protestant Era,* trans. J. L. Adams (Chicago: Univ. of Chicago Press, 1957).

8. Paul Tillich, *The Shaking of the Foundations* (New York: Scribners, 1948), 79.

9. Buber, *I and Thou,* 7.

10. Karl Barth, *Church Dogmatics,* trans. G. T. Thomson and Harold Knight (Edinburgh: T. & T. Clark, 1956), I, Pt. 2, 42. 14. This is true, in particular, of two critiques of the generally accepted view of the I-Thou, I-It conceptuality. In a suggestive article, "I-Thou and I-It: An Attempted Clarification of Their Relationship," *Journal of Religion,* 43 (July 1963): 193–209, W. Taylor Stevenson wanted to bring the I-Thou and I-It relations into "closest union"(207); he maintained that Buber does not do this. Nevertheless, Stevenson was chiefly interested in interpersonal relationships. He argued for an "extension of the area within which the I-Thou relation is present and effective, although without the normative characteristics of exclusiveness and intensity" (197). Harvey Cox moved in a similar direction in his *Secular City: Secularization and Urbanization in Theological Perspective* (New York: Macmillan, 1965), 48, 263ff., when he suggested that the I-Thou relation does not describe all authentic interpersonal relationships. Cox then refers to what he calls the "I-You" relation. Cox is not directly concerned with the relationship between persons and nature, however.

11. Cf. Dietrich Bonhoeffer, *Ethics,* ed. Eberhard Bethge, trans. Neville Horton Smith, (New York: Macmillan, 1955), 112: "The life of the body, like life in general, is both a means to an end and an end in itself. To regard the body exclusively as a means to an end is idealistic, but not Christian; for a means is discarded as soon as the end is achieved. It is from this point of view that the body is conceived as the prison from which the immortal soul is released forever by death. According to the Christian doctrine, the body possesses a higher dignity. Man is a bodily being and remains so in eternity as well."

12. Martin Buber, "Brother Body," *Pointing the Way: Collected Essays,* ed. and trans. Maurice Friedman (London: Routledge & Kegan Paul, 1957), 20–24.

13. Barth, *Church Dogmatics,* II, Pt. 2, 267.

14. Buber, *I and Thou,* 135: "The description of God as a Person is indispensable for everyone who, like me, means by 'God' not a principle (although mystics like Eckhart sometimes identify him with 'Being') and, like me, means by 'God' not an idea (although philosophers like Plato at times could hold that he was this): but who rather means by 'God' as I do, him who—whatever else he may be—enters into a direct relation with us in creative, revealing, and redeeming acts, and thus makes it possible for us to enter into a direct relation with him. This ground and meaning of our existence constitutes a mutuality, arising again and again, such as can subsist only between persons. The concept of a personal being is indeed completely incapable of declaring what God's essential being is, but it is both permitted and necessary to say that God is also a person."

15. The same is true for Tillich. He is well aware that the I-It relationship is not the only relationship to nature possible for persons. Hence Tillich has available to him the fundamental analogical terminology for depicting humanity's relationship to the living God.

16. Buber himself puts the question: "If the I-Thou relationship requires a mutual action which in fact embraces both the I and the Thou, how may the relation to something in nature be understood as such a relationship?" (*I and Thou,* 124).

17. Martin Buber, *The Knowledge of Man: Selected Essays,* ed. Maurice Friedman, trans. Maurice Friedman and Ronald Gregor Smith, (New York: Harper & Row, 1965), 106.

18. The problem is not obviated even if we see the creative divine word as speaking through the tree, as Buber is inclined to suggest, as when he says: "God speaks to man in the things and beings whom he sends him in life" (*Mamre: Essays in Religion* [Melbourne: Melbourne Univ. Press, 1946], 103). As Buber says, that kind of divine speaking is indirect (*At the Turning: Three Addresses on Judaism* [New York: Farrar, Straus & Young, 1952], 57). It surely differs markedly from the immediacy and the intensity of the divine speaking apprehended in the speech between the divine I and the human Thou.

19. Buber, *I and Thou,* 124ff.

20. Ibid, 124.

21. At first glance, it might seem helpful to invoke a doctrine of panpsychism at this point. Karl Heim did that, and, in a sense, Teilhard moved in the same direction with his construct of the "within" of every creature. But a doctrine of panpsychism does not really solve the problem before us. It only postpones the basic questions. For we would then have to ask: in what sense is the tree psychic? In what sense is the tree psychic when one's relation to it lacks the mutuality and the speech that are characteristic of the psychic relation with the human Thou? Buber's cautious agnosticism would again seem to be the better way. Cf. his *I and Thou*, 8: "The tree will have a consciousness, then, similar to our own? Of that I have no experience. But do you wish, through seeming to succeed with yourself, once again to disintegrate that which cannot be disintegrated? I encounter no soul or dryad of the tree, but the tree itself."

22. This discussion of Buber draws on investigations I first undertook more than thirty years ago. See my article "I-Thou, I-It, I-Ens," *Journal of Religion* 48:3 (July 1968), 260–73. Recently Sallie McFague has also highlighted Buber as a figure of import for ecological theology. (See her book *Super, Natural Christians: How We Should Love Nature* (Minneapolis: Fortress Press, 1997), 100ff.). Rather than seeking to revise or clarify Buber's phenomenology, however, McFague chooses to set it aside as inadequate.

23. For the "mystical, existential, dialogic" periodization of Buber's development, see Maurice S. Friedman, *Martin Buber: The Life of Dialogue* (Chicago: Univ. of Chicago Press, 1955).

24. See Friedman, *Martin Buber*, Pt. 2.

25. I will not probe into the question whether the I-Ens relation is in some sense prior to the I-Thou relation, as the I-Thou relation precedes the I-It relation, according to Buber; or whether it is in some sense given with or a derivative of the I-Thou relation. On the priority of I-Thou to I-It, see Friedman, "Introduction," *Martin Buber*, 22ff.

26. This is not to deny that the I-Ens relations with the first has elements different from the second and third. Fabricated nature is nature taken up into or stamped by the world of human spirit. Hence the I-Ens relation in this respect merits special attention. But such detailed analysis is not possible here.

27. Buber, *I and Thou*, 1.

28. Cf. Buber, *I and Thou*, 12: "In face of the directness of the relation everything indirect becomes irrelevant."

29. The point here is that the I-Ens relation is characterized by a perduring kind of contemplation that comes to rest, as it were, in the entity contemplated. A different kind of seeing, perhaps best denoted by the word *observation*, is involved in the I-It relation.

30. Cf. John Calvin, *Institutes of the Christian Religion*, ed. John T. McNeil, trans. Ford Lewis Battles (2 vols.; Philadelphia: Westminster Press, 1960), I:21: "While we contemplate in all creatures, as in mirrors, those immense riches of his wisdom, justice, goodness, and power, we should not merely run them over cursorily, and, so to speak, with a fleeting glance; but we should ponder them at length, turn them over in our minds seriously and faithfully, and recollect them repeatedly."

31. It might be said that the progress of natural-scientific knowledge, with its disclosure of the intricate workings of nature, inhibits the development of the I-Ens relation. In a sense this is true. But the creative scientist, as distinguished from the technician, always proceeds in his or her work with a sense of wonder and humility. For a discussion of the spontaneity of nature, from a theological perspective, see my study *Brother Earth: Nature, God, and Ecology in a Time of Crisis* (New York: Thomas Nelson, 1970), 134ff.

32. The literature on this subject is virtually infinite. Among others, the following works are instructive: Immanuel Kant, *Critique of Aesthetic Judgment*, trans. James C. Meredith (Oxford: Clarendon Press, 1911); E. F. Carritt, *The Theory of Beauty* (London: Methuen, 1914).

33. On the differentiation between the beautiful and the sublime, see Kant, *Critique of Aesthetic Judgment*, 90; Carritt, *The Theory of Beauty*, 241 ff.

34. John Muir, *The Writings of John Muir* (8 vols.; Sierra ed.; Boston: Houghton Mifflin, 1917–18): "One Thousand Mile Walk," 406. As the quotation indicates, the I-Ens relation can distinguish between a person and a constellation of natural entities as well as a person and an individual entity—even the whole universe. Cf. "Travels in Alaska," 6, in the same work, in which Muir observes that "the whole universe appears as an infinite storm of beauty."

35. John Calvin, *Commentaries on the First Book of Moses Called Genesis*, trans. John King (Edinburgh: Edinburgh Printing Co., 1847), I:85.

36. Martin Luther, *Werke* (Weimar Ausgabe), XIX:496; cited by Heinrich Bornkamm. *Luther's World of Thought,* trans. Hart. H. Bertram (St. Louis, Mo.: Concordia, 1959), 182.

37. Muir, *Writings,* "One Thousand Mile Walk," 301.

38. Muir, *Writings,* "The Mountains of California," I:161ff.: "Few indeed, strong and free with eyes undimmed with care, have gone far enough and lived long enough with trees to gain anything like a loving conception of their grandeur and significance throughout the seasons."

39. These moods are respectively concomitant with entities that are sublime and beautiful.

40. Herman Melville, *Moby Dick: Or the White Whale* (New York: New American Library, 1961), 405.

41. Ibid., 334.

42. Ibid., 196.

43. Calvin, *Genesis,* 106.

44. John Calvin, *Calvini Opera,* ed. W. Baum, E. Cunitz, and E. Reuss (Brunswick: Schwetschke, 1863), XXIII: 21ff.

45. Calvin, *Institutes,* I:xiv, 20.

46. Muir, *Writings,* "Travels in Alaska," 21.

47. This remark was made to a graduate colloquium at Harvard Divinity School, 1962.

48. I employ this formulation so as to leave open the question concerning a general divine revelation in the natural world, which is somehow prior to or independent of the revelation of God in Jesus Christ. That is an important question, but not one that needs to be addressed here.

49. Calvin, *Calvini Opera,* XXXVIII: 59.

50. Calvin, *Genesis,* 57.

51. Martin Buber, *Ten Rungs: Hasidic Sayings,* trans. Olga Marx (New York: Schocken, 1947).

52. Buber, *Mamre,* 105.

53. Cf. Friedrich Schleiermacher, *On Religion: Speeches to Its Cultured Despisers,* trans. John Oman (New York: Harper, 1958), 88: "Every finite thing, however, is a sign of the Infinite, and so these various expressions declare the immediate relation of a phenomenon to the Infinite and the Whole. But does that involve that every event should not have quite as immediate a relation to the finite and to nature? Miracle is simply the religious name for event. Every event, even the most natural and usual, becomes a miracle, as soon as the religious view of it can be dominant. To me all is miracle."

54. Muir, *Writings,* "Our National Parks," 328.

55. Muir, *Writings,* "Travels in Alaska," 84. Cf. his "Mountains of California," 196ff.: "In the morning everything is joyous and bright, the delicious purple of the dawn changes softly to daffodil yellow and while.... The birds begin to stir.... Innumerable insects begin to dance, the deer withdraw from the open glades and ridge tops.... the flowers open and straighten their petals as the dew vanishes, every pulse beats high, every life cell rejoices, the very rocks seem to tingle with life, and God is felt brooding over everything great and small."

Chapter 6

1. Larry Rasmussen, *Moral Fragments and Moral Community* (Minneapolis: Fortress Press, 1993).

2. Ibid., 152.

3. Ibid., chap. 8.

4. Ibid., 169.

5. See my essay "The Mission of the Church: Reflections along the Way," *Lutheran Quarterly* 23, no. 4 (November 1971): 366–87. Regarding the cultural problematic of postmodernism, Robert Jenson has instructively written in "How the World Lost Its Story" (*First Things* 38 [October 1993]: 19–24), 22: "Throughout modernity, the church has presumed that its mission was directed to persons who *already* understood themselves as inhabitants of a narratable world.... But this is precisely what the postmodern church cannot presume. What then? The obvious answer is that if the church does not *find* her hearers antecedently inhabiting a narratable world, then the church must herself *be* that world[, first and foremost in liturgical praxis].... In the postmodern world, if a congregation or churchly agency wants to be 'relevant,' here is the first step: it must recover the classic liturgy of the

church, in all its dramatic density, sensual actuality, and brutal realism, and make this the one exclusive center of its life."

6. Erwin Panofsky, *Gothic Architecture and Scholasticism* (New York: Meridian Books, 1957).

7. Ibid., 44f.

8. Ibid., 45.

9. Otto von Simson, *The Gothic Cathedral: Origins of Gothic Architecture and the Medieval Concept of Order,* Bollingen Series XLVIII (Princeton, N.J.: Princeton Univ. Press, 1956), chap. 3 and 4.

10. Von Simson, *The Gothic Cathedral,* 103.

11. Georges Duby, *The Age of the Cathedrals: Art and Society, 980–1420,* trans. Eleanor Levieux and Barbara Thompson (Chicago: Univ. of Chicago Press, 1981), 99.

12. H. Paul Santmire, *The Travail of Nature: The Ambiguous Ecological Promise of Christian Theology* (Philadelphia: Fortress Press, 1985), chap. 1.

13. Duby, *The Age of the Cathedrals,* 99f.

14. Ibid., 100.

15. See Santmire, *The Travail of Nature,* chap. 5.

16. Ibid., chap. 6.

17. See Frank C. Senn, *Christian Liturgy: Catholic and Evangelical* (Minneapolis: Fortress Press, 1997), chap. 7.

18. Lynn White Jr., "Natural Science and Naturalistic Art in the Middle Ages," in *Religion and Technology: Collected Essays* (Berkeley: Univ. of California Press, 1978), 33 (quoted by Senn, *Christian Liturgy,* 241).

19. Martin Luther, "That These Words of Christ. . . ," *Luther's Works,* ed. Helmut Lehmann, vol. 57 (Philadelphia: Fortress Press, 1961), 57f. See Santmire, *The Travail of Nature,* chap. 7.

20. WA 23:134.34-23.136.36. Cited by Heinrich Bornkamm, *Luther's World of Thought,* trans. Martin Bertram (St. Louis: Concordia, 1958), 189.

21. Robert W. Jenson, *Visible Words* (Minneapolis: Augsburg, 1978).

22. Luther, "That These Words of Christ. . . ," 57f.

23. For a review of Moltmann's view of the world in God (panentheism), see Steven Bouma-Prediger, *The Greening of Theology: The Ecological Models of Rosemary Radford Ruether, Joseph Sittler, and Jürgen Moltmann* (Atlanta: Scholars Press, 1995), 114–19.

24. Sallie McFague, *The Body of God: An Ecological Theology* (Minneapolis: Fortress Press, 1993).

25. *Lutheran Book of Worship* (Philadelphia: Fortress Press, 1978), 122.

26. See Thomas J. Talley, "The Creation Theme in Eucharistic Prayer," in *Creation and Liturgy,* ed. Ralph N. McMichael Jr. in honor of H. Boone Porter (Washington, D.C.: Pastoral Press, 1993), 13–27.

27. *Lutheran Book of Worship,* 69. Eucharistic Prayer C in the current Episcopal *Book of Common Prayer* proclaims similar themes, yet with a more contemporary sensibility: "At your command all things came to be: the vast expanse of interstellar space, galaxies, suns, the planets in their courses, and this fragile earth, our island home" (quoted by Frank C. Senn, "'The Care of the Earth' as a Paradigm for the Treatment of the Eucharistic Elements," in McMichael, ed., *Creation and Liturgy,* 248.)

28. Dietrich Bonhoeffer, in his own terms, affirmed the Zwinglian point that the church *is* the body of Christ. See *Christ the Center,* trans. Edwin H. Robertson (San Francisco: Harper and Row, 1978), pp. 58f.: "Just as Jesus Christ is present as Word and in the Word, as sacrament and in sacrament, so he is also present as Church and in the Church. . . . The Church is the body of Christ. Here body is not only symbol. The Church *is* the body of Christ, it does not *signify* the Body of Christ. When applied to the Church, the concept of body is not only a concept of function, which refers only to the members of his body. It is a comprehensive and central concept of the mode of existence of the one who is present in his exaltation and humiliation." For a review of Bonhoeffer's fundamental christological insights in this connection, see Clifford J. Green, *Bonhoeffer: A Theology of Sociality,* revised ed. (Grand Rapids: Eerdmans, 1999).

29. My language here is deliberate: the glory of the ubiquitous, risen Lord in the whole cosmos is revealed to the faithful in this moment. This is not yet to say that the cosmos *is* the body of Christ. That kind of statement, if it can be considered at all, biblically speaking, could only be made eschatologically, regarding the consummated new heavens and new earth that are yet to come, when the Son will turn over his rule to the Father, and God will be all in all (1 Cor. 15:28).

30. One urban congregation, located in what some think of as "the slime and grime" environment of northwest Baltimore, has attempted to create such an exemplary, proclamatory inner-city garden. The eighty-eight members of St. John Lutheran Church have planned a "sanctuary garden project" with six components: flower gardens, vegetable gardens, a meditation garden, a wildflower bed, a micro-vineyard and a prayer labyrinth. Low-income children from the neighborhood are being attracted to this imaginative ministry. (See Linda Nansteel Lovell, "A Sanctuary Garden Sows Seeds of God's Love," *Seeds for the Parish* [Chicago: Evangelical Lutheran Church in America, 1999], 12:6, 1.)

31. The idea of a consonance between the affirmations of faith and the findings of the natural sciences has been explored suggestively by Ted Peters. See the volume he edited, *Cosmos as Creation: Theology and Science in Consonance* (Nashville, Tenn.: Abingdon, 1989).

32. Much work must still be done to develop such ideas. Some preliminary suggestions have been made by Paul F. Bente Jr. "A Proposed Creation Cycle of Eight Sunday Worship Services" (Landenberg, Penn., 1998. Available from Bente at 75 Good Hope Rd., Landenberg, PA 19350-9645).

33. A number of helpful resources are available to support good liturgical preaching in this respect. Reference has already been made to the sermon of Paul Tillich, "Nature, Too, Mourns for a Lost God," in *The Shaking of the Foundations* (New York: Scribners, 1948). Many of Joseph Sittler's works offer rich material for homiletical reflection: for example, *The Care of the Earth and Other University Sermons* (Philadelphia: Fortress Press, 1964); and, more generally, *The Anguish of Preaching* (Philadelphia: Fortress Press, 1966). Ecojustice themes are highlighted in the volume edited by Dieter Hessel, *For Creation's Sake: Preaching, Ecology, and Justice* (Philadelphia: Geneva Press, 1985). George L. Murphy, et al., have provided ecologically and cosmically relevant exposition of the common lectionary of the church in *Cosmic Witness: Commentaries on Science/Technology Themes* (Lima, Ohio: CSS Publishing Co., 1996) as has Jennifer M. Phillips, *Preaching the Creation throughout the Church Year* (Boston: Cowley Publications, 2000). Cf. also J. Michael Scheid, "A Theology of Nature and Its Implications for Christian Worship," (Ph.D. diss., San Francisco Theological Seminary, 1997).

Chapter 7

1. Ernest Becker, *The Denial of Death* (New York: Free Press, 1993).

2. These trends have been around for a long time. See the discussion of nature in American life in my *Brother Earth: Nature, God, and Ecology in a Time of Crisis* (New York: Thomas Nelson, 1970), chap. 1. See further, my essay, "Nothing More Beautiful than Death?" *Christian Century* (December 11, 1985), 1154–58.

3. Annie Dillard, *Pilgrim at Tinker Creek* (New York: Bantam Books, 1974), 6.

4. Annie Dillard; *For the Time Being* (New York: Alfred A. Knopf, 1999).

5. See Plotinus, *Enneads* VI 9.

6. The saints most to the fore in this chapter are: Brendan ca. 486–575, Columba 521–597, Columbanus 543–615, Kevin, d. 618, and Patrick ca. 390–ca. 461 Probably the best available study of Celtic Christian spirituality is Philip Sheldrake, *Living between Worlds: Place and Journey in Celtic Spirituality* (London: Darton, Longman, Todd, 1995). Sheldrake also supplies helpful suggestions for further reading. In addition, see Lisa M. Bitel, *Isle of the Saints: Monastic Settlement and Christian Community in Early Ireland* (Ithaca, N.Y.: Cornell Univ. Press, 1990); Kathleen Hughes and Ann Hamlin, *Celtic Monasticism: The Modern Traveler to the Early Irish Church* (New York: Seabury, 1981); Liam de Paor, *Saint Patrick's World: The Christian Culture of Ireland's Apostolic Age* (Notre Dame, Ind.: Univ. of Notre Dame Press, 1993), James P. Mackey, ed., *An Introduction to Celtic Christianity* (Edinburgh: T & T Clark, 1997); and Mary Low, *Celtic Christianity and Nature: Early Irish and Hebridean Traditions* (Edinburgh: Edinburgh Univ. Press, 1997). To be ranked among the best coffee-table art-history books ever published, is Jacqueline O'Brien and Peter Harbison, *Ancient Ireland* (London: Weidenfeld & Nicolson, 1996). Also of interest and a joy to peruse: Bernard Meehan, *The Book of Kells: An Illustrated Introduction to the Manuscript in Trinity College Dublin* (London: Thames & Hudson, 1996).

7. William Butler Yeats, "The Lake Isle of Innisfree," in *W. B. Yeats: The Last Romantic*, ed. Peter Porter (London: Aurum Press, 1990), 18.

8. See O'Brien and Harbison, *Ancient Ireland,* chap. 1.

9. Williams's great hymn, "For All the Saints," gave the poem of the same title, written by William W. How, a captivating power. For the hymn and text, see *The Lutheran Book of Worship* (Minneapolis: Augsburg, 1978), 174.

10. The text can be found in Oliver Davies and Fiona Bowie, eds., *Celtic Christian Spirituality* (New York: Continuum Press, 1995), 41ff. See, further, N. D. O'Donoghue, "St Patrick's Breastplate," in Mackey, ed., *An Introduction to Celtic Christianity,* 45–63.

11. *The Voyage of St. Brendan: Journey to the Promised Land,* trans. John J. O'Meara (Buckinghamshire: Gerard Cross, 1976, 1991). See further, Thomas Finan, "Hiberno-Latin Christian Literature," in Mackey, ed., *An Introduction to Celtic Christianity,* 90. Brendan himself is a fascinating figure, as John J. O'Meara, the translator of *The Voyage of St. Brendan,* indicates. Brendan lived in an era when many Irish monks set out on journeys (Columba for Iona in 563, Columbanus for France ca. 590). His name is connected with the foundation of several Celtic monasteries. He is also reported to have visited Iona and the Orkney and Shetland Islands, as well as Britain and Brittany. Hence his attributed name, "the voyager." The epic itself was written in Ireland as early as 800. But, according to O'Meara, the story "clearly reflects such sea-journeys and visits to islands and island monasteries as Brendan himself is reported to have made."

12. Ibid.

13. Quoted in ibid.

14. William Butler Yeats, "The Second Coming," *Modern American and British Poetry,* rev. ed. Louis Untermeyer (New York: Harcourt, Brace, and World, 1955), 491.

15. Williams, "For All the Saints," 174.

16. Adomnan of Iona, *Life of St. Columba,* trans. Richard Sharpe (London: Penguin Books, 1995).

17. Sheldrake, *Living between Worlds,* 81.

18. See *New Catholic Encyclopedia,* s.v. "Relics." On the historical emergence of the "relic cult," see Caroline Walker Bynum, *The Resurrection of the Body in Western Christianity,* 200–1336 (New York: Columbia Univ. Press, 1995); (Lectures on the History of Religions Sponsored by the American Council of Learned Societies, Number 15), 104–8.

19. Umberto Eco, *The Aesthetics of Chaosmos: The Middle Ages of James Joyce,* trans. Ellen Esrock (Cambridge, Mass.: Harvard Univ. Press, 1982).

20. Ibid., 58.

21. Bitel, *Isle of the Saints,* 227f., quoted by Sheldrake, *Living between Worlds,* 69. The Celtic saints were also claimed by a vision of personal sociality insofar as many practiced the discipline of having a "soul-friend." Unique to Celtic churches, although dependent to some degree on the traditions of earlier, eastern monasticism, the institution of the soul-friend stood for a deep bond of personal loyalty and spiritual companionship. These relationships tended to last for years and were forged between men and women, women and women, men and men, clergy and laity.

22. Finan, "Hiberno-Latin Christian Literature," 70.

23. Ibid., 78.

24. H. Paul Santmire, *The Travail of Nature: The Ambiguous Ecological Promise of Christian Theology* (Philadelphia: Fortress Press, 1985).

25. See n. 5.

26. Sheldrake, *Living between Worlds,* 73. See also O'Donoghue, "St Patrick's Breastplate," in Mackey, ed., *An Introduction to Celtic Christianity,* 45–63, 50: "It is noteworthy that the Trinity, or rather the Deity, three and one, is invoked in its creative power and presence: the 'strong power' is not simply a massive overshadowing presence but a vibrant all-sustaining, all-permeating energy."

27. Sheldrake, *Living between Worlds,* 74.

28. Peter Brown, *The Cult of the Saints: Its Rise and Function in Latin Christianity* (Chicago: Univ. of Chicago Press, 1981), 125.

29. O'Donoghue, "St Patrick's Breastplate," in Mackey, ed., *An Introduction to Celtic Christianity,* 45–63, 54.

30. See Sheldrake's discussion, *Living between Worlds,* 46ff.

31. Ibid., 47.

32. Sheldrake, *Living between Worlds*, 34.

33. Cf. Esther De Waal, *The Celtic Way of Prayer* (New York: Doubleday, 1997), 44: "The Eastern idea of Christ as the head and center of the created world was well preached when Christianity was first introduced into Ireland, and there is much in the early monastic writings, above all in that great hymn of the monks of Bangor, the *Hymnus Dicat*, written between 680 and 691, which speaks of Christ's kingship as the center of life in the Trinity."

34. Finan, "Hiberno-Latin Christian Literature," 81.

35. See Hilary Richardson, "Celtic Art," in Mackey, ed., *An Introduction to Celtic Christianity*, 359–85.

36. Thomas Cahill, *How the Irish Saved Civilization: The Untold Story of Ireland's Heroic Role from the Fall of Rome to the Rise of Medieval Europe* (New York: Doubleday, 1995), 114.

37. Ibid., 110.

38. Sheldrake, *Living between Worlds*, 39.

39. Ibid., 80.

Chapter 8

1. All of the ideas adumbrated in this chapter need more detailed attention. They are intended to be suggestive of a direction, rather than comprehensive in scope. But I hope that the kind of approach to ethics I am proposing here will offer a basis for more inspired moral commitments on the part of the church at large. For a more comprehensive statement of a Christian environmental ethic, I refer the reader once again to the study by James Nash, *Loving Nature: Ecological Integrity and Christian Responsibility* (Nashville, Tenn.: Abingdon Press, in cooperation with the Churches' Center for Theology and Public Policy, Washington, D.C., 1991). See also the ecologically shaped social ethic proposed and well argued by Jerry Folk, *Doing Theology, Doing Justice* (Minneapolis: Fortress Press, 1991); and the older but still valuable work of Bruce C. Birch and Larry L. Rasmussen, of particular importance for many American readers, *The Predicament of the Prosperous* (Philadelphia: Westminster, 1978).

2. See my study *Brother Earth: Nature, God, and Ecology in a Time of Crisis* (New York: Thomas Nelson, 1970), chap. 1.

3. See my study *The Travail of Nature: The Ambiguous Ecological Promise of Christian Theology* (Philadelphia: Fortress Press, 1985), chap. 8.

4. Larry Rasmussen, *Moral Fragments and Moral Community* (Minneapolis: Fortress Press, 1993).

5. These "four callings" differ significantly, especially in light of their biblical specificity, from the four signs of communal enclaves suggested by Rasmussen, *Moral Fragments and Moral Community* more generally. The number four is coincidental. I identified his "four signs" above, chap. 5.

6. See the discussion by Alan Thein During, *How Much Is Enough? The Consumer Society and the Future of the Earth* (New York: Norton and Company, 1992).

7. Source: *World Watch Magazine*, January/February 1999, 39.

8. Two recent approaches to these issues are: C. Dean Freudenberger, "Bridging the Gap: Sustainable Development More Fully Considered," *dialog*, 37:1 (Winter 1998), 48–56, and Trudy Bush, "Plain Living: The Search for Simplicity," *Christian Century* 116:19 (June 30–July 7, 1999), 676–81. Also consult the Lutheran social statement *Toward Sufficient, Sustainable Livelihood for All* (Chicago: the Evangelical Lutheran Church in America, 1999). For a more thorough analysis, see Richard J. Foster, *Freedom of Simplicity* (San Francisco: Harper and Row, 1981); and John B. Cobb Jr., *Sustainability: Economics, Ecology, & Justice* (Maryknoll, New York: Orbis Books, 1992). Further, see Gary Gardner, "Why Share? A Strategy for Living That Cuts Materials Waste and Pollution Turns Out to Offer Some Important Social Benefits As Well," *World Watch Magazine* (July/August 1999).

9. See Bill McKibben, *Hundred Dollar Holiday: The Case for a More Joyful Christmas* (New York: Simon and Schuster, 1998).

10. For what follows, see Timothy Eagan, "Bid to Save Fish Puts West on Notice," *New York Times*, February 27, 1998, A 10.

11. A mandate to care for the family farm is not some escapist romanticism, as advocates of our mass technological society sometimes suggest. On the contrary, the question posed by Norman Wirzba

is telling: "How can Christians be responsible caretakers of the earth if they are not familiar with farming practices?" ("Caring and Working: An Agrarian Perspective," *Christian Century* 116:25 [September 22–29, 1999], 898. His plea is well-taken: "Agrarianism has not been adequately considered by philosophers, theologians or scientists. . . . The reason for agrarianism's marginalization is simple: agrarianism represents a fundamental challenge to the technological/industrial/capitalist worldview or ethos. Whereas *techne* is about making and controlling a world in our own image, agrarianism is about tending to or taking care of a world already given."

12. I leave open the question of vegetarianism here, with this simple caveat: in light of the biblical witness to shalom as our rightful relationship with animals, the burden of proof would seem to rest squarely on the shoulders of any Christian who chooses to eat meat, except for reasons of health or survival. This is only to touch lightly, however, on a highly complicated and advanced theological discussion about animals and animal rights. See, among others, the following: Steven C. Bouma-Prediger and Virginia Vroblesky, *Assessing the Ark: A Christian Perspective on Nonhuman Creatures and the Endangered Species Act* (New York: Crossroad, 1997); Lisa Mighetto, *Wild Animals and American Environmental Ethics* (Tucson: Univ. of Arizona Press, 1991); Andrew Linzey, *Animal Gospel* (Louisville, Ky.: Westminster John Knox Press, 1998); Andrew Linzey and Tom Regan, *Animals and Christianity: A Book of Readings* (New York: Crossroad Publishing, 1988); Thomas Sieger Derr, "Every Sparrow that Falls," review of *Rain without Thunder: The Ideology of the Animals Rights Movement,* by Gary L. Francione *First Things,* 77 (April 1998): 60–64; Richard Alan Young, *Is God a Vegetarian?* (Chicago: Open Court, 1998); Stephen H. Webb, *On God and Dogs: A Christian Theology of Compassion for Animals* (Oxford: Oxford Univ. Press, 1997). For a comprehensive theological approach, see especially Jay B. McDaniel, *Of God and Pelicans: A Theology for Reverence for Life* (Louisville, Ky.: Westminster John Knox Press, 1989).

13. Of the many new sustainable communities that have been developed in the U.S. in recent years, one of the most impressive is the Civano project in Tucson, Arizona. Driven by the theologically shaped Catholic vision of a former inner-city community organizer, Kevin Kelly, Civano is pedestrian-friendly, with tree-lined walkways and gathering places for citizens of every age. This development offers housing that uses a minimum of potable water and that maximizes passive solar options. Most impressive, the community's codes require adherence to a strict energy and building code that will result in enough energy savings to prevent one billion pounds of carbon emissions from entering the atmosphere over the next two decades. While this project is not within the reach of most low-income families, it does exemplify a highly imaginative, environmentally responsible approach to the construction of new communities for the middle-class and upper-middle-class housing market. The question then is: Can theologically inspired Christian developers find a way to create similar projects for low-income people?

14. A model for such structures is the Environmental Sciences Building at Oberlin College, Oberlin, Ohio—an attractive, self-contained (energy use and waste disposal) building developed by an entire community, academic and residential, inspired by the Protestant vision of an Oberlin professor with a passion for environmental design, David Orr.

15. See, for example, Jane Holtz Kay, *Asphalt Nation: How the Automobile Took over America and How We Can Take It Back* (New York: Crown Publishers, 1997). And, still worth consulting: Barry Commoner, *Making Peace with the Planet* (4th ed.; New York: Pantheon Books, 1990), 99ff.; and Barry Weisberg, *Beyond Repair: The Ecology of Capitalism* (Boston: Beacon Press, 1971), chap. 5: "Oiling the Machine: Automobiles and Petroleum." More generally, see James Howard Kunstler, *The Geography of Nowhere: The Rise and Decline of America's Man-Made Landscape* (New York: Simon and Schuster, 1993).

16. See *EcoCity Cleveland* (Special Issue), fall 1998.

17. Anthony M. Pilla, "The Church in the City" (Cleveland: Archdiocese of Cleveland, 1993).

18. Anthony M. Pilla, Christian Faith and the Environment: Reverence and Responsibility (Cleveland: Archdiocese of Cleveland, 1990).

19. G. M. Hopkins, "God's Grandeur," *Modern English and American Poetry,* ed. Louis Untermeyer, (New York: Harcourt, Brace, and World, 1955), 429.

20. Oscar Cullmann, *Immortality of the Soul or Resurrection from the Dead? The Witness of the New Testament* (London: Epworth, 1958), 44ff.

21. John Calvin, *Institutes of the Christian Religion,* ed. John T. McNeil, trans. Ford Lewis Battles (2 vols.; Philadelphia: Westminster Press, 1960), 1.5.5.

Index

Eiseley, L., 3
Engel, J. G., 129 n.11
Engel, J. R., 129 n.11
Elder, F., 4
environmental movement, 1–2
Erikson, E. H., 76
Erickson, K. P., viii, 129 n.1
eschatology. *See* theology, creation-history
evil, radical, 21–22, 59. *See also* sin, original

Fackre, G., 139 n.9
Falk, R., 2, 129 n.3
Finan, T., 100, 108, 113, 146 nn.11, 22, 23;
    147 n.34
Folk, J., 147 n.1
Foster, R. J., 147 n.8
Fowler, R. B., 132 n.24
Fox, M., 6, 10, 17, 18–25, 27, 28, 46, 58,
    65, 75, 135, nn.5, 7–21, 25; 140 n.24
    and Augustine 18, 21
    and Joachim of Fiore, 20
    cosmic christology, 18–19
    creation spirituality, 20
    fall-redemption theology, 18
    original blessings, 19–20
    theology of, 18–25
Francione, G. L., 148 n.12
Francis of Assisi, St., 12, 15, 19, 25, 67, 92,
    124, 125
French, W. C., 134 n.3
Fretheim, T., 8, 34, 131 n.21; 136 n.16;
    137 nn.17, 18, 29
Freudenberger, C. D., 147 n.8
Friedman, M. S., 142 nn.23–25

Gardner, G., 147 n.8
Gilkey, L., 131 n.16; 135 n.30
God
    immanence of, 57, 72, 81–82. *See*
      also christology, ubiquity of
      Christ
    and creation-history, 55–60
    as person, 58, 63–65, 67, 73, 141
      n.14

as the living God, 67
as the loving God, 56–57
cosmic purpose of, 57–58
Gogarten, F., 63, 140 n.3
Gore, A., 45–47, 53, 138 nn.1–6
gothic architecture, 77–78
great chain of being, 54, 77–79, 81–82
Green, C., 144 n.28
Gregory of Nyssa, St., 137 n.21
Gustafson, J. M., 130 n.13

Hall, D. J., 130 n.15
Harbison, P., 145 n.6; 146 n.8
Hamlin, A., 145 n.6
Hauerwas, S., 139 n.9
Haught, J. F., 138 n.8
Hefner, P., 131 n.16; 139 n.9
Heim, K., 63, 142 n.21
Hiebert, T., 131 n.21
Hopkins, G. M., 126, 148 n.19
How, W. W., 146 n.9
Hughes, K., 145 n.6
Hultgren, A. J., 139 n.10; 140 n.23
Hume, D., 103
Huxley, A., 24

Ingram, P. O., 139 n.11
Irenaeus, St., 9

Jacob, E., 137 n.33
Jensen, F., 129 n.5; 131 n.18; 133 n.30
Jenson, R. W., 82, 129 n.10; 143 n.5; 144
    n.21
Joachim of Fiore, 20
Johnson, E., 132 n.22
Jones, L. G., 139 n.9
Joyce, J., 105, 106

Käsemann, E., 24
Kant, I., 141 nn.32, 33
Kay, J. H., 148 n.15
Kelly, K., 148 n.13
Kevin, St., 145 n.6
King, U., 139 n.9

O'Brien, J., 145 n.6; 146 n.8
O'Donoghue, N. D., 111, 146 n.29
Oelschlaeger, M., 139 n.11
O'Meara, J. J., 146 n.11
Origen, 26, 35
Orr, D., 4, 129 n.7; 148 n.14

Pannenberg, W., 131 n.16
Panofsky, E., 77, 144 nn.6–8
Patrick, St., 97, 98, 100, 114, 145 n.6
Paul, St., 13–15
personalism, 61–65
    anthropocentric, 62–63. *See also* Teilhard de Chardin, Pierre, theology of, personalism
    ecological, 68–73
    Tillich, P. and, 63–65
Peter, St., 15
Peters, T., 130 n.12; 133 n.31; 145 n.31
Perrin, N., 24
Phillips, J., 145 n.33
Pilla, A., 125, 148 nn.17,18
Plotinus, 145 n.5
Polkinghorne, J., 8, 131 n.20

Rahner, K., 9
Rasmussen, L., 74–75, 76, 118, 130 n.13; 143 nn.1–4; 147 nn.1, 4, 5
Reich, C., 1, 22, 135 n.22
Regan, T., 148 n.12
Richardson, H., 147 n.35
ritual. *See* worship
Robbins, F. E., 137 n.19
Royal, R., 131 n.15.
Ruether, R. R., 130 n.14; 134 n.3

Santmire, H. P., 132 n.24; 134 nn.37, 40; 134, nn.1, 2; 134 n.3; 135 nn.26, 27; 136 n.1; 137 n. 24; 138 n.40; 138 nn.43, 44, 45; 138 nn.7, 9; 139 n.12; 140 n.18–23; 141 n.5; 142 n.31; 143 n.5; 144 nn.15, 16, 19; 145 n.2; 146 n.24; 147 nn.2, 3
Scheid, M., 145 n. 33.

Schleiermacher, F., 143 n.53
Scroggs, R., 139 n.10
Senn, F. C., 144 nn.17, 18, 27
Sheldon, J. K., 129 n.11
Sheldrake, P., 103, 108, 109, 112, 114, 145 n.6; 146 nn.17, 21, 26, 27, 30, 31; 147 nn.32, 38, 39; 147 nn.38, 39
Simkins, R. A., 136 n.5
sin, original, 21–22, 58–59, 135 n.20
Sittler, J., 8, 9, 23, 131 n.18; 135 n.24; 138 n.45
Sobosan, J. G., 130 n.13
Stendahl, K., 14, 134 n.42
Stevenson, W. T., 141 n.10
Stewart, C. Y., 132 n.24
Suger of St. Denis, 77–78
Swimme, B., 130 n.13

Talley, T. J., 144 n.26
Teilhard de Chardin, P., 10, 46, 47–60, 62 , 65, 70, 77, 78, 81, 115, 132 n.26; 140 nn.13–17; 142 n.21
    abolition of nature, 53, 55
    biogenesis, 50
    christogenesis, 52
    christology, cosmic, 52
    cosmic drift, 49, 51
    cosmogenesis, 50
    dominion, human, 55
    evolutionary anthropocentrism, 50, 54–55
    homogenesis (noogenesis), 50
    law of complexity-consciousness, 49–51
    the Omega Point, 51–52
    orthogenesis, 48–49
    personalism, 50, 55
    theology of, 46–60
    the "within" and the "without" of matter, 48, 51–52, 56–57
theology
    anthropocentrism in, 55, 161–65
    "apologists," 7, 130 n.15; 130 nn.25–26
    and the city, 24

and creation/creation history, 56–60

and evolution 48. *See also* Teilhard
de Chardin, Pierre, theology of

ecological/cosmic, 46–47

eschatology, 24. *See also* biblical
interpretation, creation-history

fall-redemption, 18–19, 58–60

and interreligious encounter, 45–46,
139 n.11

metaphor of ascent, 78–79, 81

metaphor of fecundity, 78

new paradigm in, 10–15

the Omega world, 56

public, 133 n.28

"reconstructionists," 6, 130 n.13;
132 nn.23–24; 132 n.3

"revisionists," 7–10, 131 nn.18–21;
132 nn.23–24; 132 nn.25–26

and science, 7–8, 91, 131 nn.16, 17;
138 n.11

and story, 46, 133 n.30; 143 n.5

See also nature, theology of

Thiemann, R. F., 133 n.28

Thomas Aquinas, St., 35, 77, 81, 117

Thoreau, H. D., 3, 16, 17, 18, 20, 24, 94,
96, 101, 107, 134 n.1

Tilberg, C. W., 129 n.5; 131 n.18

Tillich, P., 3, 10, 61, 63–64, 67, 72, 102, 129
n.6; 140 n.1; 141 nn.6, 8, 15; 145 n.33

Toolan, David S., 130 n.13

Trible, P., 39, 40, 137 nn.23, 26, 29, 30,
34–37; 138 n.39

van Gogh, V., vii, viii

von Rad, G., 36, 131 n.22, 137 nn.25, 27

von Ranke, L., 56

von Simson, O., 77, 144 nn.9–10

Vroblesky, V., 148 n.12

Ward, B. K., 129 n.8

Watt, J., 1

Weisberg, B. 148 n.15

Westermann, C., 31, 136 n.3; 137 nn.28,
34, 37; 138 n.38; 138 n.46

White Jr., L., 10–15, 80, 144 n.18

Williams, R. V., 99, 146 n.9; 146 n.15

Wilkenson, L., 130 n.15

Wirzba, N., 147 n.11

Wordsworth, W., 24, 96, 97

worship, 74–92

baptism, cosmic meanings, 85–87

as constituting the church, 74–75

eucharist, cosmic meanings, 52,
87–91

and gardens 90, 145 n.30

and the gothic spirit, 77–81

real presence of Christ 80, 88–89

revelation of ubiquitous Christ, 89,
144 n.29

sacraments as "visible words," 82–83

and the Word, 91–92

Worthing, M. W., 140 n.15

Wright, G. E., 32, 136 n.4

Yeats, W. B., 97, 98, 101, 110, 145 n.7; 146
n.14

Yoder, J. H., 136 n.9

Young, R. A., 148 n.12

Zwingli, H., 88